Praise for *Taming the Dragons of Change in Business*

In his latest book, Dick Stieglitz brilliantly leads us through the confusing and threatening maze of change in business. H ble *steps of how to not just survive change, b* ont *and leading it. This is a* who wants to move powerfully

Martha Borst, Best Se
Your Survival Strategies

Dick Stieglitz has distilled millions of dollars of mistakes and triumphs into a valuable, easy-to-read book with great stories. Every point is a winner. If you are looking to accelerate your business or career in a changing world, this is the book for you.

Jim Schleckser, CEO, CEO Project

Dick Stieglitz has thrived in a world of change and his book reflects wisdom from the school of hard knocks. One caveat though: Dick is quite modest in presenting his advice as tips. Don't believe it for a minute! Those ten tips are guiding principles that need to be part of your core DNA to succeed in the relationship economy.

Cyrus Taylor, PhD, Dean of the College of Arts & Sciences
Case-Western Reserve University

Dick Stieglitz delivers rubber-meets-road experience for anyone who is building a business in these changing times. He also provides valuable insights to the challenge of helping government agencies change. Plus he gives you a great read—he tells stories well. This book is well worth your time. Not that I have an opinion.

Mark Amtower, author of *Government Marketing Best Practices* and radio host of *Amtower Off Center*

The biggest risk in business today is the pace of change. New technologies and regulations mean that business people are constantly assimilating new information in order to make prudent decisions. Taming the Dragons of Change in Business *provides practical advice that can be used by professionals at every level to thrive in a world of change.*

James A. Kaitz, CEO and President,
Association for Financial Professionals

Taming the Dragons of Change in Business *is a practical book with insights Dick Stieglitz learned from decades as a successful business leader. The take-aways are simple, useful, and profound. It's a must-read for anyone who wants greater success and a more meaningful life in a rapidly changing world.*

Bob Busch, CEO and President, Busch Change Solutions Inc.

Things that worked for leaders in the past may no longer work for them in the future. Taming the Dragons of Change in Business *provides practical tools for how leaders need to think, how they need to be, and what they need to do to excel in the new world ahead.*

Archie Tinelli, PhD, Executive Leadership Coach

The rate of change is accelerating everywhere, even in the Federal government market. Taming the Dragons of Change in Business *provides insights that will help any leader position his organization to compete successfully in such a challenging world.*

Jeff Copeland, CEO, ImmixGroup

Taming the Dragons of Change in Business *is a must-read if you're a leader committed to being your best, achieving meaningful success, and exceeding your transformation goals. Dr. Stieglitz is a wise and seasoned executive who provides a fountain of tips on how to get real, get ready, and get rolling with change.*

Marta Wilson, PhD, CEO, Transformation Systems, Inc.
and Author of *The Transformation Desktop Guide*

Taming the Dragons of Change in Business *delivers a different perspective on change and success, one that enables readers to face change with power, clarity, and hope. I look forward to sharing this book of direction and wisdom with my clients who are working to become successful in today's world, or are already there and want to expand their success.*

Heather Ramsey, Certified Professional Co-Active Coach

Taming the Dragons of Change in Business *is dead-on. You will learn the key lessons for success in today's changing business world! If you want to succeed by adapting to change, building relationships, and enhancing your customers' experience, this is a must-read!*

Peter Giardini, President, The Club, LLC.
Editor, *Real Estate Mastermind* Newsletter

Motivating and inspiring with ten areas of real differences today that can help you sort out winning ideas for investments. Makes you think about the future differently!

Alan V. Rogers, Major General (Ret), USAF & Angel Investor

Master the new rules for achieving success in the global relationship economy

Global competition, acquisitions, new technologies, and downsizings have produced a business environment of perpetual change. Facing such changes, the success you enjoy today can actually hold you back from achieving greater success tomorrow. But you can leverage change to your advantage if you know the new rules of the global relationship economy.

Are any of these common changes affecting your workplace:

- Your role has changed substantially, or you have a new position
- The technologies you've used for years are being replaced
- Your company was recently sold or may be sold in the near future
- Workers in China or India can do what you do for half the cost

These changes frequently incite ferocious resistance—dragons that can hinder your growth. But change itself isn't the dragon. It's your reaction to change that could limit your success. This book will help you tame those dragons, and take charge of your destiny in today's changing business world.

This book presents 10 easy-to-understand tips that work in a world of never-ending change. The tips lie in three areas:

- *Part I – Beliefs:* Changing how you look at yourself, your career, and change
- *Part II – Relationships:* Changing how you treat your colleagues, customers, strategic partners, and competitors
- *Part III – Actions:* Changing the goals you set for yourself, and the actions you take to achieve them

In the past, your skills made you valuable. But today, your value is *who you know* and how you can help others achieve their goals. That concept is the foundation of the global relationship economy where creativity is rewarded more highly than productivity. Knowing the new rules is the key to your future success.

The astonishing changes happening today are a source of unlimited opportunity for those who anticipate, embrace, and exploit the emerging new possibilities. *Taming the Dragons of Change in Business* provides all you need to do just that!

TAMING THE DRAGONS OF CHANGE IN BUSINESS

How to Thrive—Not Just Survive—
in the Global Relationship Economy

TAMING THE DRAGONS OF CHANGE IN BUSINESS

10 Tips For Anticipating, Embracing, and Using
Change to Achieve Success

Richard G. Stieglitz, PhD

Potomac, Maryland

Acuity Publishing
9812 Falls Road #114-157
Potomac, Maryland 20854-3863
301-365-9031, Fax: 301-365-9041
Info@AcuityPublishing.Com

This publication is designed to educate and provide general information regarding the subject matter covered. It is not intended to replace the counsel of other professional advisors. The reader is encouraged to consult with his or her own advisors regarding specific situations. While the author has taken reasonable precautions in the preparation of this book and believes the facts presented within the book are accurate, neither the publisher nor author assumes any responsibility for errors or omissions. The author and publisher specifically disclaim any liability resulting from the use or application of the information contained in this book. This information is not intended to serve as emotional or therapeutic advice related to individual situations.

Publisher's Cataloging-In-Publication

Stieglitz, Richard G.

Taming the dragons of change in business : 10 tips for anticipating, embracing, and using change to achieve success / Richard G. Stieglitz. -- 1st ed. -- Potomac, Md. : Acuity Pub., c2008.

p. ; cm.

ISBN: 978-0-9820500-3-3

At head of title: How to thrive--not just survive--in the global relationship economy.

1. Organizational change--Management. 2. Corporate reorganizations--Management. 3. International trade. 4. Success in business. 5. Leadership. I. Title.

HD58.8 .S75 2008   2008907639
658.4/06--dc22   0901

Printed in the United States of America.

Cover and book design: Patricia Bacall

This book is dedicated to the mentors, colleagues, partners, and competitors who helped me tame my dragons so I could succeed in a business world that increasingly depends on effective relationships.

Also by Richard G. Stieglitz, PhD

Taming the Dragons of Change
*10 Tips for Achieving Happiness & Success
When Everything Around You Is Changing*

CONTENTS

NOTE FROM THE AUTHOR

The most significant change in the business world today is that it has become a relationship economy. Sociologists say we are connected to everyone in the world through six degrees of separation. In the past, most of us have operated in the first degree: We conducted business with people we knew well. But today's relationship economy gives us tools to operate in the second and third degrees. The super-successful people you know already do this. Opportunities flow to them because they connect with people who are connected to other people who help them. Of course, the relationship tools we have today that have no historical parallel are the World Wide Web, BlackBerrys, e-mail, YouTube, and other collaboration devices that allow us to contact anyone anywhere at any time.

The relationship economy has brand new rules. Intelligence, education, and determination alone were sufficient for success in the industrial and information eras. But today's relationship economy values and rewards *what you know* AND *who you know* more than any skill you possess. The new reward system may seem unfair at times. But if you don't constantly expand *what you know* and *who you know*, you risk becoming a commodity—a human robot stuck in a dead-end job that could be offshored to India or China, or replaced by a computer. On the other hand, the inescapable changes of the relationship economy are producing a rapidly flowing river of new possibilities that could carry you to higher levels of success.

During the last twenty-five years, everything has changed. Several times. Capitalism has become a roller-coaster ride of thrilling climbs and frightening falls. In the late 1970s, the U.S. economy was criticized as bloated, unproductive, and destined to fall far behind Germany and Japan with their superior business cultures and product quality. But it didn't happen. By the 1990s, the U.S. economy was red-hot, the Soviet Union had disintegrated, and the U.S. was back on top as the acknowledged leader in what seemed like a never-ending technology boom. The world depended on the United States to rev the engine of global growth and prosperity.

It was a dizzying comeback! But as we high-fived ourselves for creating an economy that produced government budget surpluses, things started to fall apart. A decline in the communications industry burst the dot-com bubble, terrorists destroyed the World Trade Centers, manufacturing and service jobs moved offshore by the thousands, the price of oil skyrocketed, and the mortgage market had a meltdown. Before the end of the first decade in the new millennium, the U.S. economy was in trouble again.

We could drink several bottles of California wine (the strong Euro and weak dollar make French wine too expensive) while we debated whether the U.S. Congress, free trade, Exxon-Mobil, unions, or General Motors was to blame for the decline. In my opinion, it wasn't so much that the U.S. economy faltered as it was that several countries began competing with us on even terms. For example, the economies of China and India are booming because of low labor costs even as they, like us, struggle to pay for an unquenchable thirst for oil.

The exciting reality is that jobs around the world are changing! But for many in the U.S., the changes are painful. In a survey taken during the 2008 Presidential Election, more than 80 percent of all respondents said they weren't satisfied with how things were going. They wanted changes that would improve the U.S. economy and used the campaign to search for a candidate who could make it happen. But there was no consensus on what changes to implement. For example, citizens in Detroit, Toledo, and other Rust Belt cities fanatically believed that changing the North American Free Trade Agreement (NAFTA) would bring some of their old jobs back home. Others felt that slowing the pace of change would give the U.S. time to regain its position as the leader of the globally connected economy.

Unfortunately, there won't be any slowdowns. In fact, every facet of our lives will continue to change—and in the business world, change is on steroids! A tsunami of new technologies, acquisitions, reorganizations, outsourcings, and offshorings floods our workplaces. And even when these changes don't affect us directly, we still wonder what will happen next.

On the other hand, rapid change has advantages. Many people prosper by riding the upside of change, and you can too. The purpose of this book is to show you how to use change to expand your success. First you must realize that it is your reaction to change, not change itself, that determines your success or failure. When you fear, deny, or resist change, you spend precious energy wrestling emotional dragons that fill your head and your heart. Even though the dragons are purely in your imagination, they're quite capable of destroying your success. However, by taming the dragons of change that are inside you, you transform change into an asset for your organization and your career.

This book is written for leaders whose purpose is to transform their organizations to succeed in the relationship economy. However, those leaders must first tame their own personal dragons of change before attempting to tame the organization's dragons. So I blended the two perspectives and included vignettes to address organizational and personal change. Whichever change (or both) you are seeking, this book will be highly valuable to you.

While the strategic, sales, and operational sides of business have been analyzed in many books, *Taming the Dragons of Change in Business* deals with the people side—specifically how to get the most from yourself; your ideas; and your relationships with customers, co-workers, strategic partners, and competitors in global markets. This book is a must-read for you if:

- Your company was sold in the last two years or it might be sold in the next two years;
- Your role has changed substantially, you have a new job, or you plan to switch careers or jobs in the next two years;
- People in China can do your job for a fraction of your pay;
- The methods, tools, and technologies you've used for years are being replaced; or
- Your organization, after reorganizing and acquiring new tools, will be expected to produce much more than it does today.

If one or more of these is true for you, you are experiencing the effects of the relationship economy. But you have exciting new opportunities to succeed if you tame the dragons related to such changes.

To succeed in the new economy, you'll need the same tools as you did in the past: education, training, creativity, and determination. But you will also need much more. The ten tips in this book are the "more." They're rules-of-thumb that power the relationship economy, and they will power you toward success too.

Dick Stieglitz

THE CHANGING WORLD OF BUSINESS

*The astonishing changes you are experiencing today
are a source of unlimited opportunity when you
embrace and exploit the emerging new possibilities.*

Between 1980 and 2000, almost 50 million private sector jobs in the United States were abolished. At the same time, roughly 80 million new jobs were created, a net gain of 30 million jobs. When you examine the churn, you will find dying companies that can't compete, and many unplanned and unwanted job changes. But you also will find a cornucopia of industries that were born based on new relationships and technologies. Ancient nautical maps were inscribed *Cave Hic Dragones* to warn sailors about the dragons that lurked in uncharted waters. A similar warning should be on the business and career plans you prepare to navigate the uncharted waters of today's new business world.

People and organizations in virtually every sector of the economy are working together more creatively than ever before. This seismic but largely undetected change moves us from a production-based industrial economy to an economy fueled by synergistic relationships and innovative ideas. Such a relationship economy promises to deliver worldwide prosperity (yes, even in Africa, which could be the next source of low cost labor) and wealth to organizations and people who make it happen. But you must be willing to change and adapt to succeed in the new environment.

> Global connectivity has produced an economy based on ideas and relationships.

The relationship economy is powered by devices like cell phones, the Internet, and BlackBerrys that enable us to communicate with anyone, anywhere, at any time, and on any subject. It used to take days or weeks to acquire resources to execute an idea, but today it can be done in a few hours using the Internet. These devices accelerate the pace of change and the proliferation of new ideas.

1

The industrial age was linear. Any change in organization, tools, or processes produced a proportional increase in output because changes generally didn't leverage each other or spread rapidly. By contrast, the relationship economy is geometric. New phenomena can appear from nowhere and change everything. Your success can multiply overnight just by coupling a small new idea with an increase in the number and effectiveness of your relationships.

Change never stops happening. When you grasp that simple reality, change becomes an asset. You start to anticipate tomorrow's change instead of struggling to react to yesterday's change. You join the small minority of people who recognize the early signs of change and use change to unlock the treasure chest of new opportunities. In the relationship economy, the keys to that treasure chest are *what you know* and *who you know*.

> Change happens. When you embrace that reality, you instantly add change to your toolbox of success strategies.

Today everyone is a knowledge worker. *What you know* is just as vital in the manufacturing, transportation, and service industries as it is in the traditional knowledge fields of engineering, medicine, and law. The days are gone when workers were highly paid to skillfully do the same task day-in and day-out. Those tasks are now performed by machines, or soon will be offshored to Mexico, India, or China, where skilled labor is much less expensive. Inexpensive transportation and high bandwidth communications have connected skilled laborers in faraway lands to our markets and transformed the world of business.

Knowledge and skills are different. Skills change slowly since they are learned through training and practice. Unfortunately, some skills may not be in demand in tomorrow's world. Knowledge, on the other hand, changes rapidly. Today, the life cycle of a new idea from inception to history may be a few years. In some fields, just days or weeks. Of course, skills are still useful, but you also must refresh *what you know* continuously. You must share your knowledge with people who need it and acquire new knowledge at the same time.

Networking (*who you know*) has always been career-enhancing, but in the relationship economy it is survival. Using cell phones and e-mail, the average worker exchanges knowledge with nearly five times as many people per day as workers did thirty years ago. Cash may have been king in the industrial age, but today *who you know* and *what you know* rule!

Relationships are precious assets to be treasured and cultivated, and time is scarce. We get the same twenty-four hours each day as our grandparents did, but more activities compete for our time. Therefore, when you meet someone, deliver value by helping them:

> Networking is a survival skill in the relationship economy.

- Recognize an opportunity or problem that they have missed;
- Discover a strategy that they didn't know before; or
- Broker a solution that they can't do by themselves.

You also have the right to expect the same value when someone asks for time on your busy calendar.

One question I'm often asked during presentations is, *"Dick, what dragons are you taming to achieve success in the relationship economy?"* The short answer is that I'm less controlling, more collaborative, and more giving in relationships—at least I try to be that way. Let me explain. It's hard for me to break out of my nuclear engineering box. As a PhD nuclear engineer and U.S. Navy submarine officer, I look at life as if it were a nuclear reactor. A reactor is a simple machine. It has control rods that regulate power by localizing a fission reaction in a super-critical mass of enriched uranium in the reactor vessel. Insert the controls rods, and the reactor will shut down. Remove the control rods, and the reactor will generate more power. But if you remove the control rods too far or too fast, the reactor might explode.

Several people who cared about me said that my compulsive need to control others was a dragon. But control made sense, and it seemed to work. Control everything and don't take any chances. For example, I founded and led a company using a control paradigm. I kept my hands tightly on the control rods because I was afraid the company might explode and fail. I manipulated people so they did things my way, and my way produced top results—at least at the start. Operating that way, the company quickly grew to fifteen employees and $3 million in annual revenue. But it got stuck there because that was all the reactor volume I could control. Control might have been an effective style in the industrial era, but I was proof it didn't work in a rapidly changing and organizationally flat relationship economy.

My company never exploded, but it didn't generate as much income as it should have. The peaks and valleys in our growth curve correlated directly to progress in taming my control dragon. Oh sure, market conditions influenced our results. But, in general, the company grew when I allowed my capable staff to perform, but it was flat when I missed the signs of change and forced others to do things *the right way* (the way I learned years ago). You may not have a revenue curve to quantitatively reflect the effect of your behaviors, but your gut will tell you whether your career is advancing or stagnant.

My second breakthrough was learning to collaborate with co-workers, customers, partners, and competitors. As I tamed my control dragon, I was surprised at the extraordinary amount of collaboration that was required to succeed in the relationship economy. I'm comfortable developing a strategy, analyzing financial statements, or directing a big project. However, I've found that success depends more on having productive interactions with others than on how well I am able to plan, analyze, or direct operations. I learned that developing and sustaining relationships with the best and brightest people are essential for success in the relationship economy.

> Developing and maintaining relationships with the best and brightest people are essential.

I was my own worst enemy when it came to collaboration. As the boss, I knew the cliché, *"People are our most valuable asset."* But the *do-it-myself* dragon made me work at a burnout pace and expect others to do the same. I operated in hero-mode with very little, if any, collaboration. I was shocked when an employee resigned to work for a different company. Eventually, I learned that everyone is a free agent in today's relationship economy, and effective collaboration occurs when every member of the team feels valued.

My third breakthrough was acquiring a willingness to help people without an expectation of getting something in return. *Quid pro quo* (what will I get in return?) was a dragon in my relationships. Today's astonishing rate of change places intense demands on people at every level, from clerk to CEO. We face challenges that were unimaginable a few short years ago. Simply stated: *We can't succeed alone.* I found I need to help others when they ask without wasting time negotiating a price for the help. *Pay it forward!* I'll help you today if you need it, and I'll receive help when I need it. However, the way the relationship economy operates, the help I receive may not come from you, and the help you give may go to somebody else.

The relationship economy depends on people willingly helping each other. That's where *what you know* and *who you know* merge. Most of us enjoy helping others and connecting them with people who also could help. We like being valued and respected, and receiving accolades for our team's success. I encourage you to yield to the natural human desire to help others because giving such help will lift you to new heights. If you're surrounded by people who are helpful, optimistic, and entrepreneurial during times of change, it's because you set that tone.

> We can't succeed alone! Let's help each other without wasting time negotiating a price for that help.

Our personal and professional lives are inseparably entwined. A change in one occurs in parallel with ongoing changes in the other. Consider the following examples of change challenges:

- Your family is growing and your house is too small, but your job doesn't pay enough to afford a larger house.
- You've enjoyed extraordinary success up to now, but a bundle of joy at home has changed your priorities.
- You find yourself underemployed in the relationship economy, but you have no idea where to go next professionally.
- You've worked for the company a long time and feel a sense of loyalty, but prospects for substantial growth are dim.
- You have an idea that will flourish in the relationship economy, but you're reluctant to risk what you have to pursue the idea.
- You are an executive responsible for leading your organization through change, but you wonder if you can make it happen.

One of these challenges may be awakening dragons in you today. But the need for change isn't a dragon. The dragon that limits your success is your response to these kinds of change challenges.

Social scientists claim the pace of technological and cultural change is accelerating. They forecast that the amount of change we've seen in the last ten years will occur again in the next five years. One natural reaction is to resist changes that push you out of your comfort zone. A new job, new technology, new boss, or new challenge all feel uncomfortable. You may wish change would go away so "normal" can return. But change isn't going away. You can ignore, resist, or fight change; or you can adapt and use it to succeed. Either way, the world around you will continue to change.

> You can resist change or use it to succeed. Either way, the world will continue to change.

Recognizing that change is inevitable, the purpose of this book is to help you integrate change into your plan for success. *Status quo* may have been a useable strategy in the past, but it's a death spiral in a rapidly changing world. If you try to maintain *status quo* today, you'll soon find yourself behind competitors who have already assimilated yesterday's change and are creating tomorrow's change. One surefire strategy for success is to be a reliable source of positive changes in your industry and your organization.

As I reviewed things that worked in my career and personal life, I found that they fell into three areas of change. Those areas are the three major parts of this book:

- *Part I* addresses **Beliefs** about abundance (tip #1), opportunity (tip #2), and investment (tip #3). These tips will help you see how your beliefs are affecting your organization and career.
- *Part II* addresses **Relationships** in terms of communications (tip #4), diversity (tip #5), and collaboration (tip #6). These tips will help you improve relationships with co-workers, customers, strategic partners, and competitors.
- *Part III* addresses **Actions** in terms of purpose (tip #7), planning (tip #8), innovation (tip #9), and execution (tip #10), since small changes in your goals and the actions you take to achieve them could easily produce big changes in your results.

You may already know a few of the ten tips contained in this book. If so, great! Those tips will be refreshers. Other tips may be new or feel uncomfortable. In any case, I invite you to consider each tip carefully without immediately accepting it or summarily rejecting it.

The ten tips will expand your understanding of emotions that occur when unexpected or unwanted changes enter your workplace. The tips will help you tame dragons that limit your success by giving you new ways to think about change, to improve relationships, and to take action in the face of career-altering changes. The ten tips will put you among those who prosper *because of* the rapid changes happening today in the business world.

Part I

BELIEFS

The Foundation for Success

OVERVIEW

We each erect an imaginary box in our minds and operate inside that box. The box is imaginary because the walls are built from how we believe things are, not necessarily how they really are. These beliefs can be as deeply entrenched in our minds as the Colorado River is in the Grand Canyon. Unfortunately, if you remain in your box of beliefs, you'll miss possibilities that are outside the box. The relationship economy has moved many of the walls. So in order to succeed, you must be willing to let go of any belief that stands in the way of your success.

To understand your walls, analyze the judgments you make in statements that begin with: *"I can't," "The world is,"* and *"You are."* These statements sound like facts, but they're really just your beliefs, the walls of your imaginary box. In the past, an epiphany may have lifted the curtain to reveal the real *Wizard of* Oz behind one of your beliefs. In those rare moments of clarity, you seize the power to change your life. The vignettes in this introduction to Part I, Beliefs, will help you expand your box by taming the beliefs dragon. The introductory vignettes are followed by the first three tips:

Tip #1 **Abundance** – *Be Abundant in Your Attitude*
Tip #2 **Opportunity** – *Answer When It Knocks*
Tip #3 **Investments** – *Pay It Forward*

I THINK I CAN

Ability is what you're capable of doing. Motivation determines what you will do. But attitude determines how well you do it.
—Lou Holtz, Football Coach

When I was thirty-nine years old, I held the title of director with a large aerospace firm and directed a staff of 130 people. That summer, I attended a director's meeting at company headquarters and was the youngest director present. I left feeling it would be years until I would be promoted to vice president. My job was routine and didn't challenge me, but the position was very comfortable. I was well paid, received substantial annual bonuses, and drove a company car.

I described my position to a friend and he asked me a question that I had never asked myself. He asked, *"Could you run your own company?"* I answered, *"I think I can,"* and began to plan how I would gather the resources and relationships required for success. Within a year, I quit my job and started my own company. If I had responded, *"No, I don't think so"* or *"I'm not so sure,"* the possibility would have died right there.

You may want to change something about your organization, how you relate to customers and co-workers, your job, or your growth potential. *"I think I can, therefore I can"* may not always be true. But the *I-think-I-can't* dragon always is a dead-end street. Why would you try if you knew (really, it's *believed*) you couldn't succeed? Believing in the possibility of success is an essential prerequisite for success.

> **Belief in the possibility of success is an essential prerequisite to success.**

The more life experiences I accumulate, the more I realize that beliefs are the foundation of success. They're more critical than skills, education, resources, or even relationships. They're more important than past successes or failures, or what other people say or do. For the most part, your beliefs will determine whether you fail or succeed in today's relationship economy. Success should be easy then, since you have full control over your beliefs. Or do you? Each day you have a choice to keep or re-examine your current beliefs. Choose wisely.

THE BEST PARKING SPOT

Your beliefs set boundaries on your success. Take charge of those beliefs and set your goals where you really want them.

Recently, I had lunch with my cousin. As I pulled into the shopping center where the restaurant was located, the parking lot looked full. So I grabbed the first empty space in the last row. As I walked to the restaurant, I saw my cousin park his car in the front row only fifty feet from the restaurant's front door. I exclaimed, *"Wow! You got a great spot. I didn't think parking would be open in the front row."* He responded: *"I was lucky."*

Driving back to my office after lunch, it occurred to me that luck had little to do with him finding the perfect parking spot. Instead, my cousin had imagined the possibility of a front row space and found it while I had surrendered to the dragon of low expectations. If I had thought differently, I might have found a front row parking space too. How many people settle for the first available position in a back row of the business world instead of stretching themselves to look for a challenging front-row opportunity?

During the twentieth century, people learned valuable skills through years of intense education and training. By age twenty-five, their lifelong career was pretty much determined. While most fields in today's relationship economy still require education, they also require much more. First and foremost, they require new beliefs. They require you to hold high expectations about how much is possible. Success in the twenty-first century requires you to expect more of yourself and those around you.

Your beliefs determine what you see as possible or impossible, and possibilities that you miss altogether. You and I may look at the same reality and see different things. Neither of us sees the whole picture. We may be missing fantastic opportunities. For example, how much has your current organization been changed by new technology, new relationships, international competition, or the merger-mania that are common today? Do you see those changes as big problems or big opportunities?

TWO-DOLLAR CUP OF COFFEE

The relationship economy is changing business fundamentals. Ideas that seemed ridiculous just a few years ago are succeeding spectacularly today.

Not too long ago, coffee was twenty-five cents a cup, and free with breakfast. Recently I paid $2 for coffee when my wife and I went to Starbucks. Including tax and tip, our bill was more than $5 for my grande Verona plus her skim milk, decaf, double-Splenda, extra-hot latte. The server called her drink a *"latte, no fun"* when he shouted the order to the woman who prepared our beverages.

I didn't particularly want coffee at three o'clock on a spring afternoon, but I enjoyed having a comfortable place to sit and talk. My wife and I sat on the patio next to a woman who answered e-mails on a PC while she drank her coffee. What Starbucks really sells at almost ten times the previous cost of a cup of coffee is an environment: outdoor tables, indoor couches, and a wireless network that suits the relationship economy. Today, people want wireless connectivity to be available like coffee. And, in the age of the *mobile me*, they'll pay for that convenience.

Business fundamentals are changing in the relationship economy, and Starbucks is just one of the many wildly successful ideas. Bottled water is another example. I bought a case of twenty-four twelve-ounce bottles on sale for $4. That's roughly fifteen cents for a glass of water, which has been free for my entire life.

Similarly, Amazon.com sells a relationship that you can't buy at the corner bookstore. They add value in the book reviews, unique advice, and recommendations they give to customers. Amazon.com will ship a book to your door, of course, but you'll pay a premium. When you visit the company's Web site, you connect to a relationship partner that understands you more every time you make a purchase or an inquiry, and people are willing to pay for that!

By changing your beliefs, you can find opportunities like these too. I wonder what lucrative business opportunities might be hidden in the astronomical price of gasoline or the large number of experienced baby boomers who will soon enter semi-retirement? Hmmmm.

CLOSE THE WAREHOUSES

*The significant problems we face today cannot be solved with
the same kind of thinking that created them in the first place.*
—Albert Einstein

A large Defense agency buys items that the military services all use. Twenty years ago, it stored $250 billion worth of stock and was the world's largest warehouse operation. Its storage, shipping, and spoilage costs grew until someone asked, *"Why do we have warehouses? Let's ship direct from suppliers to users and close our warehouses."* The idea met staunch resistance because the change would force many workers to find new jobs. Critics said, *"America needs the warehouses to protect our security."* But that argument died under the microscope of a business case analysis.

Today, warehouses are closed and the inventory is below $100 billion. The agency now says its business is managing relationships, not goods. Once the agency stopped believing that warehouses were necessary, it lifted the barrier to efficiency improvements and cost savings. Transformational thinking often changes relationships, like shipping goods directly from suppliers to users with no middleman. In today's relationship economy, such supply chains are widely used.

To increase your success, change your beliefs about people and things. Old beliefs can be the dragon that keeps organizations and people stuck in a rut. But where do such beliefs come from? Over the years, experiences molded your beliefs about how the world is. For example, my beliefs were, and to some extent still are, shaped by:

- A scientific education that causes me to believe that the solution always lies in getting the right formula and data;
- Ten years in nuclear submarines where I believed that perfection was expected and anything less than perfect had to be fixed; and
- Early success when I started my own company, which led me to believe that I could succeed all by myself.

What beliefs do you cling to that may be getting in the way of the new strategies and new relationships required to expand your success?

THE COMFORTABLE
STATUS QUO

Status Quo *will give you more of what you have today. If you already have everything you want, change isn't necessary.*

As their sons approached school age, my daughter and son-in-law were concerned about the low quality of public schools and high cost of private schools in San Francisco. They looked for a new house, and their anxiety grew as they realized that there were no affordable houses in areas with quality schools. A friend moved to North Carolina, so they looked at new houses there. But would my son-in-law find a job that paid enough? That, of course, assumed he would be required to change jobs.

New technologies enabled a new relationship between my son-in-law and his job. They moved to North Carolina, bought a house three times as large for the same price as their California house, found good schools, and my son-in-law kept his same job and worked over the Internet. Before the Internet and high-bandwidth communications provided new options, the decision to move to North Carolina would have been more difficult and risky.

We feel that we make decisions objectively, but our beliefs limit the options we consider and thereby perpetuate *status quo*. We say we want more, but to change *status quo* we must do things that are uncomfortable. Since *status quo* is comfortable, there always seem to be more reasons to do nothing. In the world of business where the sin of commission (doing something) is criticized more often than doing nothing (not changing), *status quo* is generally a safe choice.

Status quo may be the best choice. But don't choose *status quo* just because it's comfortable and safe. Once you understand the often fatal attraction of the *status quo* dragon, you can tame it by:

- Looking at *status quo* as the future. Is it really what you want?
- Reviewing your goals and asking if *status quo* will achieve them;
- Honestly considering alternatives other than the *status quo*; and
- Not defaulting to *status quo* if you can't choose an alternative.

Status quo will give you more of what you already have. If you have everything you want for tomorrow, then *status quo* is okay.

SIX BLIND MEN

*Test your beliefs about the world continuously since
they are merely hypotheses about people, markets,
and technologies that could change at any time.*

The story of six blind men who *see* an elephant illustrates that each of us has only part of the answer to the challenges we face. Each man described what he felt with his hands and visualized in his mind:

- The first man caught the tail and reported: *"It's a flexible broom that's bushy on one end and moves with a sweeping motion."*
- The second man hugged a leg and said: *"You're wrong. It's a tree trunk that's so thick I can't get my arms around it."*
- The third man grabbed the trunk and shouted: *"No. It's got to be a fire hose. Can't you feel the water spray?"*
- The fourth man gently felt the tusks and said: *"Let's be careful. It has a spear that's pointed at the end."*
- The fifth man laid his hands on the elephant's side and lamented: *"Where do we go now? We'll never get around this wall."*
- The sixth man tugged at an ear and said: *"You're all wrong. It's a flat and flimsy blanket."*

Each of the six men was right in what they felt but incorrect in their perception of the overall size and shape of the elephant.

Since the relationship economy changes so quickly and you only see part of it, collaboration is more important for success than ever before. When you achieve success, don't stop questioning what is happening around you, because fixed beliefs become dragons when they replace analysis. Your beliefs aren't etched in stone. Instead, they are merely hypotheses about people, markets, and technology that can change in an instant.

Some beliefs might be so insightful that they last a long time. But every belief eventually becomes obsolete. At the corporate level, it happened to Polaroid and Xerox, who believed the market for their products would never end. And it will happen to you and me if we act like one of the six blind men and fail to hear, assimilate, and respond to the messages that shifting events and relationships send to us.

HOW MUCH IS POSSIBLE?

"Everything that can be invented has already been invented."
—Charles Duell, Director of the U.S. Patent Office, 1899

"Babe Ruth is making a big mistake by giving up pitching."
—Tris Speaker, Baseball Hall of Fame .300-hitter, 1921

"Who the heck would want to hear actors talk?"
—Harry Warner, CEO, Warner Brothers Pictures, 1927

"I think there's a world market for about ten computers."
—Thomas J. Watson, CEO, IBM, 1943

"There's no reason for anyone to have a computer at home."
—Ken Olsen, CEO, Digital Electronics (DEC), 1977

"640K of computing power should be enough for everyone."
—Bill Gates, Chairman, Microsoft Corporation, 1982

These are famous quotes from six experts in their respective fields. Despite their individual achievements, we might call them "six blind men" because the quotes show that they had only partial insights even in the fields of their substantial expertise. If men and women who are acknowledged to be world-class visionaries can't see the full picture because it is beyond human imagination, is it reasonable to believe that you and I know the limits of what is possible even for ourselves and our organizations?

What is the biggest goal you have set for your organization and yourself in the relationship economy? Do you believe you see the full measure of your potential? As large as your goal may be, consider the possibility that what you could achieve is well beyond what you currently envision. As you move toward today's goal, you'll begin to see larger possibilities and ways to achieve them.

The closer you get to your current goal, the easier it will be for you to see the next level of what's possible. At first glance, that may seem obvious, but the implications are significant. Because only by moving steadily toward your biggest goal can you discover the next level of what is really possible. To achieve the highest potential for your organization and yourself, first achieve the full potential that is possible today.

CLOSING THOUGHTS ON BELIEFS

Think for yourself and allow others to enjoy the same privilege.
—Voltaire

I left the Navy in part because my next assignment would have been in Washington, and I didn't want to leave Charleston, South Carolina. However, after looking for an opportunity for a long time, I accepted a job in Washington and have enjoyed this fascinating city ever since. That major change in my career illustrates the three themes of this section:

- *Our beliefs set boundaries on our success.* I thought I wanted to stay in Charleston, but the best job offer I received there was in ship design, which is a dying industry today.
- *Our beliefs limit the options we will consider.* Opportunities are far more plentiful in Washington than Charleston. If I stayed in Charleston, I probably wouldn't have started my own company.
- *Each of us has just part of the answer to any challenge.* In 1976, I had no clue about the limitless opportunities that would become available in applying computer technologies.

You'll probably face several big decisions like this in your career too. Your beliefs will shape your decisions. Since each decision builds on the result of previous decisions, your beliefs will ultimately determine the success you'll have or not have in your lifetime.

Your beliefs create boundaries that affect your career choices and your ability to switch from one field to another. The beliefs grow into self-inflicted dragons when your current position doesn't satisfy your future needs. Consider the following self-inflicted beliefs that stop people from pursuing more enjoyable, financially rewarding, and challenging opportunities:

- I must stay in my job until my children graduate from college (or my mortgage is paid off).
- I must live in this region to be close to my family, friends, and recreational activities.
- If I continue to work hard, I will get bonuses and promotions.
- There is nothing else that I'm qualified to do.

- This is the only job that pays what I need to live.
- I don't have the time, energy, or desire to start over.
- I like the people I work with and don't want to leave them.
- My job is comfortable and I can do just enough to get by.
- I have sweet memories of past successes in my current job.
- I'll still succeed even if my industry changes dramatically.

Review these beliefs. Put a check next to each one you think is true. Pencil in any beliefs you have that I didn't list. Then place a star next to what you feel are the one or two most non-negotiable beliefs. For each of those, list the positive and negative consequences of the belief on your career and your life. Your beliefs aren't right or wrong, good or bad. Rather, how they shape your decisions and your results makes them helpful or makes them into dragons.

In my big career changes—which included leaving the Navy to work in industry and later resigning from a large firm to start my own company—I had to deal with several core beliefs. When I left the Navy, my salary doubled, but when I began my own company, it was cut in half. One stable factor in both career changes was relationships. The same people who supported me in one position were there for me in the next. In fact, the number of relationships has more than tripled in my career. Now that I am retiring, I must confront my beliefs again to shape my new life. However, having done it twice before makes it easier for me to embrace a major change and use it to expand my success.

> You created your beliefs, so you can change them if that's what it will take for you to succeed.

The relationship economy will force you to consider changes more often than ever before. I don't mean just changing jobs within a field; I mean taking the risk to begin a whole new career. Your parents may have faced a career-change decision once or twice in their lives. But the business world is changing so rapidly, and new opportunities arise so frequently, that you may face ten or more career-change decisions in your lifetime. To switch from one field to another, you'll find that you must confront your beliefs. Remember, you choose those beliefs to start with, so you can change them to achieve success in the global relationship economy.

ABUNDANCE

Tip #1 – Be Abundant in Your Attitude

OVERVIEW

Living in an attitude of abundance is a creative and effective life strategy. You will receive more of the success and happiness you want with abundance thinking than with scarcity thinking. Abundance thinking is the belief that there's plenty for everyone, so you and I willingly help each other achieve our respective goals. On the other hand, scarcity thinking is the belief that opportunity and resources are scarce, so I'd better get mine before you get yours.

The scarcity dragon is very clever. It will trick you into thinking that you're winning a competition when in fact you are damaging vital relationships. The sixteen vignettes in Tip #1 will show how thinking abundantly produces synergy, innovation, and win-win solutions; how an attitude of scarcity fosters independence and competition, which are barriers to success in the relationship economy; and how there really can be enough for everyone!

GIVER'S GAIN

Abundance thinking lubricates business transactions,
while scarcity thinking acts like sand in the gears.

I joined a Business Networks International (BNI) group to build my consulting practice. BNI's philosophy is *Giver's Gain*: refer business to others during weekly meetings, and eventually I'll receive referrals in return. The philosophy works! In one case, for example, a lawyer in the group referred me to a CEO with a start-up. The CEO became my client for strategic planning services, and I referred him to a CPA for accounting services. The CPA, in turn, referred the CEO to an estate planner and an insurance agent in the group. It was win-win for everyone, especially the CEO, who was able to get his business and estate up and running in record time.

BNI is designed to be a second-degree-of-separation operation, although referrals often extend to the third degree. For example, I was referred to a business broker who later referred me to a client who was preparing to sell his company. Super-successful business women and men (for example, Oprah Winfrey, Donald Trump, Warren Buffet, and Bill Gates) intuitively know *Giver's Gain*. Two-off, three-off, and even four-off deals come to them by the dozens. They pick-and-choose deals that fit in their long-term strategies. Instead of viewing referrals as a bothersome rip-off, they see referrals as a way to help others. After all, a small piece of a rapidly growing pie can become the most valuable of all. The sly dragons that hold us back, of course, are doubts that giving will really bring more in the long term and a fear that we might give more than we receive.

In the long run, win-win transactions are the only ones that produce abundant success. The other choices make one party, or both parties, into losers because one party tries to win at the other party's expense. Consider the following alternatives to win-win transactions:

- *Win-Lose Transaction.* When capable people meet in a win-lose transaction (*I win, you lose*), they both lose because some of their creativity is spent to protect themselves from the dog-eat-dog competitor. Win-lose strategies divert energy from goals and re-direct it toward competition. In a win-lose transaction, one party wins and the other loses; but in total they achieve less than they would if they worked together. Unfortunately, an unrelated third party sometimes wins, and then they're both losers!

- **Lose-Win Transaction.** A lose-win transaction (*I lose, you win*) usually leaves the person who sacrifices his success for the other's success feeling empty and angry. Such transactions are surprisingly common among people who care intensely about others. Furthermore, the recipient of the special treatment may feel guilty about "taking advantage" of their partner. Lose-win is not a relationship that motivates either party to achieve greatness as an organization or as an individual.

- **Lose-Lose Transaction.** Lose-lose transactions are least effective of all. A person compromises their possibilities and tries to make his transaction partner lose too. It's surprising how often people fall into the lose-lose bear trap. Lose-lose happens when a person feels sorry for himself and passes the misery to others. The adage *misery loves company* is appropriate for lose-lose transactions.

You may ask, "*Why would anyone pick any of these transactions?*" I agree. They are ludicrous choices when you could choose a win-win relationship. But the *opportunity-is-scarce* dragon sees competition (a *win-lose* transaction) even when there isn't any, and tries to push you away from a win-win relationship toward one of these less favorable alternatives.

> People who are competitors today could become strategic partners who expand tomorrow's success.

Organizations and people who you view as competitors today could be transformed into strategic partners who will multiply your success tomorrow. The relationship economy moves too fast to invest time in relationships with organizations and people who demonstrate again and again that they aren't win-win players. Be a win-win business partner yourself no matter what, and you'll find that you'll attract people who share that value.

WHO IS YOUR COMPETITION?

*In the relationship economy, more so than ever before, all
parties must achieve their goals or the relationship will die.*

Parking spots at United Auto Workers (UAW) headquarters are marked: *Union Made American Cars Only*. The sign symbolizes the fierce competition UAW members feel toward their adversaries, the big three U.S. automakers and foreign automakers. On the company side, General Motors (GM) displayed its competitive juices when it rejected an alliance with Nissan and Renault, claiming, *"We're big enough and strong enough to fight on alone."* However, the recent retirement buyout offers by GM and other U.S. automakers have been a jolting reminder of the declining importance of the U.S. automakers and unions in the global market.

Even as GM's market share and UAW membership shrink, the market share and employment of foreign automakers with non-union plants in the U.S. are expanding. The UAW fought hard to win high wages and benefits for its members and retirees, and memories of those victories are dragons that appear at today's negotiation tables. While the U.S. automakers and unions battled each other, foreign automakers quietly stole market share. One blog contributor tacitly summarized the situation by saying, *"If you can't find a new job for the same pay as your old job, you were overpaid!"*

Only mutually supportive relationships survive. Is it possible for a company to thrive while its employees and suppliers struggle? Is it possible for employees to succeed while their company fails? Is it possible for a company or its employees to win while their customers suffer? What alternatives do the U.S. automakers and the UAW have today? The answer is the same work-together alternatives they had years ago when the market share of foreign automakers was of minor consequence, except now those alternatives are more painful since the companies are near bankruptcy and many workers are unemployed.

Competition may have been an acceptable behavior during the industrial age, but the global relationship economy treats cutthroat competition harshly. Things change so fast that, while organizations focus their mind share on vicious competition, other companies search for and implement creative solutions that quietly steal market share. The prosperity and survival of large organizations in the relationship economy require management and workers to tame their competitive dragons long enough to explore entirely new business models. The new models usually involve changing the relationships among organizations that were once considered to be adversaries (e.g., dealers, suppliers, and foreign automakers). It's a risky approach, and some business experiments will inevitably fail. But by remembering they that are teammates rather than competitors, workers and management will learn from the setbacks and try other approaches until they find something that works for everyone.

> Tame your competitive dragons long enough to explore new business models for partnering.

On a personal level, are you and I in competition for new opportunities? If you answer *YES*, our relationship will proceed based on the belief that: *"There isn't enough for both of us, so I'd better get mine before you get yours."* We'll try to out-maneuver each other, and some opportunities may actually disappear because of our conflict. However, if with an attitude of abundance you respond *NO*, then you and I will cooperate to pursue new opportunities based on a belief that our future success will be shared. In my experience, the few times my attitude of abundance has been exploited by a win-lose competitor are negligible compared to the help I have received from others, the unexpected opportunities that have come my way, and the peace that abundance thinking has produced in my life. Isn't that the kind of abundance you want in your life too?

MONKEY TAILS

*Scarcity may have increased value in the industrial
age, but cooperation and reputation are the source
of sustained success in the relationship economy.*

Friends purchased a forty-two-foot sailboat that was custom-made in Taiwan. During construction, the boat's builder paid to fly them to Taiwan to review construction plans, make outfitting choices, and meet the shipyard's craftsmen. Before the proud new owners visited the shipyard, the craftsmen were told that they were building a dream for the couple they would meet. Nothing was too much trouble or too good for the boat.

When construction was finished, the boat was shipped to Annapolis, where the new owners lived. They invited friends to a party where the boat was christened *Monkey Tails*. The celebration wasn't dampened by the torrential rains that fell on the day of the party. Great food and music helped. The president of the shipbuilding company visited the U.S. to attend the party and present the boat to prospective buyers in Annapolis. The boat received accolades among Annapolis' sailing aficionados, and the story of the abundant construction process spread throughout the harbor.

In the industrial age, the scarcity dragon might have pushed the boat builder to charge for every change the owners requested in an effort to maximize profits. Instead, an attitude of abundance during construction built synergy between the boat's builder and owners. In the connected relationship economy, that synergy created a buzz in Annapolis that paved the way for future orders in a lucrative new market for the boat builder, and added to the owners' pride in their new sailboat.

An attitude of abundance is believing that all parties in a transaction can achieve their objectives, and finding ways to make it happen. By cooperating with others in ways that might be considered soft by industrial-age standards, you build a reputation that will be a source of sustained success in the relationship economy.

THE AWAKENING

Our expanding abundance has awakened a desire to help others and pointed the quest for prosperity in new directions.

For my company's Christmas party, employees and their significant others met in a hotel in tuxedos and evening gowns. After an hour of cocktails and hors d'oeuvres, twelve stretch limousines picked up our group of seventy people and took us to see the national Christmas tree and *The Awakening* sculpture at Haines Point. Next, the limos drove us to Pentagon City Mall where each person was given a brand new one hundred dollar bill with written rules for how it could be spent.

The rules allowed everyone thirty minutes to spend the money. We could only buy things for ourselves which, as it turned out, was difficult because many people wanted to buy a gift for somebody else. The leader took out a stopwatch and said, *"Ready. Set. Go!"* Seventy people in formal attire rushed through the mall spending new hundred dollar bills. Several mall shoppers wanted a job at the company. That holiday party became part of the company's abundant folklore.

Shopping malls are symbols of material abundance. What is remarkable about Pentagon City Mall is that it's unremarkable. Today it is a mall world. There's probably a similar mall within ten miles of where you live. This wasn't always the case. When I was a young boy in the 1950s, there were no malls. Shopping meant driving store-to-store searching for an acceptable item at a fair price. But the material abundance we enjoy today has created a paradox: Goods alone are not enough. Prosperity has awakened a strong desire to help others and to preserve our planet.

The relationship economy is taking the quest for abundance in new directions. That a product is affordable and functional is not a sufficient reason to buy it. It also must be produced in a way that preserves the environment and does not exploit workers. Some people haven't embraced the new direction yet. But the relationship economy is moving to reward those whose goods and services are essential to society and kind to our planet. Are you part of that new awakening?

BUDGET SHORTFALL

In the relationship economy, success accrues to those who
find innovative ways to transform scarcity into abundance.

An Ohio high school earned a prestigious *Innovations in American Government* award for transforming a budget shortfall into a landmark learning program. The curricula required computers for 2,000 students, but the budget allowed just $100,000 for computer support. The first reaction was to abandon the curricula, but school officials and parents tamed the *no-way-out* dragon by forming a student-led company to provide the needed services. Class schedules were restructured to offer industrial courses in computers and network fundamentals. Students supported the school's computer system and received hands-on experience at the same time.

Starting as freshmen, students could elect classes in software, Web design, and network maintenance. Roughly 10 percent of freshmen, 25 percent of sophomores, and 30 percent of juniors and seniors selected the program, which included one class every day and extra time before or after school. The students also learned customer service and business management skills. Local businesses hired new employees from the student-led company, and the computer training increased the college acceptance rate.

The school's solution to a budget shortfall defies fundamental rules from the industrial age. First, that scarce skills are hard-to-find and expensive. And the corollary, when scarce skills become plentiful, they will be devalued. The relationship economy, as illustrated by this high school's innovative program, is reversing scarcity-based rules. In the relationship economy, value is driven by abundance. For example, e-mail, cell phones, and BlackBerrys are valuable because they are abundant. Everyone is connected. The devices allow communication with anyone at almost any time. Success in the relationship economy goes to those who transform scarcity into abundance. Abundance thinking will create abundance.

FREEWARE

*In the relationship economy, sharing your knowledge
and your relationships is a prerequisite to success.*

In the late 1990s, Jim Barksdale, Netscape's CEO at the time, incorporated abundance thinking in a clever and unorthodox business strategy. He announced that Netscape would distribute *Navigator,* its top revenue generator, free over the Internet. Even back then, freeware wasn't unusual. However, what was unusual was that Netscape made *Navigator* source code available with no restrictions.

Before the relationship economy, scarcity dragons made such ideas unthinkable. An industrial age board of directors would never have approved the plan to give away their core product. But Netscape did exactly that. Every copy of *Navigator* downloaded by a user made all the other copies more valuable. AOL bought Netscape a year later for six times the company's stock price at the time that *Navigator* was offered as freeware. How much did the freeware add to Netscape's value? No one knows, of course, but it was more than zero.

Netscape is totally gone today, but give-it-away-free strategies have become common. Two current examples are the free Web searches we perform with *Google* and other search engines, and the *Java* code Sun Microsystems gives away to promote its servers. Once a product's indispensability is established, add-on products and services grow in value. Every copy of a relationship product (e.g., a BlackBerry, iPhone, search engine, or Web site) adds value to all the other copies because it expands the relationship circle. Therefore, giving away such products makes business sense.

The relationship economy introduced freeware as a viable business model. If relationship products and services grow in value when more people use them, and if costs decrease as they become more plentiful, it follows that the most widely used relationship products and services should be free! The business challenge in the relationship economy is simple: Make a relationship product that's indispensable to millions of users.

CAVEMAN WITH E-MAIL

*Ultimately, your ability to work effectively with
others will determine your success or failure.*

In 1998, my company joined a team to take an exciting new Internet security product to market. The product had great potential because it was scalable across the entire World Wide Web. Our task was to determine the distribution strategy. Our staff invested hundreds of hours to identify distribution channels, estimate costs, evaluate the risks, and quantify return on investment. We gave the patent holder the information we prepared at our expense. They chose to do channel distribution themselves—not an unreasonable business decision in my opinion. But, after making that decision, they made offers to lure away the key people who developed the distribution plan.

My reaction when the employees told me about their job offers was a test of our *win-win* corporate value. The employees naturally were attracted by the lucrative offers and stock in the company that held the patent. How should I handle the situation? My legal dragons told me to sue. But that was *lose-lose:* We would both waste valuable resources in a legal battle that had no positive outcome. Altruistically, another voice proclaimed we should continue to help them. I liked the idea, except it had a *lose-win* feel. We considered taking a competing solution to market, but that *win-lose* approach would surely create cutthroat competition.

It's easy to be *win-win* when everyone else is *win-win*. The challenge is to be *win-win* when others aren't—to find a *win-win* solution or walk away from the deal. This time we walked. The promising technology never got to market because the patent holder behaved like a caveman who was happy to have the only e-mail address in existence. Without relationships to distribute the product, they went bankrupt a year later. They had violated a fundamental rule of the relationship economy: *Achieve ubiquity as quickly as possible.* As Netscape demonstrated, one way is to give the product away to increase its value. If I had the chance today, I would recommend that strategy as the channel distribution program.

LESS CAN BE MORE

Win-win *relationships build synergy while a* win-lose *attitude drives others to compete ruthlessly for every new opportunity.*

To reduce costs, a federal agency requested proposals from industry to combine work previously performed by three companies including mine. The winning strategy seemed to be obvious: The three companies should unite in a prime-subcontractor relationship and submit just one proposal to make the client's choice easy. Teaming arrangements like that are common in government contracting. We immediately teamed with one of the other companies, but the third company refused to tame the *we-want-it-all* dragon. They submitted a competing proposal to get more than one-third of the $30 million contract.

With two excellent proposals to pick from, the government's choice was difficult. Some members of the selection panel wanted our team, and others wanted the third company. The client took eighteen months to decide. We won the contract, but everybody lost. The client lost the expertise of the third company. The third company lost all the work they previously performed. And we lost because, during the long evaluation period, a fourth company was awarded a $10 million software development project that probably would have been added to our contract if our three companies had teamed together.

For most of my career, I behaved like the third company. I believed that hoarding opportunity and knowledge gave me strategic power. I was painfully wrong for a long time, and that scarcity dragon severely limited my company's growth. Today, I willingly share my knowledge and expertise with others because sharing produces better results in the long run than what I may or may not win in any single transaction. Nothing is more valuable in the relationship economy than a consistent record of *win-win* transactions with your business partners. That reputation will preserve and extend your network, and ensure your future success.

MOST VALUABLE PLAYER

The most valuable player isn't really valuable
until he (or she) plays on the winning team.

Terrell Owens, often called TO, was a star wide receiver for the San Francisco Forty-Niners. When his contract ended, he signed with the Philadelphia Eagles as a free agent. In his first year on the Eagles, the team was conference champion, but it lost the Super Bowl. TO blamed the quarterback for the loss. The following year, he was suspended for "conduct detrimental to the team" after blasting the team's front office and quarterback during a TV interview. The Eagles released the superstar in the middle of the second year of his contract.

When he was released, TO had more receiving yards than the rest of the Eagles combined. He was angry that his teammates and the team didn't adequately recognize his one hundredth touchdown. The Eagles missed the playoffs in the season that TO was released, despite having a powerful team even without him. The following season, TO played for the Dallas Cowboys. As of this writing, the Cowboys have yet to win a playoff game since TO joined the team. Some sports fans believe that TO is winning. But, even though he is arguably one of the most talented wide receivers in the history of pro football, no team has won a Super Bowl with TO as a player.

The ultimate recognition in the NFL, of course, is winning the Super Bowl. No matter what their record the previous year, each July players report to summer camp hoping that *this will be the year.* They know the team with the best individual talent often doesn't win the Super Bowl (or Major League Baseball's World Series as the New York Yankees demonstrate). Since team victory is the highest reward an individual can achieve, all individual praise and awards are empty if the team loses. The real Most Valuable Player always plays on the winning team.

In the relationship economy, the business world is much like sports. Success is a team event. The scarcity dragon entices you to believe that you can win by yourself, that you aren't receiving enough recognition or rewards for the results you produce, or that your teammates don't contribute their fair share. But if you embrace that dragon, you may behave in ways that damage crucial relationships. On the other hand, a supportive, *win-win* attitude by a star contributor motivates the team to reach its highest potential and strengthens the relationships needed to achieve consistent, year-after-year success.

Win-win thinking fosters an environment in which everybody achieves their organizational and personal goals. It produces a dynamic upward spiral where one success creates possibilities for additional successes. It is axiomatic that success produces confidence, and confidence produces success in a reinforcing cycle. Therefore, *win-win* thinking increases your chances of being a repeat or three-peat winner in business!

> A star contributor motivates the team to consistently achieve its highest potential.

Win-lose thinking, on the other hand, usually produces open conflicts. Each competitive action escalates the response of the other party in a deteriorating spiral. For example, if I compete vigorously against you, you will naturally respond by competing vigorously against me. If I win, my team might high-five itself saying, *"We beat you! That's business."* But that behavior puts you and me into an ongoing scenario in which we not only don't help each other, we also actively attempt gain advantage by thwarting each other's plans.

Confrontational *win-lose* attitudes by competent organizations can lead to *lose-lose* results. In the long term, everyone receives less in *win-lose* transactions. However, if I look for ways to help you and you look for ways to help me, we both succeed at levels that are measurably higher than either of us could achieve on our own.

SHARING

*The relationship economy offers creative ways to
share resources with amazing varieties of people
around the globe, limited only by our imaginations.*

I was copied on the following e-mail from one government executive to another in the same federal agency:

"Calm down. No one is trying to cut you out of anything. Words like unprofessional and cutthroat are a bit strong since proposals just went into the e-business office. Ours was a last-minute idea submitted at the eleventh hour. We obviously surprised you, and I apologize for that. You have my full assurance that if the e-business office funds our proposal and not yours, we'll work with you and other stakeholders to ensure the resources are invested as a unified plan for our agency."

The e-mail went on to outline how the two proposals, which seemed competitive, could be the foundation of a new agency-wide strategy.

In the end, neither proposal was funded, mostly because they competed with each other. A single, integrated proposal likely would have been one of the six proposals that got $2 million in seed funding. It's not at all surprising that the executive who prepared this e-mail has been promoted three times in the last nine years and now serves as a top executive in another agency. The individual who was angry and sent the original e-mail remains in the same position and is still trying unsuccessfully to tame the *need-more-resources* dragon.

If you see resources as scarce, you'll fight to ensure you get your share. Usually your opponents (could they be partners?) react by competing with you. In this case, competition produced two losses when teamwork may have produced victory. On the other hand, if you see resources as abundant and willingly share them as this executive offered to do, you just may attract more resources. Even when your creative efforts to share fail, you will still receive credit for trying, and that credit may be a deciding factor in obtaining additional resources for tomorrow's needs.

WHAT DO YOU WIN?

Do you sometimes think of opportunity as being a scarce commodity and compete to get your fair share? Actually, it's relationships that are the rare and fragile commodity.

My company engaged a software consultant who produced creative solutions and had impeccable technical credentials. He finished most projects on time, and his software was thoroughly tested. What more could we ask for? Unfortunately, few people got along with him. He insisted on being right, and frequently took legal action to get his way. He was critical of co-workers and demanded a disproportionate share of the work. The client wondered if we should replace him, even though that action might have been detrimental to the project. We didn't use him on other contracts because, despite his superior technical skills, he was a relationship liability.

Like the consultant, the scarcity dragon sometimes tells you, *"They will take it away unless you protect yourself."* When you listen to that dragon, you surrender to the belief that opportunity is scarce. You feel you must be smarter, stronger, and quicker than everyone else in order to win. But what do you win, and what do you lose? My compulsion to win usually is focused on financial results whereas the things I risk losing are trust, respect, and peace. Ironically, when I compete vigorously for financial things, I sometimes lose them too.

Like air and water, opportunity is among the most replaceable commodities on Earth. New opportunities are created every day of the year. Yet, many people treat opportunities as if they were rare and do competitive, unnatural, and even illegal things to win them. Actually, relationships are the rare and fragile commodity. Months, sometimes even years, are necessary to create relationships that prosper through successive opportunities. At the organizational and personal levels, maximize the opportunities you give to others. Help the people around you build their success on your success. Make success into a shared experience today and there will be more success tomorrow.

GRAINS OF SAND

*"There is nothing so useless as doing efficiently
that which should not be done at all."*
—Peter Drucker

To prepare for my first nuclear submarine overhaul, I worked with the shipyard's planning department. Several months before ship arrival, we planned the work package, issued job orders, and ordered material. Two metrics that we monitored closely were the number of job orders issued and material items ordered. The planners knew this, so to make their quotas, they issued job orders for simple tasks like shore power and pure water that were common to every overhaul. Just before the ship arrived, I found that job orders for complex repairs and long-lead items hadn't been issued. There were only a few such job orders, but they were time-consuming to prepare. As a result, critical jobs were delayed while we waited for late-ordered material.

If you're like me, you feel overwhelmed by the variety of tasks that demand your time each day—and the demands are growing! Time is constantly on your mind as you rush through a day's schedule. But if you allow yourself to become obsessed with doing more and doing it faster, time scarcity becomes a dragon.

In reality, time is abundant. You have enough time for every task you must do, if you do the most important things first. Everyone gets 86,400 seconds every day, but some people let them slip through their fingers like grains of sand on a beach. For example, some claim the Web is the biggest waste of time ever invented. Speaking for myself, I sometimes spend hours in curiosity-driven Web research, e-mails, and (I'm embarrassed to admit) *Free Cell.* However, the Web also saves me time providing a wealth of information at the click of a mouse, while ten years ago it would have taken me hours to find (or maybe not find) the answer at the local library.

In the relationship economy, time is a precious, irreplaceable asset. Those who use it wisely will be handsomely rewarded. For executives and service-oriented businesses, time is the core resource. Success requires you to work smarter, not longer. Rather than looking for ways to work harder, focus on completing the tasks that matter.

RUNNING OUT OF KNOWLEDGE

The useful lifetime of knowledge is shrinking, so it's urgent that you continuously refresh and expand your knowledge.

My older brother and I were driving on a parkway when the car's engine coughed and died. We had run out of gas. When we got home, my brother told our father he was so intent on driving that he forgot to stop for gas. Filling a gas tank is obviously an essential task. Just as obviously, you must refill your knowledge tank continuously to succeed in the relationship economy. Unfortunately, some people cram their calendar full of activities and say, *"I don't have time to learn."* Like my brother who ran out of gas, the *I'm-so-busy* dragon will cause them to run out of knowledge while the relationship economy passes them by.

The basis of jobs is changing. Industrial age workers sold their hours to one employer at a time. By comparison, workers today can market knowledge-based services and products to almost anyone in the world concurrently. An increasing number of today's workers are free agents who participate in projects on an *ad hoc* basis, contribute knowledge, and move on when a project is over. In such a dynamic environment, organizations are challenged to build a workplace that attracts the best and brightest, and workers are challenged to keep their knowledge current.

History demonstrates that when international communications and trade expand, standards of living increase rapidly. For example, living standards bloomed in thirteenth century Italy when Marco Polo initiated trade and communications with eastern cultures. His travels stimulated 400 years of world exploration. Rapid economic growth occurred again in the early twentieth century when the agriculture-based economy was replaced by international trade in manufactured goods. Another large-scale exchange of knowledge is happening today in the global relationship economy. Just as it would have been futile to resist the shift from an agricultural to industrial economy, it is foolish to ignore the shift to a knowledge-based economy. Seems like a no-brainer, but are you refreshing your knowledge base or running out of knowledge?

EIGHT BILLION DOLLAR CHANGE

*Sweeping change provokes ferocious resistance dragons
and makes a people-driven approach essential to success.*

In 2000, the Navy began to deploy a secure enterprise network called the Navy-Marine Corps Intranet (NMCI). The ambitious project was scheduled to take five years with a cost of $8 billion. NMCI took longer and cost more than estimated, not because of technological problems, but because resistance dragons provoked by the fundamental change weren't tamed until several years into the project.

For example, NMCI reduced one Navy CIO's staff from 140 to thirty-five people. The NMCI contractor was surprised when the CIO's staff resisted the project. No government employees were laid off, but many switched to new jobs. After four years, the NMCI Project Manager said, *"We're behind because we viewed NMCI as a technology project, when it really is a sweeping change to how people do their jobs every day."*

Businesses face the same dragons that impeded NMCI when they try to change to succeed in the relationship economy. Change is a high-performance engine with both logical and emotional cylinders. To attain peak performance, all cylinders must fire in order. When any cylinder misfires, the engine sputters. Strategy, workforce, process, and technology are the logical cylinders. Any change in one affects all four, even though it's easy to fall into the trap of viewing a project as strictly about new technologies or a workforce reorganization.

The logical cylinders of change get plenty of attention. But emotional cylinders like the following are often neglected and allowed to grow into dragons:

- Attachment to what exists today;
- Uncertainty of what the future will be after the change;
- Reluctance to invest the resources required to change; or
- Fear that the change will fail.

You may add emotions to this list, but these natural human responses to change occur in almost every organizational or career change. Plan for them when you are making a change.

ECONOMIC STIMULUS

*Which is best: your way or mine? Could there be a third
way that combines the best of your ideas with the best
of mine? We'll find that alternative only if we look for it.*

In early 2008, Congress passed and the President signed into law an
economic stimulus package intended to prevent recession. One would
think the Democratic and Republican parties would be proud of their
joint achievement and share credit for an important legislative action. But
instead, Democrats repudiated the package because it had insufficient benefits
for the elderly or unemployed, while Republicans disavowed the package
because it didn't make tax cuts permanent. The bill was a compromise, and
compromises are not *win-win*. Both parties feel like they made significant
concessions and try to recover those losses in future transactions. That's why
Congress fights the same battles over and over and over again.

Which is best: Your way or mine? We could argue about it for days,
weeks, months, even years without producing anything of value. What if
there was a third alternative that's better than your way or my way? But we
won't find it until we stop arguing and search for an approach that integrates
the best of your ideas, the best of mine, and new ideas we'll discover when
we start working together.

Are opportunity and resources abundant? Those who say *YES* deal
with issues in one way, but those who say *NO* behave differently. With an
attitude of abundance, you willingly share opportunities and resources with
me, and I willingly share them with you since we both believe *your success
is my success*. On the other hand, the scarcity dragon claims, *"There isn't
enough for everyone, so get yours first."* We compete rather than help each
other, and potential solutions go by unnoticed. An attitude of abundance
believes a third alternative exists and is committed to finding it. Not my
way, not your way. But a better way, a more abundant way than either of
us could create alone. Not a compromise, but an exciting approach that we
both can embrace whole-heartedly.

CLOSING THOUGHTS ON ABUNDANCE

Opportunity is abundant, so abundant that mankind has built four quadrillion dollars of assets in just 5,000 years.

At the beginning of recorded history, about 5,000 years ago, there were essentially no public or private assets. But in the year 2000, the assets on planet Earth were valued at four million trillion dollars, a million times the U.S. federal government's annual budget. That was the estimated replacement cost of private, corporate, and public roads, bridges, buildings, computer and communication systems, shopping malls, factories, airplanes, ships, trucks, cars, and homes.

If opportunities and resources are as scarce as many believe, how did mankind accumulate such mind-boggling abundance in only fifty centuries? The answer is, on average, each generation of men and women built more than was destroyed by natural disasters and wars, and produced more than it consumed. Those of us alive today are the fortunate beneficiary of more opportunities, more resources, and more assets than any previous generation has ever enjoyed.

We begin the relationship economy with abundance almost beyond comprehension. Man's early inventions, like fire and the wheel, were the basis for further inventions and creative applications. Each invention increased the possibility of other inventions until we have today's flood of technologies, machines, business opportunities, and recreational activities. The progression of mankind isn't linear; it's geometric.

Our ancestors gave us a huge gift. However, to whom much is given much is expected. Our obligation is to extend the relationship economy to everyone including, for example, people in Africa, the Dark Continent, who have never tasted prosperity. This is a pragmatic rather than altruistic goal because when more people participate in the world economy, we create more opportunity for our children and grandchildren. It's likely those people will be the next source of low cost labor and new markets. Will we harness our abundant opportunities and resources for the good of all mankind, squander them, or destroy them with the dragons of competition and war that an attitude of scarcity produces?

OPPORTUNITY

Tip #2 – Answer When It Knocks

OVERVIEW

Opportunity rarely knocks loudly at the front door and shouts, "*I'm here!*" It usually enters quietly through a side door appearing to be an unwanted change or a failure. Do you recognize them as opportunities and let them in?

When an unexpected event or change occurs, it's natural to be disappointed, confused, and maybe even a bit angry. You can embrace those dragons if you want to, or you can tame them by looking for opportunities in adverse situations. Instead of cursing a setback or change that you couldn't avoid, be thankful for it. Gratitude will allow you to exploit events and changes that you otherwise might judge to be bad.

The fifteen vignettes in Tip #2 will help you consciously and consistently convert unexpected changes and unfortunate events into business opportunities. They'll enable you to be optimistic no matter what happens, to make the best of every situation, and to recognize alarms as early indications of change. Do that and you will succeed handsomely in the relationship economy.

PASSED OVER

When it seems like the door to opportunity has
been slammed in your face, a new opportunity
is probably just beginning. Look for it.

In grade school, I read every book I could find about the Navy and submarines. Since my dream was to join the Navy and become an admiral, I competed for and won a Navy ROTC scholarship and was commissioned as a naval officer. But after nine years of service, I was passed over for promotion to lieutenant commander, the equivalent of Army major. Nine out of ten officers in my category were promoted. At thirty years of age, the Navy was telling me that I would never be an admiral. I was devastated and didn't know what I would do with my life.

I was promoted the following year, but my career in the Navy was doomed. So I started looking for a job. Westinghouse rejected me at Oak Ridge National Lab, and the accident at Three Mile Island Nuclear Power Plant shut down the civilian nuclear power industry. I didn't see anything else I could possibly do. Desperate, I considered any vacant job near my house, even if it had nothing to do with my credentials.

After three months, relationships came through for me. My boss, a Navy captain, recommended me to a company in Washington for a position that used my education and Navy experience. In that job, I learned to write proposals to government agencies and supervise large contracts. Then I became vice president of a computer company and learned how to manage a small business. Eight years out of the Navy, I started my own company to help government agencies change.

None of the success I enjoyed in business would have been possible if the Navy hadn't passed me over for promotion, although being passed over didn't feel like an opportunity at the time. Opportunity sometimes arrives in packages that we don't like at first glance. My life-changing opportunity was disguised as a devastating failure, and I almost didn't recognize it. I almost threw it away. Don't throw your opportunities away just because they aren't what you expect or want.

CHEAP SHIRTS

When the unexpected happens, as it often does, you can let it set you back or you can fit it into your plan.

On my Saturday morning trip to the shopping center, I noticed a new dry cleaning store advertising: *"Shirts $0.50 Each."* I generally pay $1.50 per shirt at my regular dry cleaner, so I seized the chance and dropped off five dress shirts for laundry, and a suit and three pair of pants for dry cleaning. Later in the day, I saw that my regular dry cleaning store was empty. Apparently, other people were attracted to the new store's low price too. The following Saturday, I picked up my shirts and dry cleaning. But when I wore them, I found the shirts were not starched how I like them and two shirts had pressed-in wrinkles.

On my next visit to the shopping center, my old dry cleaner had a window sign that read: *"We fix shirts that were pressed for $0.50."* I smiled as I walked through the door and gave them my shirts and dry cleaning. Next door at the food store, several people laughed about the ingenious way they regained customers who had problems like mine. My regular dry cleaner discovered a clever way to respond to the price-cutting strategy used by his new competitor. If he had surrendered to the *you-can't-do-that-to-me* dragon and tried to compete on a price basis, he probably would have lost his shirt!

We build a foundation for growth with knowledge-gathering and networking activities. They prepare us for the epiphanies that often occur after what seems to be a negative event. When something changes or goes wrong in your workplace, as it sometimes does, you have the choice to let it be a setback or to fit it into your plans for the future.

On an organizational level, the relationship economy requires you to know your competition as well as you know your own business and to convert that knowledge into opportunity. Snoop around by visiting your competitor's Web site, talking with their employees, or interviewing some of their customers. The things you will find out may be shocking. To discover new perspectives and sharpen your strategy, ask probing questions and make the most of the answers. And do it several times each year.

BELTWAY SNIPERS

Use the power of your expectations wisely.

In October 2002, the Washington area experienced a rampage of fifteen sniper attacks. After the first attack and succeeding attacks, eyewitnesses reported on TV that the single sniper drove a white van. Over three weeks, ten people were shot to death, several others were wounded, and police were swamped with reports of white vans driven by a man with a rifle. When the pair of snipers was arrested, police found they actually drove a blue sedan with the backseat removed to allow one of them to fire the rifle while the car was in motion.

If nobody had seen a white van, why did so many people think they had? How could they see something that never existed? The incident shows the power of expectations. People thought they'd seen a white van because they had heard the news. Expectations of seeing a white van with a sniper became so high that honest, well-intentioned people claimed to have seen what didn't exist.

Expectations are powerful. They affect what you find in the world around you—and what you miss. The phenomenon frequently occurs in the physical realm, but it is also common in the intangible realm of relationships and business opportunities. You will find opportunity when and with whom you expect to find it. Therefore, expectations can be dragons. If you expect opportunities to decline in a changing business world, they will. On the other hand, if you expect to find opportunities, you will. The opportunity or lack of opportunity you find will match your expectations. So your expectations become your reality.

That creates a predictable business cycle: Expectations affect your beliefs, your beliefs cause you to recognize or miss opportunities, the opportunities you find determine your success, success changes your expectations, and so forth. This cycle has always existed, but its periodicity is shorter in the relationship economy since opportunities have short lives. Am I suggesting that you and your organization can achieve success in the relationship economy simply by changing your expectations? Absolutely!

IS THAT OPPORTUNITY KNOCKING?

Things will get better despite our efforts to improve them.
—Will Rogers

A man came to my house to refinish the wood floors. He was founder and president of his company, which was recommended by neighbors. We began talking about the challenges of owning a small business and I asked, *"How did you start your business?"* He said his last employer went bankrupt unexpectedly. One day he had a full slate of jobs and the next day he was unemployed. He said he learned the floor business working with a series of companies, and he decided to transform his misfortune into opportunity. He contacted customers who had recently received price estimates, hired workers who also were unemployed, and he was in business. That event was four years before our meeting. Today his business is thriving.

Opportunity sometimes arrives in ugly packages—for this man it was the bankruptcy of his former employer. Would you call that an opportunity if it happened to you? Too often, the dragons of change make *"Oh no, what now?"* our first reaction to a change. We may be angry about or afraid of the change. The downsizings, reorganizations, and mergers common in today's business environment have left people confused, discouraged, and suspicious. If you let them, those dragons will cause your performance to deteriorate and opportunity to evaporate in your organization. Those dragons also can cause you to miss lucrative business opportunities that are embedded in the change.

It's easier to recognize new opportunities if you are thankful for everything that happens, even the pain and uncertainty of an unwanted change. Instead of judging a change to be good or bad, look at it as an opportunity. Exploit the positive aspects of the change no matter how small or obscure they may be. You set the mood around you by what you say and how you act. What is your attitude toward unexpected changes? Do you consider them to be opportunities or problems? Attitudes are contagious. Is yours worth catching?

WHEN ALARMS RING

A paradox of the relationship economy is that even
victories may be an alarm that things are changing.

My company won a million-dollar government contract in full-and-open competition. It was a sizable contract for us but relatively small by government contracting norms. As the incumbent, we were heavily favored to win the award because of our track record and relationship advantages over the competitors. The companies we beat were IBM, Booz Allen Hamilton, BearingPoint, and two companies that I had never heard of before.

As I enjoyed the victory celebration with our happy proposal team, an alarm went off in my head: *Why are those huge companies bidding against my small company? And how much threat are the two companies I never heard of?* The market for the change management services my company offered was evolving and, until that moment, I had missed the indicators of change. One paradox of the relationship economy is that victories can be an alarm that the world is changing. In my case, both large and small companies were entering my market because the government's budget for change was growing.

Even though you are successful today, that success itself may be a sign of change. There also could be other signs of change in your market, organization, and career that say, *"Be careful, your world is on fire."* Customer complaints, a dip in the number or size of orders, a new competitor, a talented employee who resigns. Each of these is an alarm that may be false or may be real. It's easy to rationalize such results with trite explanations. But what would you lose by treating these indicators as fire alarms, taking a close look at what you are doing, and changing your actions if appropriate?

Maybe you should pay more attention to the subtle alarms in your market. Don't let the *everything's okay* dragon cause you to miss a change or lull you into false security until your world crashes and burns. It's more effective and profitable to lead market change than to chase the leaders while you extinguish organizational fires that were caused by missing a significant change.

DARK MATTER

*You get subtle messages that something is wrong long before
you find a tangible problem. Pay attention to those messages.*

For decades, scientists have known that the laws of gravity discovered by Isaac Newton and updated by Albert Einstein are flawed. The issue is that the universe doesn't contain enough visible matter to generate the gravity required to keep galaxies from flying apart. So scientists hypothesized the existence of a mysterious, undetectable substance they called *dark matter*, even though they couldn't produce *dark matter* in the lab. Recently, scientists studying data from the long-ago collision of two galaxies found indisputable evidence that confirmed the existence of *dark matter* and measured its contribution to the force of gravity.

The relationship economy exhibits many phenomena that can't be explained without the business equivalent of *dark matter*. Ventures succeed that, according to all the old rules, should fail while Fortune 500 companies are having difficult times. That's why a periodic, frank review of your performance and actual results is essential, even though organizations and people never like looking in a mirror.

An effective review must have two parts: a self-assessment and feedback from those who know you. On the self-assessment side, ask your team: (1) *Are we making progress toward our goal?* and (2) *Is the goal what we should be doing?* Get similar feedback from external sources like customers and strategic partners. Don't shut your eyes to potential early alarms by giving into the *I-don't-need-feedback* dragon and refusing to perform a self-assessment or to obtain external feedback.

The alarms should ring if your self-assessment doesn't align with the external feedback. Listen to that alarm, which can go either way. The external feedback sometimes says you are doing better than you think. Most times, you think you're doing fine, but the external feedback says you have challenges. Exploit the opportunities that exist in differences between how you see yourself and how others see you.

SALES PREVENTION TEAM

Whether you're in sales or not, you are. In the relationship economy, you are always selling yourself and your ideas.

I canceled my American Express card after thirty years, and I did the transaction in less than ninety seconds through an automated customer interface. It was the easiest and most productive transaction I had with the company in a long time. It also was an example of technology run amok. I interacted with a computer when I should have worked with someone who could help me. Canceling the card should have been an alarm to company officials, but they missed it. They still have no idea why a thirty-year member would cancel his account, and they are likely to continue the business practices and service offerings that caused me to cancel in the first place. They have very effective sales prevention mechanisms.

In interviewing candidates for positions in my company, including accounting and administration, I asked questions like:

- In your last job, how were you involved in sales?
- How did you help the sales team be successful?
- How can you help expand sales to new and old customers?
- How will you promote the company to your friends and family?

Every candidate must see how they directly affect sales. Since repeat business was 90 percent of revenue, every customer contact must be done in excellence. Our goal was not just to retain a customer; we also wanted them to tell other customers about our excellent service.

You still may say, *"I'm not in sales."* If you believe that self-limiting dragon, an alarm should ring because in the relationship economy you're always selling yourself or your ideas. Look for opportunities to sell. They're often disguised as problems. You are a walking advertisement for the importance of what you do today and what you are capable of doing tomorrow. Why would anyone buy you? If you don't sell yourself, your career and your organization are likely to atrophy and you might be replaced by an automated customer interface. In short, no sales equates to no growth. Don't let yourself be a player on the sales prevention team.

QUIET ALARMS

*The absence of something that's always been present may
be the first alert that a new opportunity is coming your way.*

During the Cold War, submarines were found by detecting the noise they radiated into the ocean. However, today's submarines are so quiet that they create a noise hole. That is, the ocean is unusually quiet when a submarine passes through because the fish leave and ambient fish noises disappear. But an astute sonar operator will sense the presence of a submarine by the reduced noise levels. Similarly, the absence of things normally present in your business world is usually an early indicator that a change is happening—your first alert that new opportunities are coming your way.

For example, today there are fewer small business set-aside competitions in government than just a few years ago. That wasn't a problem for my company, since we didn't compete for set-asides anyway. But the *everything-is-okay* dragon wins when I ignore such phenomenon. What's happening is that the government is bundling multiple projects into new mega-contracts. That makes partnering with other companies more vital for success than ever before.

To assess the "quiet alarms" in your field, make a list of the changes that have occurred over the past two years. The changes may be new technologies, merger mania, former competitors collaborating, reduced or increased demand, high or low unemployment, etc. Those changes indicate how the relationship economy is already affecting your markets. If you ignore those changes and believe that everything will be okay, you may be missing a huge opportunity—or threat.

Label each change on your list as "T" if you view it as a threat to your future success or an "O" if you see it as an opportunity. But the changes themselves don't determine your success; rather your ability to transform "Ts" into "Os" is what will make you successful. If you're successful today, then you have beliefs that are working for you, and you might not be ready to change. But fixed ways of doing business can't work forever in the rapidly changing relationship economy. Get a jump on change by exploiting the "Os" and making the "Ts" into additional "Os."

THANKS FOR THE TICKET

Break the chain-of-events in response to small alarms to prevent disasters that can destroy a business or a career.

D riving home from work one day, I received a speeding ticket on the George Washington Parkway for traveling seventy-two in a fifty-mile-per-hour zone. I was angry about getting the ticket and for being delayed twenty minutes while the police officer went through his routine. As I signed the ticket, he lectured, *"I'm giving you this ticket because I care about you. I hope it increases your awareness of the dangers you face and the responsibility you assume when you drive a car."*

At the time, his statement infuriated me! It obviously was a canned speech. Nobody enjoys getting a speeding ticket, but as I drove home at exactly fifty miles an hour, I thought to myself, *"Maybe he just prevented me from wrecking my car. Maybe he saved my life and other lives, even the life of a child like one of my young grandsons."* I committed myself to pay attention to the alarm the officer had set off, which transformed getting a speeding ticket into a useful experience.

The relentless pace of change in the relationship economy sets off more alarms than ever before. Unfortunately, it's easy to miss or ignore them. You might react defensively when someone tries to help by pointing out a dangerous behavior or a potential risk, and you may get angry about the minor consequences of a small error when you could be grateful for the opportunity it provides to avoid a major disaster.

Of course, you want things to run smoothly, and most of the time you escape minor errors with minor consequences. Then, from nowhere, disaster strikes, and you get angry because the consequences of the error seem incongruous with size of your error. You may have forgotten the small alarms that you missed along the way and the little lessons you ignored until there was a big price to pay. Don't let the dragons of annoyance and anger prevent you from hearing the little alarms and breaking the chain of negative events when the stakes are small.

EIGHT MISTAKES

*You already know what to do about your biggest
challenge. What stops you from doing it?*

D uring a monthly one-to-one with the chairman of my CEO group, it
was obvious to both of us that our lackluster sales growth in changing
markets was a major issue for my company. The chairman asked me
what action I thought would solve the problem. I responded that we needed
a sales manager. He then asked, *"Do you know anyone who can do the job?"*
The dragon of several past failures clouded my thinking: *"I've hired eight sales
managers in my career, and they've all failed to produce. The only person I know
who might be able to do the job is a guy who left the company five years ago."*

The chairman then asked, *"Why don't you call him?"* It was a direct solution, one that I hadn't allowed myself to consider because of my feeling of
failure when he left the company five years earlier. But I called the former
employee later that day, and sixty days later he rejoined the company. In
his first full quarter, sales increased over 20 percent, and he started training
the staff in business development.

I had hired eight people who failed as sales manager, but what had
I learned from those experiences? Instead of embracing those lessons, I
allowed the dragon of past failures to block taking action. My results were
deteriorating and I desperately needed a solution, but I was afraid to fail
again. Actually, I had the opportunity to try again knowing more about
what to look for in an effective sales manager than I had known in any of
the previous eight hiring attempts.

When asked if he made mistakes, Jack Welch, the legendary former CEO
of General Electric, said, *"I could fill a room with them."* So the challenge isn't
whether or not you'll make mistakes in the fast-paced relationship economy.
Mistakes are a natural consequence of taking action. The real challenge is
how much will you learn from your mistakes and how fast will you fix them.
Each mistake you make gives you additional knowledge and experience to
use in your future decisions. Just be sure you learn from your mistakes and
don't repeat them!

SAND TRAPS

When you find yourself in the sand traps of business, the question is: How many strokes will it take to get out?

In a recent golf match, I was two strokes over par after seven holes—a great round of golf for me. On the eighth hole, a par four, my drive was down the middle, but my iron shot caught the sand trap left of the green. *"Not a problem,"* I thought. I'll pop the ball up, let it roll to the hole, and save par. But I took too much sand and my shot didn't clear the top of the trap. My next shot in the trap was more difficult, but I still tried to hit the perfect shot and roll the ball up to the hole. Again I took too much sand. Frustrated on my third shot from the trap, I aimed to the middle of the green, cleared the trap, and two-putted for a triple bogey. Why didn't I do that on my first shot and take a bogey rather than try a spectacular but risky recovery from the sand trap?

The relationship economy offers a variety of sand traps to challenge you. For example, you may face getting out of a:

- *Getting Help* Sand Trap: Your project is having problems. Do you ask for help or quietly try to solve the problem yourself?
- *Relationship* Sand Trap: A customer or co-worker is angry. Do you address the issue or wait for it to blow over?
- *Integrity* Sand Trap: You received the decision you wanted but then found new information. Do you reopen the issue and tell the whole story, or keep quiet and exploit the favorable decision?

These are opportunities to *fix the problem now*. Maybe the solution is less than ideal and even a little embarrassing. Maybe it won't put you where you'd like to be, but at least taking the appropriate action will fix the problem and avoid potentially worse consequences. Chip out of the trap and take your two putts for a bogey!

Dragons will encourage you to eliminate problems by denying that they exist, by making excuses and blaming others, or by taking a convenient but risky way out. In golf, the maxim is: *Don't let one bad shot ruin your whole game*. In other words, don't risk further harm by hoping that the problem will fix itself. Take action to fix it now!

A CROOKED STICK

Opportunities in the relationship economy may not look like you imagine them. Make the best of each opportunity, even if it isn't what you were expecting.

I went into the woods near my house to find a talking stick to use in my men's group. The ideal stick would have been about six feet long, an inch and a half in diameter, and straight. I searched for two hours, but I couldn't find a stick that met my specifications. Without cutting a tree, the sticks that were straight were too short, and those that were the right diameter and length were crooked.

Finally, in frustration, I picked a stick that was about the right length and diameter. It had a nice feel but several severe bends. As I trimmed the dead bark, I concluded that searching for the perfect stick was like searching for opportunity in the relationship economy. I keep looking for the perfect opportunity, but all I find are situations that fall short of my specifications. When I took the stick to the men's group, they fell in love with it despite what I called defects. They said, *"The stick has character. Let's use it!"*

The frustration I felt at not being able to find the perfect stick was the difference between my expectations for the stick and the reality of the sticks available in the woods that day. I wanted to change reality (i.e., find an ideal stick), which was frustrating and unproductive. I tamed the frustration dragon when I changed my expectations to match the sticks that were available in the woods that day.

I'm not suggesting by any means that you reduce your expectations for opportunity in the relationship economy. Quite the contrary, there are many reasons why your expectations should be sky-high. But you may be confronted with business opportunities and career positions that are substantially different than what you expect. Make the best of such situations and don't miss a rewarding new opportunity or advantageous new project just because it doesn't have the precise characteristics you think it should.

TOUGH DAYS

*Making the best of every day, even the tough days, will put
you way ahead of most people in the relationship economy.*

One day, I had a particularly tough time at work. I participated in three back-to-back meetings that failed to accomplish their objectives. The profit on the previous month's income statement was half of what I had expected. I signed a termination agreement with a senior employee that we shouldn't have hired in the first place. And we were notified that we lost a multi-year contract I expected to win. The twin dragons of disappointment and loss raged inside me. It was challenging to look at those developments as opportunities, let alone make something positive of them.

This particular day may have been a little unusual but the truth is such days occur all too often. There are five things I do to tame my frustrations on days like this, and they might help you to tame your dragons too:

- *Slow down* and enjoy each task that you do instead of rushing to finish everything on your work list.
- *Congratulate co-workers* who make a difference in the company or your life. Tell them how much you appreciate what they do.
- *Encourage the people around you*, especially those who face a challenging project or have experienced a recent setback.
- *Assign tasks that workers will enjoy* and explain how the tasks will benefit their careers and be important to the company.
- *Work on a project you like* and ignore tasks on your work list that you hate doing. Indulge in a little procrastination.

Besides improving your organization or project, these attitude shifts also will increase your productivity and bring peace into your life.

The tempo of the relationship economy sometimes seems like a Monday-through-Friday string of tough days, and it may carry over into the weekends too. It's easy to get tangled in the relentless barrage of tasks that you must do, and be disappointed when the results and appreciation are less than you expect. But success lies in making the best of each day, especially the tough ones.

BEANIE BABIES

Resiliency in the face of disappointing setbacks and unwanted changes is essential in long-term success.

A friend of mine sold Beanie Babies as a hobby to earn extra cash. One weekend, he participated in a fair in Virginia and lost money. The fair was poorly advertised, attendance was down, and there were fewer competing Beanie Baby vendors than usual. It was his third weekend fair in a row where his sales didn't cover the costs of the fair and a night in a hotel. Where was the opportunity in this deteriorating market?

When we discussed his result, he said, *"Beanie Babies are past their peak."* It was hard for him to acknowledge that, especially since he owned hundreds of Beanie Babies. But in doing so, he had tamed a dragon and started to change. It was the first time he faced the new reality: Selling Beanie Babies at fairs was no longer a profitable business. He didn't curse his misfortune; instead, he was thankful for the new insight and unexpected tax write-offs.

In the relationship economy, changes like the decline in the popularity of Beanie Babies are common. While my friend mourned the lost of the extra income, he learned a valuable lesson and sold his remaining Beanie Babies profitably over the Internet at lower prices and lower overhead. If you are resilient, changes that initially appear to be failures can easily be turned into successes. You can do this in the relationship economy by:

- Recognizing changes in the environment around you;
- Getting over them quickly—taming the dragon of loss;
- Being willing, even eager, to try something different;
- Keeping the solution simple and focused on your goals; and
- Being accountable to yourself for both your old and new results.

What is the most significant challenge you face today? In what area of your professional life are your results considerably less than you'd like them to be? Those areas require resiliency. They require you to look at things differently and change your approach to achieve greater success in the future.

CLOSING THOUGHTS ON OPPORTUNITY

When the business world gives you lemons, make lemonade.
Cultivate the ability to transform problems into opportunities.

At a critical point in the growth of my company, a key manager who also was our most productive salesman quit. I was shocked by the loss and worried about the future. I thought, *"How will we ever replace him?"* The other executives felt the same. Grief and concern were etched on their faces. As the leader of the company, I needed to tame my dragons and guide the team past the loss and toward future success.

I went to the grocery store, bought three lemons, and with a red felt-tipped pen marked them: *shock, loss,* and *worry.* During our next staff meeting, I tossed a lemon to each of the three remaining key managers with the invitation *"Let's make lemonade."* With a positive rather than defeatist attitude, we formed a relationship with the departing employee's new company. He became the sales manager for a software product that we marketed. The new relationship worked because he knew our capabilities, and we knew him well. His leaving actually created an opportunity that hadn't existed before.

Think of the most lucrative professional opportunities you've experienced. If you're like me, you will find that those opportunities either grew: (1) by chance when a situation worked out differently than you expected, or (2) by pursuing an innovative solution to what initially looked like a major problem. Remember those opportunities the next time that something doesn't work out the way you wanted or you discover an unexpected new challenge. Make the new challenge into an opportunity.

Time, energy, and creativity aren't like other resources. If you don't use them today, they're gone forever. Each day, ask yourself, *"How will I spend my time, energy, and creativity?"* Don't focus on the past by rehashing history. Instead, live in the present by finding future opportunities even as you resolve today's problems. When life gives you lemons, make lemonade for you and your team.

INVESTMENTS

Tip #3 – Pay It Forward

OVERVIEW

When you invest, you defer current consumption in order to increase future consumption. The consumption might involve resources, time, or even relationships. For example, consider a loan. When I loan you money, I forego today's consumption to increase my consumption when you repay the loan. Conversely, you increase today's consumption but reduce future consumption when you repay the loan with interest. Investments involve risk (you may not repay the loan), so the art of investing is balancing risk with reward. Consuming today also has risks.

Your consumption level today is the result of investments you made or didn't make in the past. So the vignettes in Tip #3 encourage you to take long shots in addition to conservative investments, to consider the changing rules of the relationship economy in investments, and to invest in yourself (you already have the only body you'll ever get). By "paying it forward" to build relationships, increase your knowledge, and strengthen your organization, you are building the probability of higher future consumption levels!

FEEDING THE CALVES

*Continuously feed the calves (new ideas) that could be
a source of tomorrow's success, even as you enjoy the
milk from the cows that produce today's successes.*

I worked on a dairy farm as a teenager. My job was to round up the cows, herd them into the barn, and help with milking. While we attached milking machines to the cows, the farm's owner spent his time feeding the calves rather than working with the cows or the lone bull. I asked him why, and he said, *"These calves are my future. You milk the cows while I invest in the future."* His point is particularly relevant today in the relationship economy.

Individually and as leaders of organizations, our natural tendency is to protect and expand today's success: We *milk the cows* but often neglect the calves. Most organizations train and incentivize their people to improve today's results. For the most part, everyone in business and government— from executives to administrative and accounting personnel—performs tasks whose purpose is to improve today's results. It is difficult to divert time and resources away from practices and products that produced yesterday's success in order to risk investing in practices and products for the future.

Since the life span of success in the relationship economy is shorter than ever, you must continuously identify and nurture ideas that can be the source of tomorrow's breakaway success, even as you milk the products and services that are producing today's success. It is prudent to divert a small portion of your attention each day to invest in the future.

Make no mistake about it: Delegating today's tasks so you can focus on tomorrow is easier said than done. The urgency dragon will draw you away from tomorrow and warn you not to divert resources and mindshare from today's success to untested ventures that may prove to be worthless. Do you have the extraordinary discipline and creativity required to invest in tomorrow's success when it might compromise today's success?

WIN A LOTTERY

Try things that will make your biggest dream come true.

The odds are 156 million to one in the Mega-Millions lottery game, which I play every now and then. I won $600 once by matching four of the six numbers. Just two numbers away from the big jackpot, which I wished I had won. Wouldn't it be nice if we could achieve our biggest goals just by wishing for them? Wish for a blockbuster new product, an exciting promotion, or a market-sweeping acquisition and *POOF* they happen. But wishing isn't enough. Investments and risk-taking are required.

To win the prize you want, you must risk buying tickets in a lottery that will deliver that prize. Consider the following lotteries that many people want to win:

- The ***Take-an-Idea-to-Market*** Lottery. An innovative service, gadget, or product. The cost of a lottery ticket is believing in a crazy idea, and working day and night to sell it.

- The ***Invest-in-a-Startup-Company*** Lottery. Maybe you already work for a small company, or you know one that could be the next Google. The cost of a lottery ticket is passionately investing your time, effort, and cash in that small company.

- The ***Start-Your-Own-Business*** Lottery. The cost of a lottery ticket is taking a cut in pay, risking your savings, and leaving no stone unturned in the search to find and satisfy customers.

- The ***Write-a-Best-Seller*** Lottery. The cost of a lottery ticket is endless hours of writing and editing. And when the book is ready to publish, you also invest endless more hours to market it.

Are you investing in lotteries like these? Like a conventional lottery, you can't win the prize unless you buy the tickets!

The relationship economy is a gigantic collection of lotteries. But the *risk-aversion* dragon in your head will tell you that investing in them is too big a risk. But you'll never hear words like those from a successful entrepreneur. If you aren't buying tickets in high-reward lotteries, then you aren't giving yourself a chance to win the big prize you really want. What success lottery do you want to win? Are you investing in tickets for that lottery?

THE PRODUCT LOCATOR

A missed investment in the relationship economy is a missed opportunity, but it happens faster than in the industrial age!

In 1938, Chester Carlson invented and patented xerography, but he couldn't find investors for his idea. IBM turned him down because they thought the process would replace carbon paper, a small market. Finally, eight years later, the Haloid Company, which later became the Xerox Corporation, took a risk and bought rights to Carlson's patent. The company released its first photocopier in 1958 and, by 1965, had over $500 million in annual revenue. Needless to say, by saying *NO* to Carlson, IBM missed a lucrative opportunity. Are you saying *NO* to the Xerox opportunity of your career?

I did. In 1992, when the Internet was young, my company won a Defense Department research contract to develop software dubbed the *Product Locator*. The *Product Locator* retrieved maintenance manuals, parts lists, and inventory data for military systems without users knowing where the data was stored. Our Google-like *Product Locator* used screen sweeps to retrieve data from remote systems and present it to users. It worked! We owned rights to commercialize the software but didn't invest to take the product to market. If we had, by the year 2000 our company may have become what Google is today.

The *take-the-first-step* dragon made me cautious, which was a good thing. I looked at several possibilities. But one seemed too hard, another cost too much, and a third took too long. I didn't get any help because my vision was limited to what my company could do alone—another dragon! If we had taken the risk, the likely reaction to our first try would have been: *"That's ugly!"* So we'd get help and work on it more. The second try would have been better, but still not what we wanted. Finally, on about the third try these things usually begin to look pretty good. But I didn't tame the dragons and take the first step.

Invest in success by pursuing a risky opportunity. Often you'll find the investment takes more time than money. Reluctance to take a long shot may be what is keeping you and your organization stagnant. Ask yourself: *What risk must I take to achieve my biggest goal?*

FANTASYLAND

*The relationship economy offers a fantasyland
of possibilities, so invest to create a clear vision of
your success and the path you'll take to get there.*

L egend says that Walt Disney insisted on building the Fantasyland castle first when constructing the original Disneyland theme park in southern California. His project manager, architects, and construction schedulers all said that approach would take longer and be much more expensive. But he insisted: *"I want everyone who is building this park to see that castle all day, every day, so they will understand why they work here."* Walt Disney invested the funds to build the castle first, and his strategy paid off in the daily motivation the castle provided to accelerate construction of the multi-faceted theme park.

A portion of your investments, especially time investments, should be in intangibles like the magical image of a Fantasyland castle. Such investments create a stimulating vision of the future to guide your team's daily decisions and actions. The investments may take the form of off-site meetings to help your staff understand the goals, the strategy, and the contribution expected from each of them. That focus provides context and creates the passion needed to conquer the challenges and persevere through the setbacks that will inevitably occur along the path to success.

Teams do their best work when they can see what they are working toward. Therefore, leaders who articulate a clear vision for tomorrow accelerate the climb to the top of the success ladder. What is the vision of your Fantasyland in the relationship economy? If you don't have one, invest the time and effort to find one. Start by critically examining your current relationships with customers, competitors, co-workers, and suppliers. Ask yourself how you could take those relationships to a whole new level. Walt Disney gave us more than an entertaining collection of theme parks and movies. He also gave us an example of how to take visionary risks to succeed.

CHOICES

Your success is a series of choices, one after the other.
Your choices can be based on comfort, safety, or growth,
but the relationship economy favors decisions for growth.

On his last day, an employee stopped by my office to thank me for the advice I had given him three years earlier when he started with the company. He reminded me that I suggested he invest in company stock as *"the best savings account you'll ever open."* He said: *"When I heard your recommendation, I didn't want to invest. But today I'll cash-in over $100,000 in stock. I invested $16,000 over the last three years. That's a six-to-one return! Now my wife and I will buy a house when we move."* He added that the payroll deductions were a lifestyle change. He had purchased a Ford Escort instead of the BMW he really wanted in order to afford to buy stock. His choice was to invest in growth, albeit a somewhat risky choice.

Success is a series of choices, each new choice building on the previous choices. The choices may be influenced by the dragons of:

- Fear—which encourages you make *safe* choices,
- Comfort—which persuades you to make easy choices, and
- Self-indulgence—which allows you to make extravagant choices.

There also are choices to invest in growth, which often feel risky and uncomfortable. Making the choice to invest in growth (instead of fear, comfort, or self-indulgence choices) will move you steadily toward success in the relationship economy.

The relationship economy generously rewards choices for growth and penalizes decisions based on fear, comfort, and self-indulgence. Frequently, choices for growth involve risk, and success for such choices is never guaranteed. However, in the long run, successive choices for growth bring you into contact with new opportunities and new relationships. Are you stretching to invest in growth for you and your organization?

LESSONS

*Valuable lessons are everywhere. Some tell you
what to do and others tell you what not to do.*

During the late 1970s, I was vice president of a small company that provided accounting systems for home builders. Most of the time, we went to their offices and installed the first computer system that their staff ever used. During my two years with the company, I learned many valuable lessons about accounting, budgeting, cash flow, sales, project management, and people. It was an employee-owned company that went bankrupt shortly after I left. I lost the $30,000 that I invested in stock, but I learned a lot. At the time, I had no idea I would start my own company. But when I did the lessons were worth way more than the money I lost. It was a good investment after all!

The Certified Public Accountant (CPA) on our staff took me under his wing and taught me accounting. I was surprised but grateful for the time he spent mentoring me, even though we weren't friendly outside the office. I'll never forget the day he yelled at me because I said that I looked at debits as positive and credits as negative. He said, *"No! Erase those damned engineering concepts from your head!"* I listened because I wanted to learn how a business should be operated financially. He taught me the importance of attention-to-detail and a reliable accounting cycle by saying repeatedly, *"Routine things must happen routinely!"* Those lessons alone were worth $30,000!

Are you absorbing the lessons that are all around you today in your workplace and in many of your social activities? You may never start your own company, but the lessons will be invaluable in your future opportunities. Some lessons will be positive (*what to do*), and others will be negative (*what not to do*). Tame the dragon that curses the negative lessons, because those lessons are often the most valuable of all. For example, understanding what caused that small company to go bankrupt (lack of budgeting process and mismanaging cash) was possibly the most valuable lesson I've ever learned—and it only cost $30,000, about the same as year of college tuition.

FREE AGENTS

The relationship economy has changed the rules. Among the most fundamental changes is that everyone is a free agent, free to pursue the most attractive opportunities.

After an absence of eleven years, Joe Gibbs returned as head coach of the Washington Redskins for the 2004 season. But the NFL's rules had changed since Gibbs retired and built a successful NASCAR team. Defenses were more complex and pass patterns more intricate. People wondered if Gibbs could adapt to the new complexities and rule changes fast enough to win the Super Bowl during his five-year contract. The most significant rule change of all was free agency, a major change in team-player relationships. The Redskins signed many expensive free agents, but Coach Gibbs wasn't able to build the team chemistry that produced three Super Bowls. The Redskins struggled to reach the playoffs twice in his first four years, but he resigned before the fifth season without a Super Bowl victory.

The rules of the relationship economy are like free agency in the NFL. You are a free agent; I am a free agent; and our customers, colleagues, and suppliers are free agents too. Last year's strategy may have worked well enough to get you to the business equivalent of the Super Bowl. But new investments in relationships are necessary today to achieve continuing success. Look at relationship rules differently than you did in the past. As the coach of your career and organization, you must adjust to the free agent nature of the relationship economy or risk being disappointed in your future results.

The keystone rule for success in the relationship economy is that you must build relationships with free agents around the world so they trust you in future transactions. Pay it forward by caring about your partner's success and meeting your commitments in every transaction. Tame the *what-have-you-done-for-me-lately* dragon that tempts you to extract the last ounce of gain from each transaction. The more giving you are, the more your relationship partners will trust and value you. They will look at you the same way you look at them and say, *"I know I can count on her in this transaction."*

THE CHANGING RULES

An impressive resume is vital in the relationship economy, but your synergistic relationships and unique knowledge will determine your success.

Iinterviewed a highly qualified candidate for a senior position. He had a record of setting and achieving goals, and his credentials were flawless: Dean's List at a top university, master's degree earned at night, and important assignments at other consulting companies. He assumed that his resume put him on the inside track for management, and he thought that he was ready. What he didn't understand was that credentials are the price of entry in the relationship economy, not a guarantee for success. His weakness was that he had not invested in building relationships or acquiring new knowledge.

He was interviewing because his prior company was sold to a larger firm. He found himself competing for his old job against people who could do that job for a lower salary. That wasn't a contest his ego dragon would let him fight. Even with an impressive resume, he lost his job to someone who was less qualified on paper. It was a mystery to him how that happened, and he didn't understand when I explained it. In the end, we didn't hire him because he lacked client contacts and unique knowledge that would justify the high salary he wanted.

Relative to your current job, ask yourself: *"Would my boss hire me today if I interviewed for this job? Do I provide my organization with unique knowledge and relationships? Do I produce results?"* If your answer is NO, you may be spending too much time "doing" your job and not enough time investing to expand your knowledge base and nurture new relationships. On the other hand, maybe you should begin looking for a new organization now if your position "still has a year or two left." Coasting in a dying position will leave you way behind the market. We live in a time when knowledge and relationships are more valuable than seniority or advanced degrees. For some, that is great news. For others, it is an unwelcome change in the old rules. Are you adapting to the changing rules of the relationship economy?

THE BEST AX MEN

*Enduring success accrues to those who create change
or lead the implementation of change in their industries.*

Cavemen invented the ax in prehistoric times to cut down trees for firewood. The best ax men got the firewood they needed with the least effort. Over the centuries, the durability and cutting power of the ax improved immensely. When men began to build houses from logs, the ax became a vital tool in construction. The best ax men had the nicest homes and were the highest paid in their trade.

Then the chainsaw was invented. The axes in use at the time were the best in history and the first chainsaws were unreliable. Some of the best ax men ridiculed the chainsaw and refused to use it. The *I'm-the-best* dragon left them unwilling to change. But after a while, even the best couldn't earn a living with an ax. Men who might have been mediocre with an ax but were adept at using a chainsaw became the leaders of the logging industry.

Today's relentless technological advances are transforming industries as severely as the chainsaw changed logging—the auto industry, travel, textiles, computers, and pharmaceuticals to name a few. (Cobol programmers and Banyan network technicians are the axmen of the computer industry, for example.) Old ways of thinking in these industries still work, maybe better than ever. But it's just a matter of time until the "best ax men" in these industries who delay investing in new techniques and offerings go out of business.

Change is inevitable in every industry, including yours. A radical change usually begins with a new tool, a new technique, or a new product that seems cumbersome or strange at first. When you see such changes in your industry, remember these tips:

- Investigate and pursue the opportunities presented by change;
- Remain flexible as the change matures;
- Be the source of creativity and support for the change agents; and
- Proactively lead change within your organization and industry.

You may think you're among the best ax men in your industry today, but tame the *I'm-the-best* dragon in order to continue your success.

SATELLITE REPAIRS

Know when to hold 'em, and know when to fold 'em.
—Song by Kenny Rogers

In 2006, NASA reversed a 2004 decision and said that it will launch astronauts to repair and upgrade the Hubble Space Telescope in 2008. The repair team will conduct several spacewalks to enable Hubble, first launched in 1990, to continue recording images until the new telescope is launched in 2013. Officials said that 40 percent of NASA's scientific discoveries over the past sixteen years are credited to Hubble. Maryland's congressmen pushed the repair mission since the Hubble program supports about 1,000 Maryland jobs.

Eventually, everything becomes obsolete. Governments ignore this fact more frequently than businesses. Government's reluctance to end programs is a dragon that, despite tax increases, ensures there will never be enough funding for vital new projects. Business leaders are falling into the same trap when they react to poor results by investing more in old product lines (like Hubble repairs) instead of applying the resources to accelerate change. But since businesses can't tolerate mediocre results for long and still stay in business, they generally end failing programs faster than governments. All organizations must increase their willingness to abandon the old to survive and grow in the relationship economy.

One key to success in the relationship economy is *knowing when to fold 'em*, as Kenny Rogers sang in his hit song titled "The Gambler." Resources, especially creative minds, are so scarce that you must invest them in tomorrow's opportunities. The resources to build tomorrow can only be found by de-emphasizing projects that are declining today. Organizations that don't invest in tomorrow will be overrun quickly by those that do. Don't be among the organizations that are unwilling to let go of past successes and, as a result, can't find resources to invest. Reduce the resources and brainpower consumed by current successes in order to invest in new opportunities and new relationships for tomorrow.

THE VIKINGS ARE CHANGING

The future is already happening. Are you
seeing and exploiting the new possibilities?

A VISA television ad shows Viking warriors dressed in battle gear pillaging credit card holders to steal their identities. According to the ad, VISA's security features have put the Vikings out of business and forced them to find new work. The ad concludes by showing the Vikings, still in full battle gear, selling Christmas trees and ringing the bell for the Salvation Army.

Many people follow the old career paradigm of building skills in their current industry. That approach served our grandfathers well when industries evolved slowly, and it helped them survive economic ups and downs. But that paradigm is a dragon in a world that changes quickly. Technology has transformed some industries and eliminated others. Adding skills to meet short-term changes in your field can be a death spiral. On the other hand, investing to expand your knowledge in adjacent areas will add to your success. It's the only approach that prepares you to exploit changes in the next ten years that are projected to be twice as significant as changes during the last ten years.

With change becoming a routine part of business, predicting the future is a popular pastime. We celebrate predictions that come true but don't spend enough time analyzing life-altering changes that we miss. For example, how could we have anticipated the collapse of the housing market or astronomical rise in oil prices that seem to have caught us by surprise? Predictions are useful only if we apply them to alter our direction, hopefully in advance of the change.

The future is already happening. I won't attempt to predict any specific changes since they'll be history (or not) by the time you read this. But you can be sure the future will have economic shifts (could it be a meteoric fall in oil prices?), demographic shifts (e.g., the growing influence of baby boomers), and new technologies. How will trends like these change your workplace? Invest resources in opportunities in those areas to ensure your future success.

THE KING

Your health is your most valuable asset. Are you investing wisely to care for that asset? Are you investing in health care as a business opportunity?

Elvis Presley, known as the "King of Rock and Roll," died in August 1977 at his Graceland Mansion of heart failure caused by prescription drug abuse. He was forty-two years old. For months the world mourned his passing, and we still enjoy his hit songs today. I will never forget his first electrifying appearance in 1956 on *The Ed Sullivan Show*. I was eleven and wanted to be like Elvis. But if I had lived like he did, I would have been dead for twenty years now. Health is an irreplaceable asset; therefore, preserving your health must be a high-priority investment. It's very difficult to succeed in the relationship economy or to help your family if you are unhealthy. Without health, success is empty.

Taking care of yourself is more than just eating healthy; exercising; and avoiding drugs, alcohol, and smoking. It also requires you to take out the garbage in your life. That is, eliminate activities that cause anger, stress, and sleepless nights because they sap energy and degrade performance. What investments have you made recently in your health and well-being? Have you kept a New Year's resolution about dieting or exercise? Have you had an annual physical? Have you eliminated unhealthy stresses from your daily routine? Do your friends and family members tell you how healthy you look?

Technologies and philosophies for healthy living are plentiful in the relationship economy, but you'll benefit from them only when you use them. Health care programs may be expensive, but they're effective in preventing disease, detecting life-threatening illness early, and treating chronic injuries. Also meditation, tai chi, yoga, Pilates, and reading for relaxation are investments that bring balance into your life. You are your future. Live it in good health, balance, and success—maybe even by investing in an opportunity in the health care field.

CLOSING THOUGHTS ON INVESTMENTS

To multiply your future prosperity, invest part of your current consumption in a relationship economy opportunity.

Starting a company was the most risky investment I've ever made. It was a long shot, since statistics show that roughly one in ten companies survive the first five years. The investment was a drop in my income. My salary was half what I was paid by the large aerospace firm where I had been a director, and I gave up a company car and valuable stock options. My W2 for the first year with my company was less than half of my last year at the aerospace company. I worked tirelessly to make the long shot come through and, after twenty-two years of work, I sold my company stock. I could not have reached the success that I enjoy today without reducing my current consumption to invest in the future.

Many people have jobs that lock them into golden handcuffs of salary, bonuses, and benefits. Oh sure, they receive annual raises and other perks; and every few years they may switch companies to increase their responsibility. But working for someone else creates comfort and fear dragons that grow as income grows: comfort with how things are today and fear that you might fail to improve them. Those dragons prevent many people from taking a long shot to invest in the opportunities of the relationship economy.

You have an image of how successful you are today. You might be generally satisfied but would like to advance to a much better place in the future. Logically, you know that you must stretch to get there, but emotional resistance (the comfort and fear dragons) may stop you from risking a long shot. However, your future success will be proportional to the stretch you take today. The reward of stretching is more than just tomorrow's success. Stretching also provides the satisfaction of conquering a challenge, engenders optimism about the future, and makes you a leader in the relationship economy. Are you stretching today for the success you want tomorrow? Is it a long shot?

Part II

RELATIONSHIPS

Building Blocks of Success

OVERVIEW

Your value in the relationship economy is the concepts you understand, the things you stand for, your relationships, and your ability to work with others. If all you do in your career is take what you can get from your company and colleagues, your success is likely to be mediocre. On the other hand, your bosses, customers, colleagues, and competitors will value you highly if they see that you don't expect immediate *quid pro quo* for your help and contributions. By consistently building synergistic relationships and expanding your knowledge, when you move to a new position your value to your new company or team will be very high because you bring valuable allies from your previous positions.

Whether your specialty is management, service, research, sales, or administration, the quality of your relationships will determine the magnitude of your success. The six vignettes in this introduction to Part II: Relationships show you how to build organizational and professional relationships that are effective and enduring. These vignettes are followed by three tips that are essential to success in the relationship economy:

Tip #4 **Communications** *– Get Your Message Across*
Tip #5 **Diversity** *– Embrace Diversity to Expand Creativity*
Tip #6 **Collaboration** *– Collaborate, Collaborate, Collaborate*

ESTABLISHING RELATIONSHIP

You can achieve any goal you set, but not by yourself. The bigger the goal, the more relationships you'll need to reach it.

At a couples' retreat, the guest speaker taught a simple way to form a relationship with someone that you meet for the very first time. Begin the conversation with the stranger by asking, *"Hi. I'm curious,"* followed by five basic questions:

(1) *Where are you from originally?*

(2) *Have you lived there all your life? Why did you leave?*
   (Travel version of question (2): *What brought you here?*)

(3) *Do you have a family?*

(4) *What do you do?*

(5) *What was your dream when you were growing up?*

The next day, our group was riding on the resort bus when our guest speaker used the technique with a woman and her husband. After the third question, the woman said to our speaker, *"I'm a psychologist. You're trying to establish a relationship with me, aren't you?"* We all laughed heartily but saw how our speaker had successfully used these questions to begin a relationship with the couple.

You probably know the answers to these questions for family members and close friends, but do you know the answers for your co-workers, strategic partners, and major customers—people on whom you depend for your success?

The ability to build relationships is essential for success in the relationship economy. You can achieve any goal you set, but you can't do it alone. The bigger your goal, the more relationships you will need to achieve it. Therefore, the number and quality of relationships with co-workers, suppliers, customers, and competitors set a ceiling on your future success. In the industrial age, success could be sustained with relatively few effective relationships. But today many more relationships are required to succeed because the world of business is more complex and dynamic.

The only skill more vital in the relationship economy than an ability to build new relationships is an ability to preserve your old ones. Competition for new relationships is intense, and if you don't provide value to your existing relationship partners, they have many other people they can turn to instead. In the industrial age, we had to deal with local merchants who sold mediocre products or services, were hard to work with, or were unethical. However, the connected relationship economy eliminates such vendors in two ways. First, the Internet makes it easy to buy quality products and services at fair prices from distant suppliers. A new business partner is just a mouse-click away. Second, reputation spreads quickly across the Internet. The Internet is to business what the telegraph was to law enforcement in the 1800s. Everyone finds out about the bad guys pretty quickly.

Fortunately, relationships are more plentiful than ever. Just six degrees of relationship separate the seven billion people on Earth—that is, the people I know (first degree) know people (second degree) who know still other people (third degree), and so forth. By the sixth degree, I'm connected to everybody on Earth. In the industrial age, most people connected only at the first degree: typically one hundred relationships. On the contrary, the Warren Buffets, Bill Gates, and Oprah Winfreys of the world are connecting at the second and third degrees: more than one hundred times one hundred relationships! Today, global communications enable everyday people to connect at the second degree. The most successful people will often connect at the third degree. That's a lot of relationships!

> The only skill more vital for success than an ability to build new relationships is an ability to preserve your old relationships.

Building and maintaining relationships in the relationship economy demand new skills because communications devices are so different than what was available in the industrial age. The excuse *"I was busy and didn't have time to call"* isn't acceptable since there are so many ways to connect. E-mails, instant messaging, and cell phones are replacing time-consuming face-to-face meetings, and encryption keys and biometric controls have allowed digital signatures to replace written signatures on even the most sensitive legal documents. Your top business priority today is to use multiple media to expand your relationships in every dimension: company-to-company, company-to-people, government-to-government, government-to-people, and people-to-people.

SHIFT IN POWER

*The relationship between government and industry is changing
to address global challenges more efficiently and effectively.*

A government executive whom I have known for many years became executive director of a government agency whose annual budget is as large as that of a Fortune 100 company. A week before taking the new position, he asked two industry advisors and myself to suggest actions he might take during his first hundred days in the new job. I was honored by his request and worked hard to deliver my best thinking. I'm sure the other two advisors did the same. His request produced fresh insights on his new job, closer relationships, and a shared commitment to success between industry and government. The three of us as advisors had a vested interest in ensuring the strategies we recommended worked.

The relationship between government and industry is shifting to address society's major challenges more efficiently and effectively. Consider the social power that today's big businesses exercise in their worldwide supply chains: Starbucks for coffee suppliers, McDonald's for fish and beef suppliers, and Wal-Mart for consumer product suppliers. These corporate giants have power that rivals governments, and they are more effective at exercising it. They can—and often do—demand ethical practices, workplace safety, and environmental protection measures from companies in their supply chains.

Government can achieve social change faster by working with industry through win-win relationships than through new regulations. Unfortunately, the memory of abusive practices by industry in the past is a dragon that impedes new government-industry partnerships. To be sure, the move toward social consciousness by business has been uneven across industries and inconsistent among companies in the same industry. Nevertheless, mega-companies like General Electric and Wal-Mart, for example, are intensely conscious of and responsive to the voice of the communities in which they operate. If you're in industry, be patient with government agencies while they tame the mistrust dragon. If you're in government, look for ways to work more closely with industry—it could be a solution to your budget shortfalls.

FIRST IMPRESSIONS

You only get one chance to make a first impression.
—Old cliché that's even more applicable today

The day after his interview at my company, a candidate sent me a handwritten note that said:

Thanks for spending part of your "Friday" with me. I value the insights you shared, as well as the chance to swap stories. I think your company delivers significant value not only to current clients but also to future clients and the team as well. I'm looking forward to the opportunity to join the team!

We hired him and he quickly became an outstanding contributor to the client service team and the company's management team.

I wondered why I was so impressed with his note. Such notes are a standard practice. However, this one had a big impact on me: I felt understood. His reference to "Friday," even though the interview took place on Wednesday, recognized that I was in semi-retirement working three days a week. His statement about meaningful service showed he put the client first, and his reference to future clients indicated that he was prepared to help expand the company. That's a whole lot of understanding in such a short note!

First meetings plow the ground for new relationships. Most weeks, I have several meetings with someone new or to introduce two people so they can explore shared interests. I prepare thoroughly so I know what might be important to each potential partner. I visit their companies' Web sites and Google their names. I assume they have the same goal as me, so I provide background information about myself. In short, I prepare the ground to receive a relationship seed.

A valueless first meeting is a relationship killer, since there usually isn't a second meeting. I'm always punctual because nothing makes a worst first impression than being late. I start most meetings by asking, *"What are you looking for?"* to validate the opportunities and contacts I think my partner might want. Soon the conversation should shift to how they can help me. If it doesn't, I mentally begin preparing for the next partner. You only get one chance to make a good first impression.

HANDLES LIKE A PORSCHE

In the relationship economy, most of you will work with an organization, but NOT always as an employee of that organization.

I provided consulting services to a CEO whose passion was racing his red Porsche. Frustrated at his senior staff one day, he yelled, *"Why can't they be like a Porsche? Step on the gas, and they go faster. Step on the brakes, and they stop. Turn the steering wheel, and they go in a new direction."* I responded, *"Your Porsche obeys the laws of physics, but your staff responds to more complex stimuli. They have families. They have dreams. They may even have health worries. How dedicated are they to your company?"* A minute of silence followed my remarks. He had an epiphany. He saw how he treated his staff like objects that were expected to react to commands instantly and without questions, like his Porsche.

The attitude of workers toward employers, always fragile and skeptical, is changing radically in the relationship economy. Workers now see themselves as independent agents who are free to move from job to job searching for an organization that will use and expand their potential. Statistics show the number of 1099-employees (independent consultants) has more than doubled in the last three years. That trend isn't widely recognized in companies or reported in the media. For the most part, managers continue to hire workers based on their education and experience, and promote them based on seniority and loyalty.

The attitude of employers toward workers also is changing. Managers claim that *"people are our most precious asset,"* but their frustrations increase with endless employee demands for pay raises, more benefits, and less hours. Why would a company hire employees when they can hire pay-for-performance 1099-workers or offshore the work? Some companies have modified their business models to dip into the growing pool of skilled free agents to staff their most urgent and vital projects. Some employers would rather pay a consultant $100 per hour (about $200,000 a year) with no benefits than pay an employee an annual salary of $100,000 but have the headaches that go with the expectations of a full-time employee.

The parent-child dependency between employers and workers that existed in the industrial age is dying in the relationship economy. That old-fashioned management paradigm is a dragon that produces unrealistic expectations and devalues workers. Today's workers aren't content to be merely cogs in the wheels of business. They expect to have pride in the results they produce, going home every night with a real sense of accomplishment.

Success in the industrial age was driven by productivity, that is output per hour or resource unit. Management worked tirelessly to measure and improve productivity through process improvements, computer controls, and new machinery. However, in the relationship economy, productivity is the result of relationships. If you know the right people, you will reach your goals faster than competitors who might have newer technologies and streamlined processes but lack the essential relationships.

Today's employer-worker relationships are still partnerships rooted in loyalty, but the loyalty is an interdependency based on common goals and shared accountability for results. Most free agent workers enthusiastically tackle big challenges, and they accept a large stake in the outcome because tomorrow's paycheck depends on today's results. Since they often work on teams that exist only long enough to complete a single project, the results of those short-term projects are their resume and their reputation.

> **Workers depended on employers in the industrial age, but they are free agents in the relationship economy.**

Today's business priority is forming and maintaining valuable relationships. If you are leading an organization, ensure that your team focuses on increasing the quality and quantity of their relationships. You should be selecting your team members based on what and who they know, and the unique value they will deliver to your projects. If you're a talented worker in the relationship economy, don't depend on a company like your father may have in the industrial age. Free agent workers must bring relevant tools and relationships to the job every day, especially if you want to drive a red (or any other color) Porsche.

BEATING THE SLAVES

When your relationships work, you easily solve any problem.
When your relationships aren't working, that IS the problem.

About thirty minutes into the first day of a two-day seminar, a hotel server entered the meeting room quietly to refresh our coffee, fruit, juices, and croissants. The speaker interrupted his talk, walked up to her, and said:

> *"I'd like to introduce Debra. She works at the hotel to pay for nursing school and expects to graduate this June. Please give Debra a hand for helping our workshop be successful."*

We applauded and continued the workshop. Over the next two days, the service was the best I've ever seen at a hotel event. Whatever we requested instantly appeared. By investing time to learn the server's name and goals, our speaker made her feel appreciated. Five minutes of relationship building earned two days of superior service.

Beating the slaves may have been an effective motivator 5,000 years ago when the Egyptian pyramids were built, but intimidation de-motivates twenty-first century men and women. Furthermore, despite the priority that managers place on salary and perks, surveys show that compensation ranks sixth as a motivator behind:

- Recognition for extraordinary results and effort;
- Opportunities to learn and increase responsibility;
- Contributing to an important purpose;
- Stability and the promise of a secure future; and
- Challenging assignments within a person's ability.

Today, achieving success requires you to determine what motivates your relationship partners and to act accordingly.

In the relationship economy, recognizing the contributions of your relationship partners is more vital to long-term success than any other short-term action. In my experience, for every problem caused by a shortage of resources or skills, I had three problems associated with lack of an effective relationship. Every investment you make to recognize and motivate your relationship partners will deliver a huge return on investment.

CLOSING THOUGHTS ON RELATIONSHIPS

People don't care how much you know
until they know how much you care.

When my new Mercedes was due for its 1,000-mile checkup, the salesman called and asked, *"Are you happy with the car? Is there something in particular that needs adjustment during the checkup?"* I responded that the car was perfect but I didn't have time to bring it in for a checkup. He volunteered, *"No problem. I'll stop over, pick it up, and return the car afterwards."* That's exactly what happened. Two days later, a neighbor curious about the salesman taking my car asked, *"Did they fix the car?"* I answered, *"Yes, everything seems to be fine. The car is running great."* Then he asked me a strange question: *"But did you get good service?"* I told my neighbor that it was the easiest car repair of my entire life.

My neighbor's second question reflects the whole new set of criteria that determine our satisfaction with business transactions in the relationship economy. We expect more than quality products and services; we also expect good relationships. Was it easy to contact them? Do they answer questions quickly and accurately? Do they suggest ideas that I didn't think of? Did they willingly spend extra time to finish the transaction completely? Of course, servicing my car was a vital part of the transaction. But by itself, it wasn't sufficient reason to perpetuate the relationship between the dealer and me, or to spread that relationship to other potential auto buyers.

In the relationship economy, those who are creative in building relationships will be the most successful. That ability is indispensable in a world where expert knowledge can easily be replaced. When you share knowledge freely, broker opportunities, and offer imaginative solutions to others, you become more than just a service provider. When you help your relationship partners achieve results that they couldn't achieve alone and introduce them to people they never would meet on their own, you become a highly valued resource. In short, you deliver high return-on-relationship for the time they spend with you.

The relationship economy is built on technology, but its foundation is trust. Trust is an elusive quality. You can't download it and you can't buy it.

You can't force it to expand, but it can easily disappear in an instant. Business is nearly impossible if the transaction partners don't trust each other. The more transactions you have with a relationship partner, the more trust you are building.

> Vulnerability, openness, and fairness are the trust triad of today's economy, which is driven by relationships.

Trust is built and tested by the way you approach and resolve conflicts. You frequently will feel vulnerable when a trusting business relationship is growing. For industrial age managers who are in the habit of dealing in terms of numbers, power, and procedures, the trust triad of openness, vulnerability, and fairness seems like a frightening and mystical dragon. The three tips presented in this part of the book will help you tame that dragon and build trust in your relationships. The tips are about communications (getting your message across clearly), diversity (using diversity to stimulate creativity), and collaboration (achieving results far superior to any you could get by yourself).

COMMUNICATIONS

Tip #4: Get Your
Message Across Clearly

OVERVIEW

Since we communicate with more people, more often, and in more ways than ever before, no skill is more important in the relationship economy than communications. Communications has become a multimedia action that includes new channels such as e-mails; instant messaging; blogs; Web sites like MySpace, YouTube, Facebook, and Linked-In; and old-fashioned methods like phone calls (including the use of cell phones, of course) and face-to-face meetings.

While these channels and methods allow you to open new doors and pursue exciting possibilities quickly, they are not a communications panacea. They may give you more ways to exchange information, but they also provide more ways to feed the miscommunications dragon. The fourteen vignettes in Tip #4 address ways to communicate more effectively with relationship partners, to build an interactive team, to empower others through communications, and to be open and honest in communications. I hope I was able to make those messages clear!

CATCHING THE BALL

An effective communication is a message sent, received, and understood. Effective communication empowers the receiver.

The topic at a meeting of CEOs was communications. The floor of the room was covered with multicolored, three-inch diameter plastic balls. During his opening remarks, the speaker casually picked up balls and threw them to the seated CEOs with results as follows:

- One CEO wasn't paying attention. The ball hit him on the chest and dropped to the floor. (*Not listening*)
- Another CEO reached out and tried to intercept the ball intended for a third CEO. The ball fell to the floor. (*Interrupting*)
- The ball to another CEO was far to the left and was uncatchable. (*Garbled message from the sender*)
- One CEO fumbled the ball and dropped it to the floor. (*Receiver misunderstood the communication*)
- About half the CEOs focused on the speaker and easily caught the balls that were thrown their way. (*Effective communications*)

Like throwing and catching a ball, communication involves sending a message that is understood by the receiver. Effective communications cause the receiver to change in some way or take some action.

Communications—always the lifeblood of business—are more vital in the relationship economy. When the Pony Express carried the mail across the country, the trip could take weeks. The telegraph was faster, but was impractical for large messages. Today, the Internet can transmit large, complex documents instantaneously around the world. But deals are still missed; budget-busting project delays occur; and relationships are damaged by untimely, inaccurate, and incomplete communications.

Effective communications provide clear goals and direction, deliver timely information in a useable form, eliminate waiting and rework, and motivate action. How effectively are communications among your staff, colleagues, superiors, suppliers, and clients? If you have challenges in those relationships, weak communications may be the cause. Ask yourself, *"Who's dropping the ball, and how is it being dropped?"*

SPAM

Time is an irreplaceable commodity. Value your partners'
time by tailoring communications to address their needs.

When the manuscript of my first *Dragons of Change* book was completed, I wondered how well my perspectives on change would be received, so I asked a friend to review it and provide feedback. He said, *"Sure. How long is it?"* When I answered 300 pages, he said, *"TMI (too much information). I'm too busy to review anything that long."* Disappointed, I asked if he would review part of it. He said, *"Give me something to read in the bathroom. A book I can pick up, open any place, read for a few minutes, get value, and not read again for days."* Since he's a typical reader in a hectic world, the *Dragons of Change* books have been written as one- or two-page vignettes.

I learned a vital lesson from that incident: Value my partners' time by tailoring communications to suit their busy lifestyles. I used to spend hours crafting lengthy business e-mails, and was upset when nobody read them. My oral presentations were guided by the *see-how-smart-I-am* dragon. They were long and repetitive. Today, my goal in presentations is to deliver practical solutions and explain them fully. I leave out the theory and stick to what really matters to my relationship partners.

Today's new technologies facilitate garbage communications. On an average workday, for example, I receive more than 100 e-mails at four different addresses. Many people (you might be among them) receive several times that many. Roughly two-thirds of my incoming e-mails are *spam*, for me a category that includes both jokes and chain e-mails sent by friends and business associates. I delete them without opening. Half of the remaining e-mails are informational, like the news alerts that I request from Google.

I appreciate the relationship partners who send the one-in-six e-mails that contain something important because they understand the value of my time. I return the favor by respecting their time too. Do you focus on information the receiver really needs to have, or are you a spammer in your e-mail and other communications?

ASK THE UNIVERSE

Ask the Universe for what you want. It may take a while for the Universe to respond, so be patient and keep asking.

A member of my men's group casually mentioned that he wanted a more challenging job. My company had job openings, so I asked him to send me his resume. He did, but his expertise was in advertising, which didn't fit the qualifications for the consulting work my company provided to federal agencies. So I helped him polish his resume and referred him to the CEO of a public relations company. His expertise was closer, but not a match for what they wanted either. That CEO referred him to a third company where he was hired for a position with a 10 percent pay raise. In addition to patience, he used three degrees of separation to find a new position: myself, the second CEO, and the CEO who hired him.

I've mentioned before that you are no more than six degrees of separation from any person on Earth. That is, you know me, I know people who know people who know more people, and so forth. The chain touches everyone who is alive today. Networking always was important to success, but it's even more productive in the relationship economy. Don't hesitate to ask the Universe for help. The people you ask may not have what you want, but they may know someone who does. Similarly, as part of the Universe, your role is to help others. When you receive a request you can't fulfill, pass it on to someone who might be able to help.

For example, are you asking the Universe to help you achieve your biggest business goal? Does the *that-won't-work* or *I-may-look-stupid* dragon tell you such an approach is doomed? That dragon may be why you haven't achieved it yet. Don't be bashful. What have you lost if you ask for help and it doesn't come? All you need is a few of the planet's seven billion inhabitants to help, and you will probably be helping them at the same time. How many are there who might help? If you can't find one today, maybe you will tomorrow. Keep asking and be prepared for the Universe to respond in a creative way—the response may be different than what you expected.

LET RGS DO IT

The real measure of power in the relationship economy isn't how much you do individually; instead it's how much you get accomplished through an effective, interactive team.

Three years after I started my own company, a breakthrough occurred when a client said for the first time, "*Let* RGS (my initials and also part of my company's name) *do it,*" and he didn't mean me personally. The company had six employees, and we had just won a contract to help a government executive design and install computer systems at a new naval base. Up to that point, my role had been to provide a strategy for the project. But now it required a broad range of technical skills. My role changed from doer to communicator, and my success was measured by how well the team achieved the project's goals. It was an early taste of the relationship economy.

Entrepreneurs who start companies occasionally ask me how I transitioned from selling myself to building a team. It was a simple and repeatable process. First, I became a trusted advisor by helping the client plan his project and obtain funding. He routinely asked for my perspective on the major decisions. Our relationship soon was stretched in several ways: (1) There wasn't enough time for me to do everything he requested; (2) Expertise was needed in areas beyond my skills; and (3) Simple tasks had to be performed for which my hourly rate was too expensive. Each of these became an opportunity to build a team by adding new staff members. The essential first step was to communicate objectives and processes to new members of the team.

It's suicidal to try to do everything yourself in the relationship economy. Building a competent team benefits everyone. Specifically, it: (1) produces more reliable results; (2) provides surge capacity to resolve emerging issues; (3) establishes career paths for promotion; (4) enables you to focus on strategic matters; (5) enables continuity in case you're "hit by a bus"; and (6) allows you to take vacations. Those are six significant reasons for you to tame the *no-one-does-it-as-well-as-I-do* dragon and sharpen your communications skills.

BEST PLACE TO WORK

*Teams use multiple techniques to connect,
and listening is among the most effective.*

Year after year, my company received its lowest *Best Place To Work* survey score in communications. Employees thought they didn't know what was happening and the managers felt we lacked unity. Of course, those views are different sides of the same communications challenge. To improve communications, over time we instituted:

- Weekly staff meetings with an employee advocate who attended and published a meeting summary for other employees;
- Monthly "All Hands" luncheons to discuss issues and events;
- Quarterly planning off-sites with expanded participation; and
- An up-to-date Procedures & Policies Manual.

Each technique was an improvement, but communications is a two-way street: Clear messages must be sent and accurately received.

Unfortunately, only 20 percent of employees read the summary of the weekly staff meeting, and participation in monthly "All Hands" luncheons averaged 50 percent. Some project teams still complained that they didn't know what was happening, and those teams had high turnover. The executive team concluded the next step in improving communications was *listening*. So we encouraged project managers to schedule interactive discussions with their teams, and an executive participated to listen to employee concerns and respond to questions about strategy and goals. That approach fostered an understanding of the company's strategic direction and improved the survey score. But we never got close to a perfect score on the survey.

Recipients are as much responsible for communications as senders. Until the message is heard and understood, a communication has not been completed. Since the receiver hears what has been said through the filter of his understanding, the sender must use concepts, terminology, and examples familiar to the recipient. It's axiomatic that you see what you expect to see and hear what you expect to hear. Remember that axiom when you send or receive a communication.

SEVEN DIMENSIONS

The leaders and members of an effective interactive team communicate at multiple levels to achieve results.

The Federal Emergency Management Agency (FEMA) has suffered several highly visible failures. FEMA purchased 145,000 trailers and mobile homes to help Hurricane Katrina victims, and was criticized for everything from over-purchasing to not having a usage and distribution plan. Eighteen hundred homes received $4 million damage in storage. Six million prepared meals worth $40 million spoiled in the heat. Congress and agency leaders blamed bureaucracy (a synonym for poor communications) for the failures rather than face the core issues of planning, execution, and performance management. The core issue was that the FEMA team failed in several dimensions of communications.

When teams tackle complex problems, team leaders must foster communications across seven leadership dimensions:

- *Purpose:* What compelling goal are we trying to achieve?
- *Strategy:* What approach will we use to achieve that goal?
- *Motivation:* Why is the goal important to you?
- *Commitment:* What is your role in achieving the goal?
- *Measurement:* How do we know that we are succeeding?
- *Performance:* How are we doing? Are we correcting mistakes?
- *Credibility:* Does the team have confidence in its leaders?

As a leader, consciously communicate and agree on answers in each of the seven dimensions because, in the midst of challenge, the team's performance will be degraded by each dimension that's missing.

Use communications to build consensus with your teammates by highlighting the intersection of the team's purpose and purposes of individual team members. Each human being has unique purposes and concerns. When people feel that leaders are unaware of or reject their purposes and concerns, resistance dragons roar and their performance evaporates. Tame that dragon by being aware of and sensitive to the purposes and concerns of your teammates. Listening to their feedback on your strategy and plans is a great place to start!

RELATIONSHIP COACH

Superior credentials are necessary but insufficient for success.
The ability to build relationships inside your own organization
and with external organizations is also essential for success.

During a client satisfaction interview, a senior naval officer remarked to me, *"Where do you find such great people? Every time you add or replace someone on my project, the team gets better."* I answered by telling him about our candidate selection and interview processes, and our change management training program. I explained how those mechanisms deliver top-notch employees. *"But,"* I told him, *"the most important element of our teamwork is that people on your project help each other. They often exchange solutions with teams that are working on projects for other agencies that are facing similar challenges."*

In addition to coaching employees to communicate across our projects, we also encouraged government clients to work cross-agency to implement innovative joint solutions. Getting a headquarters agency to tame the *I'm-in-charge* dragon often makes the difference between active support from field activities for reorganizations and business process changes and passive—but destructive—resistance during implementation. Success in the relationship economy requires that you coordinate communications within your team, with other teams, and with other organizations.

So how can you as a leader in industry or government coach your team to achieve performance excellence? Ensuring that they have the knowledge and tools required for their tasks is a good start, of course. Next, tell them what is expected and explain the strategy with as few restrictions as possible. Give them freedom to pursue the goal within the boundaries of the strategy and your organization's rules. Periodically, take time away from the action to help them evaluate their results and performance shortfalls, if any. Lastly, point your team in the direction of new external relationships. Such new relationships often produce order-of-magnitude performance jumps and make you into a legendary relationship coach.

PUSHED TO THE EDGE

*Conflict can be a compelling motivator. Stretch yourself
and push your people—but not past the breaking point.*

D riving to a meeting with a client who was the CEO of his company, I fully expected that I would be fired. Our previous meeting had ended in conflict. In an effort to get him to change, I pushed him to the edge, but he resisted. His seventy-year-old company had shrunk to a fraction of its peak size, the market had changed, and demand was declining for the services he offered. After I arrived at the meeting and we exchanged pleasantries, I said, "*I don't know what to do next. I've pushed you as far as I should push. From here, it's up to you to take action or not.*" He answered, "*I know,*" which indicated he was finally committed to make changes. In the next few weeks, he hired two key people to strengthen the management team, diversified the company's offerings, and trained his staff in business development and quality assurance basics. Those actions reversed the decline of his company.

For many, dealing with conflict can be a dragon, and getting buy-in from colleagues is an intimidating task. Next time you face a potential conflict, use the following techniques I used in this situation:

- Establish an atmosphere of open, two-way dialogue;
- Be open and honest—say how you really feel;
- Expect and acknowledge resistance;
- Aim your communications at your audience's main concerns;
- Present your case in terms of benefits; and
- Use humor to reduce tension and open communications.

Data and logic rarely are sufficient to get others to adopt your ideas. How you present your ideas may be more important than the words you use or the ideas themselves.

When you are able to defuse explosive situations, you create rapport with colleagues. When you have rapport, something magical happens: People feel connected and empowered. To achieve rapport, tame the dragon that tells you to run from confrontation. Instead, train yourself to have constructive conversations in conflict situations.

MOOSE IN PINSTRIPES

*As a leader, justify the need for change to your
team by communicating your commitment to win.*

Mike "Moose" Mussina joined the New York Yankees for the 2001
baseball season as a free agent. He enjoyed playing in Baltimore,
but Joe Torre wooed him to the Yankees. *"Even in the midst of
the negotiations, the Orioles didn't try to change my mind,"* he said. *"My wife
would answer the phone and say, 'It's Joe Torre, Andy Petitte, or Paul O'Neil*
(Yankees manager and players). *Not once was it Mike Hargrove, Cal Ripken,
or Brady Anderson* (Baltimore's manager and players). *They didn't seem to
care what I was thinking. But even after winning three World Series, the Yankees
told me that they wanted to improve their team."*

Which team would you play for if you were the Moose? More than likely,
you would go to the Yankees because they made you feel wanted and had a
clear desire to win. A few years later, the Yankees must have forgotten their
success with Mike Mussina because, after the 2003 season, Andy Petitte (a
star left-handed pitcher) joined the Houston Astros as a free agent when
he felt the Yankees didn't care about him. However, the Yankees, realizing
their mistake, enticed Andy back for the 2007 season.

Since the need to be wanted is almost universal, leaders must acknowledge
the importance of each team member and demonstrate a commitment to
make the changes needed to win. Consider using the following techniques
to lead your team through change to victory:

- Explain what must change and why it must change in order for the
  team to win;
- Describe the end-state (the victory celebration) consistently, not just
  at the beginning but also during the entire transition period;
- Acknowledge the risks of change because people are more confident
  knowing that the risks haven't been ignored; and
- Be open and honest about details, even when it's uncomfortable.

People prefer to deal with knowns than worry about unknowns. People
eagerly support a leader who is committed to winning and has a plan to get
there. Be that kind of leader.

CHRISTMAS CARDS

High-performing teams have clear values that allow everyone
to act independently while working to achieve shared goals.

My oldest daughter worked for my company as the controller after she earned her accounting degree. It was time to order Christmas cards for our clients, and the receptionist said that I had to approve the selection. My daughter said, *"That's ridiculous. The president of a company doesn't approve Christmas cards. That's our job."* She was absolutely correct. This situation led her to discover why my company had grown quickly to $3 million in annual revenue but remained at that level for several years. The company had reached the maximum size that I could control on my own.

I'm not the only executive who wrestles with a *do-it-myself* dragon. The following statements made during meetings with other executives of small organizations indicate that the dragon is common:

- *"Everybody reports to me. It's the only way I can control things."*
- *"I thrive in chaos. People who want fixed rules frustrate me."*
- *"Everybody comes into my office and asks me what to do."*
- *"I've got to stop doing things that aren't my job."*

Do any of these statements sound like your management style? Each statement reflects the *do-it-myself* dragon. Being a center of attention for decisions may feel good, but it destroys initiative and teamwork.

I tamed the *do-it-myself* dragon by declining to participate in decisions like selecting Christmas cards. First, of course, the team had to understand the objective of distributing Christmas cards. Once that was clear, they could select cards every year without my approval! As a leader, when you consistently communicate clear goals and values, you empower everyone to act on their own without supervision or oversight. When the goals and values become habits, team members are free to create and implement their own solutions to the problems and opportunities they encounter each day. That makes your life easier and transforms work into fun for everyone.

BAD BREATH

Criticism may not be agreeable, but it is necessary.
It fulfills the same function as pain in the human body
by calling your attention to an unhealthy state of things.
—Winston Churchill

If you and I are talking and I have bad breath, please tell me openly and honestly that I need a breath mint. Don't worry about hurting my feelings. I won't like hearing that I have bad breath, of course, but I will thank you because I'll know to freshen my breath or refrain from breathing in someone else's face. As I see it, my friends tell me I have bad breath while my detractors tell someone else. When leaders accept criticism gracefully, they make it easy for others to accept criticism too. By taming your defensive dragons, even if your critics are wrong, you expand the trust in your relationships.

Open and honest communications between leaders and their team are essential for success in the fast-paced relationship economy. Pity anyone surrounded by unloving critics and uncritical lovers. If you want colleagues who will support you through changing times, competition, and personal blindness, then be open to blunt feedback and be sure that you provide direct feedback too. Open and honest communications are hard to initiate in relationships that have hidden difficult truths for a long time. There is high risk in climbing the wall of past secrets. But once you climb over that wall, open and honest communications become a habit that empowers a *can-do* attitude in everyone from top to bottom.

The lack of open and honest communications can debilitate an organization. For example, an executive in my company implored his people to "*tell me straight*" when there was a problem. But after he lashed out at project managers who reported issues, his people became afraid to report bad news. One project manager hid an overrun on a large government project rather than endure a tongue-lashing from the executive. The overrun grew larger each month until the accounting department discovered accidentally that subcontractor invoices had not been submitted for payment. As the result, the executive was fired and the project manager resigned from the company.

Avoiding open and honest feedback may seem like an easy way out, but it doesn't work very well in the long term. For example, it didn't work for the executive, the project manager, or myself in this case. Could the project overrun have been avoided if I confronted the executive about his behavior earlier? There is no way to know for sure, of course, but permitting this little issue to grow into a big one produced disastrous results for everyone concerned.

Look for opportunities to provide feedback. People lob them at you like softballs you can hit out of the park. For example, *"How are you doing?"* and *"How did I do?"* are questions that we hear nearly every day but usually answer with platitudes that do little to improve team performance. Openness and honesty are essential for success. Openness means that nothing is manipulated, inflated, understated, or conveniently forgotten. Honesty means that everything you say is the whole truth as you know it. Openness and honesty may seem hard, but they leave no room for doubt, confusion, or misunderstanding.

PROCTOLOGY EXAMS

"Lack of candor is the biggest dirty little secret in business today. It blocks smart ideas, fast action, and good people contributing all the stuff they've got."
—Jack Welch

The quarterly meetings of my company's board of directors sometimes felt like proctology exams. The board had seven members: me, the president, and five seasoned executives whose only link to the company was their role as directors. The directors' probing questions made the president and I prepare diligently for each meeting, have a plan of action to resolve performance issues, and research and present data to validate our market assumptions and performance projections.

This governance process was highly valuable because it forced us to openly and honestly face our quarterly results and projections for the future. No room for dragons here. The outside directors held us accountable to make hard and frequently uncomfortable choices. Far from resenting those sometimes painful discussions, I was grateful for the directors' counsel and their help in growing the company. They told me bluntly when I was planning to do something unrealistic or stupid—before I did it!

Jack Welch, the former CEO of General Electric said, *"Too many managers avoid making hard choices and thereby hurt not only their companies but, in the long run, the employees whom they are trying to protect."* Welch was famous for, among other things, his rank-and-yank staffing policy. He made managers rank employees annually and fired the lowest 10 percent. That may sound harsh, but Welch felt that top-grading was effective for the company and for the employees who were fired, many of whom became very successful in succeeding jobs.

Firm governance is a cornerstone of successful organizations in the relationship economy. In your organization, people at all levels must know and understand the rules under which they are expected to work. You'll know how your approach is working when you observe how the people in your organization think, talk, and behave when they pursue the goals that you have set for them to achieve.

CLOSING THOUGHTS ON COMMUNICATIONS

All of us must push our communications to the next level or risk falling behind in the relationship economy.

My visits to the dentist are a pleasure because we often swap travel stories. On the day before a vacation to St. Martin, I felt a dull ache in my jaw. Having had abscessed teeth in the past, I was worried that this might be another. I called my dentist, and he squeezed me into his busy schedule. After an x-ray confirmed the abscess, he said, *"We can do a root canal, or you can take your chances with St. Martin's dentists."* I chose to let my dentist do the root canal.

When the drilling was finished and the temporary cap was installed, my dentist handed me a bottle of pills and said, *"I picked this antibiotic because you can drink alcohol with it. I expect you'll have a Heineken or two while you're in St. Martin."* I was impressed that he had really listened to my travel stories and considered them when it was time to prescribe the medication. When I recommend him, I tell people about my emergency root canal and his perceptive prescription. His practice is successful in part because he understands that even dentists must communicate to be successful in today's relationship economy.

The most common communications at work are about travel, sports, weather, rumors, and the like. Such social conversations give us reason to talk, and when we provide details that are juicy or interesting, our contributions are appreciated. However, except as icebreakers, those subjects have low relationship value. On the other hand, our contacts and business knowledge have high value. They're useful, important, and powerful.

One gift of the industrial age was the cubicle that is common in today's office suites. They're constructed to increase productivity and limit communications. If a disturbance happens in the sea of adjacent cubicles, we poke our heads above the decorative barriers to see what has happened. By comparison, the 1970s vintage hard-walled offices seem inefficient and isolated. But they were effective for intimate one-on-one conversations and small group brainstorming.

Today, e-mail and instant messaging often substitute for face-to-face conversations. We use phones much less than we once did, and often don't recognize the face or voice of the business contacts with whom we communicate daily. In the relationship economy, such "advances" are really setbacks. They exorcize the human spirit from business and may cause us to lose touch with how people feel. They also prevent us from celebrating success and learning from failures. Unfortunately, we are even afraid to touch someone for fear of a sexual-harassment lawsuit.

> Don't assume people know that you understand, appreciate, and respect them and their goals. Tell them.

It's still easy get tangled in frustrating, circular conversations even in the relationship economy with all of its new communications devices. Whenever a change in tactics, strategy, or leadership occurs, people are challenged to sort through the differences in perspectives to re-establish a shared vision for the future. When management presents a compelling need for change, workers recall past successes. When management seeks creativity and flexibility, workers want to maintain current benefits. When management pushes for personal responsibility and teamwork, workers seek a return to the old "family" atmosphere.

Actually, managers and workers are seeking the same things. Resolution begins with communications that acknowledge different perspectives and seek shared goals. Get to really know the people in your workplace. They can't read your mind, so don't assume they know that you understand, appreciate, and respect them and their goals. You have to tell them.

DIVERSITY

Tip #5: Embrace Diversity to Expand Creativity

OVERVIEW

Embracing diversity is essential for individual success and for the health of the global economy. As a change leader, your objective should be to build a diversified team and tap into the perspectives of your colleagues as a consistent source of new ideas and solutions. By surrounding yourself with people who have varied experiences and perspectives, you will increase the likelihood that you will resolve troublesome problems, and discover and capitalize on emerging opportunities. However, to achieve diversity, you must tame the *you-aren't-like-me* dragon and engage the talents of every member of your team. The fifteen vignettes in Tip #5 show you how to use diversity to produce superior business results.

A NO-BRAINER

The twenty-first century workplace is multicultural. For leaders who grasp the implications of this reality on the future of business, embracing diversity is a no-brainer.

The host of a radio talk show interviewed an oncologist who specialized in treating bone cancer. For several years, the oncologist had breakfast on a weekly basis with a veterinarian who treated bone cancer in dogs. During their breakfasts, they exchanged treatment techniques and case results from the previous week. The interviewer asked the oncologist, *"But aren't human patients uncomfortable with receiving dog treatments?"* The oncologist responded, *"When patients face death, they're willing to try anything that might work."*

Results of these unprecedented exchanges were astounding. The diverse doctors reported the survival rate for dogs that receive human treatments more than doubled, and the recovery rate for humans who received canine treatments to augment conventional procedures increased from 70 percent to 92 percent. In this case, diversity is making the difference between life and death, plus the oncologist and veterinarian are more successful.

To executives who grasp the implications of today's multicultural workplace, increasing diversity in their organizations is a no-brainer. They know an organization that welcomes and respects employees regardless of race, age, gender, religion, sexual orientation, problem-solving style, or other traits is better able to attract top talent. They understand that a workplace that routinely taps into diverse perspectives will produce more innovative products and services, accelerate sales growth, and deliver superior customer service.

On the other hand, some executives think that diversity is a do-good program invented by liberals who push hiring quotas and promotions based on factors other than performance and ability. But most executives today are somewhere in the middle. They understand the human benefits of diversity but don't know how to use diversity to improve business results in their organizations.

Regardless of his personal beliefs about diversity, an executive would have to be blind to miss the shifting demographics of today's work force. A majority of new entrants into the work force are women and minorities, and that shift has changed the fundamentals of both domestic and international businesses. Companies are finding that homogenous teams have a substantial disadvantage when they are competing against diverse teams for new business with government agencies, multicultural companies, and consumers from multiple ethnic groups.

Despite mountains of social legislation, U.S. neighborhoods for the most part are still segregated along ethnic, racial, and income lines. But people leave those neighborhoods every morning to work side-by-side with co-workers with diverse backgrounds in businesses across the country. Therefore, business has become the frontier of diversity. New social norms for trust, respect, cooperation, and appreciation for diverse backgrounds are forged in the workplace every day. Businesses have been forced to embrace diversity in ways that society in general has yet to face, and many have increased their revenue and profits by harnessing that diversity! Organizations that embrace diverse ideas and merge them into their business processes give themselves a huge competitive advantage in the relationship economy.

> As the frontier of diversity, business is forging new social norms for trust, respect, and appreciation for people with diverse backgrounds.

Businesses today are experiencing astonishing changes that affect every aspect of their operation, and embracing diversity may be the most significant and controversial of those changes. Historically, embracing diversity has been a unique American strength. In the late 1800s and early 1900s, the immigrants from Italy, Poland, Ireland, and other European countries forced workplace diversity. Today, women, immigrants from Hispanic and Asian cultures, and openly gay women and men are challenging organizations to embrace diversity. While some of today's changes make your future uncertain, you'll find that embracing diversity will provide innovation that will build loyal relationships, increase productivity, and create a more stable business environment in which you will prosper. Is diversity in perspectives a no-brainer for you?

GOOD OLE DAYS

A change in leadership often improves short-term results because the new perspectives stimulate new successes.

I took three years to retire. The first year, I reduced my workweek to four days. The second year, I reduced it to three; and the third year to two. Finally, a month after my interest in the company was sold, I retired. When my workweek was shortened, the board of directors promoted a vice president, who had been with the company thirteen years, to president. At first, employees were concerned that his priorities and style weren't like mine. But revenue grew 20 percent in each of his first two years, and profitability remained high too. He tapped into potential that my style had failed to develop. Diversity in management style improved the company's results!

When employees lamented, *"Why can't he be like Dick," "We aren't the same company anymore,"* and *"I don't like the changes,"* they were expressing the fear many people feel when a long-tenured leader is succeeded by someone with a new agenda. While the fear of change was understandable, the hard truth is that the good ole days were gone forever. Nostalgic remembrances of a special Christmas party, a lucrative bonus, or a stimulating project had potential to grow into harmful dragons. When leadership changes occur, like changes in the weather, taming the dragons of change requires that you embrace the new reality and exploit whatever advantages it offers.

Choosing a new leader for an organization is always a gamble, but the litmus test of performance is results. There is virtually no way to prepare to lead an organization when, for the first time, you will be responsible for every result and every decision that produces results—good or bad. If my replacement had been "just like me," the company would have been weaker because he would have the same weaknesses but also less experience. Since the world changes constantly, the most effective succession choice will be the individual best qualified to meet the challenges of tomorrow. That almost always is someone with perspectives that are different from the good ole days.

IS BIAS A SICKNESS?

As sure as diversity enhances results in the relationship economy, biases eliminate possibilities and limit success.

A fifty-five-year-old man refused a job offer because his would-be supervisor seemed to be gay—he had been unemployed for a year and his family was nearly bankrupt. A woman who considered Jews to be diseased did a self-cleansing ritual after being near a person she thought was Jewish—she wanted psychiatric help but there were too many Jewish doctors. A Vietnam veteran hated Asians intensely, and avoided business and social situations where he might have to speak with them. A manager was convinced that women were weak and accident-prone, so he refused to hire them in his under-staffed manufacturing plant. Reports of irrational, dragon-like biases appear regularly in the media. But when biases reach the advanced stages illustrated in these examples, the afflicted individuals cannot succeed in a globally connected business world.

Everyone has conscious and unconscious biases that limit their success. By measuring how quickly people connect different concepts, psychologists found that biases subconsciously affect even those of us who say we don't have any. For example, Americans don't make the association between *black* and *good* as fast as they do between *white* and *good*. We feel good about ourselves when we feel good about the groups to which we belong, and we tend to have negative biases toward groups about which we know very little.

Psychologists are debating whether or not extreme bias is an illness. While biases may or may not be a sickness in the same league as alcoholism, for sure they limit success in the relationship economy. You probably don't suffer from debilitating biases such as those cited above, but you may be achieving less than you could because of your unconscious biases and be oblivious to their adverse impacts. Biases, however small they may be, cause you to project hostility toward some people. Consciously embracing diversity is an effective way to tame the dragons that your biases might create.

TO SIR, WITH LOVE

"He taught me right from wrong, and weak from strong.
That's a lot to learn. What did I give him in return?"
—Title song from the movie: *"To Sir, With Love"*

My first job after the Navy was with a consulting company. I knew nothing about consulting, but a retired Navy captain offered to be my mentor. I was thirty-one years old, while he was sixty and a veteran of the Cuban Missile Crisis. At first, the *I'll do-it-myself* dragon roared, *"What can this old man teach me?"* But I came to value his wisdom as we developed and marketed a new logistics system. I was very aggressive in trying to close deals. He saw my bias for action as a strength, but warned me that it was a weakness when I acted without being prepared. To illustrate his point, he told the story of a young bull and old bull standing at the top of a hill. The young bull says, *"Let's run down the hill and have a cow."* The old bull responds, *"Let's walk down the hill and have the whole herd."*

His message was clear. In that moment I realized there was a special bond between us, something I hadn't experienced before. We became close and openly discussed our families, our challenges, and our plans. His mentorship made business an exciting experience, one in which my head and my heart were involved. I learned an enormous amount from him, and quickly too.

As baby boomers become executives, mentoring relationships between older and younger colleagues are becoming more common in the workplace. I am surprised, however, that more organizations don't encourage mentoring as a way to infuse age diversity in their business strategy and to transfer the lessons of experience. In the relationship economy, successful people recognize the benefits of mentorship because they are genuinely concerned about mutual success.

Do you have a mentor, someone who may understand your strengths and weaknesses even better than you do? Someone who will tell you honestly what you must change to be successful? Do you give that kind of mentoring to others? You can easily mentor someone else even as you are being mentored by others.

PROMOTION BOARD

Encourage productive dissent by inviting people with diverse viewpoints into your decision-making process.

I was a member of the promotion board for managing director, the highest project position in my company. The top candidate for promotion met the prerequisites, but I was not comfortable with promoting him to the new position. In my view, he was too concerned about consensus and too slow to make decisions. His management style and priorities weren't like mine. At first, the *I'm-right-and-I'm-the-boss* dragon left me wanting to end the discussion and force a NO decision by the board.

But the candidate produced results. His group had the highest growth rate and lowest attrition. For reasons different than mine, the other two board members also had doubts about the promotion. After a lengthy debate during which we each aired the pros and cons of the promotion as we saw them, we voted to promote the candidate. He turned out to be an extraordinarily successful managing director who expanded contracts with clients and helped the clients win prestigious performance awards.

Encourage dissent by inviting people with diverse perspectives into your decision-making processes. Decisions made by acclamation aren't decisions at all. The best decisions generally are made after all viewpoints are presented and discussed, and a choice is made among alternatives that are clearly understood. If there is no disagreement, maybe the decision should be postponed until other possibilities have been identified and explored thoroughly.

Disagreement improves decision-making for two key reasons. First, a frank discussion of opposing ideas stimulates creativity and often produces alternatives that no one could have imagined prior to the discussion. Decisions without alternatives are risky indeed. And second, by promoting healthy disagreement you enable your people to voice their views and take a stand for a change that they will support. In the end, of course, decisions must be made based on *what is right*, rather than *who is right*.

HIRING DIVERSITY

Build the robust and flexible team essential for
success by hiring people with diverse backgrounds.

At my company's twentieth anniversary celebration, the question I was asked most often was, *"Dick, if you started a company today, what would you do differently?"* My answer was immediate: *"I would change my criteria for hiring people."* My dragon-like fixation on skills—that is, hiring people to fill specific positions—helped us survive in the early years, but it stunted long-term growth. My hiring decisions were based strictly on skills and experience when I also should have considered relationships, attitude, and growth potential. My criteria stunted growth because they were aimed at what we did today instead of acquiring the diversity needed to deliver new services and enter new markets.

Diversity starts with hiring. Finding candidates and conducting interviews are among the most important tasks you perform. Hiring extraordinarily qualified, growth-oriented people for every position is a given. But, in my opinion, the answer to: *"What new perspectives and relationships does this candidate bring to our company?"* should be the tiebreaker in hiring decisions.

Few companies recognize the real strategic value of hiring diversity. Most still hire using outdated industrial age beliefs like:

- Hire employees who have exceptional skills and experience;
- Hire employees to fix the organization's weaknesses; or
- Hire employees who fit the corporate culture.

In contrast, organizations that have relationship economy savvy and an eye to the future hire using criteria like:

- While experience and skill as prerequisites for interviews, hire employees (or free agents) for their relationships and teamwork;
- Place people in positions that amplify their strengths; and
- Hire people to build the culture needed for tomorrow's success.

One-size-fits-all hiring criteria are on the industrial age junk heap along with mainframe computers. Diversified hiring is the key to your future success.

GLASS CEILING

*Feminine insights are invaluable in development
of innovative solutions. Women look at business
challenges in ways that sometimes don't occur to me.*

The CEO group in which I participated was predominantly male, so I valued insights from our female CEO members especially highly. They saw issues in a different way and found nuances that I and other male CEOs missed. For example, if the issue was a strategic negotiation, the other male CEOs and I tended to focus on give-and-take competition and numbers, while the female CEOs evaluated the opponent's needs and searched for ways to satisfy them at little or no cost to us. Both viewpoints were vital in finding viable solutions.

Business still is largely a male-dominated world despite the growing number of successful women executives. The glass ceiling remains firmly in place in many organizations. My experience is that women are valuable in problem-solving discussions because they expand the range of alternatives. My *Mr. Fix-It* dragon occasionally causes me to drive to a solution before I have defined the problem clearly. When that happens, my solutions address only symptoms of the real problem. On the other hand, the inquisitive nature of women tames the *Mr. Fix-It* dragon. In general, women willingly invest extra time to ask probing questions and discover facts that otherwise might go unnoticed.

To find winning business solutions, you must see connections and possibilities that your competition will miss. To thrive in today's relationship economy, look for the missing links between seemingly disparate problems and alternatives. Connect small, unrelated opportunities to create a big breakthrough. Therefore, there is a vital need for women and men to unify their perspectives with viewpoints of the old and young, social scientists, and engineers as well as from diverse cultures. Consciously staff your team with varied perspectives. Don't exclude someone because they see things differently than you do. As a matter of fact, that may be a great reason to add them to your team!

CHECK WITH HEADQUARTERS

Give your colleagues the knowledge and authority
to make on-the-spot decisions, even though their
perspectives may be different than yours.

I n a consulting engagement, I sent the following e-mail to my client after a particularly intense discussion about her executive team:

> *DEBORAH* (not a real name):
> *I wanted to follow up on the topic we discussed today: Would you as*
> *CEO rather have your executives and project managers:*
> *(1) Make decisions and take action even if the actions they take may*
> *not be the actions you would have taken?*
>   OR
> *(2) Call on you to make the decisions because you have more experi-*
> *ence and technical expertise than anyone in the company?*

She took four days to send this response: *"It depends. In some cases I want option (1) and in other situations I insist on option (2)."*

Of course, her answer was right-on. When a decision is urgent, has only local impact, and is reversible, option (1) is best. However, if a decision is irreversible or is a bet-the-farm investment, only option (2) is acceptable. When leaders delegate category (1) decisions, they gain the time to pursue opportunities for growth. Your challenge as a business leader is to reconcile the diversities in perspective so you and your team agree on the line between option (1) and option (2). Such agreement empowers everyone to make opportunistic decisions.

While command-and-control management arguably was effective in the industrial era, it is an impotent dragon in the changing relationship economy. There rarely is sufficient time to "check with headquarters" because many huge opportunities can be won or lost in an instant of time. To achieve long-term success, train your team to operate independently, give them clear criteria for making on-the-spot decisions, and cultivate their willingness to make such decisions confidently.

NO QUOTAS

Equal Employment Opportunity and affirmative action policies rely on quotas while effective diversity policies produce results.

The admiral began the strategic planning off-site with charts that showed the race-gender profile of his management team. No one was surprised that the profile was white and male at the top. He promised to reshape the profile by accelerating promotions for women and minorities and by encouraging early retirements. The admiral ended his remarks by proudly saying this was the most aggressive diversity plan ever implemented in the Navy, and he expected every manager to contribute his best efforts to achieve the objective.

Following his stirring presentation, the off-site divided into workshops to discuss a range of topics from shipbuilding innovations to pay-for-performance. While the subjects of the workshops varied widely, the discussions were remarkably the same. Regardless of the workshop's subject, participants were stuck on the admiral's speech. Many thought that his diversity plan would fail because it mandated a different kind of discrimination and would force promotions based on criteria other than previous performance, education, and skills. No one told the admiral, but the resentment dragons resisted his change long after the other off-site discussions were forgotten.

The business case for building diversity into relationship economy organizations is compelling, but it's not a numbers game. Diversity improves results by providing measurable value in strategic areas like:

- Innovative problem solving and product/service development;
- Expanded market share that addresses demographic shifts;
- Enhanced customer satisfaction and reduced complaints;
- Accelerated recruiting and hiring;
- Improved employee morale and retention; and
- Reduced discrimination complaints and legal issues.

Diversity in perspectives drives creativity and performance advances; but diversity in gender, age, nationality, culture, and other dimensions (as appropriate to your market) fosters the varied perspectives that you will need to improve the bottom line.

HIGH TURNOVER

*Today's employees want more than compensation. They
also seek recognition, involvement, and professional growth.*

My company experienced high turnover, roughly 10 percent higher than the industry average. We analyzed the problem and were surprised to discover that 70 percent of the turnover occurred on two projects. Exit interviews for employees on those projects who left the company revealed three repeated reasons for leaving:

- *My project manager didn't appreciate me or my hard work;*
- *The project manger never asked for my ideas; and*
- *I wasn't challenged, and I wasn't growing professionally.*

Our discovery confirmed what human resource directors have known for decades: *Employees don't quit jobs. They quit supervisors.* The failure to appreciate the diverse skills, styles, and needs of workers is a common and damaging dragon in supervisor-worker relationships.

Finding and retaining top-notch workers is a strategic priority in most industries. Surveys show that compensation has decreased in importance as a motivator. Instead, people in today's highly educated work force want to be appreciated, included in important decisions, recognized for their performance, and allowed to be themselves rather then being forced into a mold. They also need to feel they are growing professionally. This is great news if you can't afford to retain your current employees or recruit new ones with high salaries and benefits. That doesn't mean salary and benefits are unimportant, but in the relationship economy they're probably less important than you think.

The connected nature of today's business world has changed supervisor-worker dynamics in another way too: Members of project teams often work in diverse locations and have minimal face-to-face contact. In that work environment, a supervisor must deal with the team solely on the basis of talent and results. There's no room for racial, ethnic, or other kinds of bias. If you find yourself supervising such a geographically diverse team, it's especially important that the team members feel appreciated and recognized, and are expanding their professional knowledge and relationships.

ORGANIZATIONAL PERSPECTIVES

Your views probably reflect the perspective of the organization you belong to. However, effective enterprise solutions require you to understand the perspectives of multiple organizations.

My first billet as a Navy officer was in the engineering department on a destroyer in overhaul. I had low regard for the shipyard because the workers took too long to complete repairs and rarely finished a job right the first time. I also was frustrated by a lack of responsiveness from the ship engineering command, who didn't respond to a single problem report that I submitted during my tour of duty on the ship. My frustrations and lack of respect were relationship dragons that made the overhaul more difficult.

During my second billet, I supervised submarine overhauls in a shipyard. I found the training, safety consciousness, and attention-to-detail of shipyard workers to be extraordinary. From prior experience, I also understood how strongly the ship's crew felt about getting the job done right the first time. But I was still frustrated that the ship engineering command took so long to resolve design issues, and also that Navy headquarters never seemed to budget enough money or time to complete a submarine overhaul.

When I left the Navy, I supported Navy headquarters and the ship engineering command as a consultant. I was impressed by the expertise of the engineers who resolved hundreds of technical issues every day and also by the diligence of managers at Navy headquarters who juggled priorities to stretch the budget to cover emergent needs. The years I spent on ships and in shipyards allowed me to understand their priorities and needs, which was important in designing enterprise change solutions that met everyone's needs.

In the relationship economy, you frequently will liaison with external organizations and other parts of your organization. If you haven't worked in those organizations, it will be challenging for you to appreciate the real needs and priorities of people who work there. Therefore, to achieve success in inter-organizational and global projects, invest the time to understand the perspectives of people in those organizations and help them understand yours.

WAKE-UP CALL

*"Thanks for the kick in my seat. I know it wasn't pleasant
for either of us, but it truly was* win-win. *It made a huge
difference in my life and the lives of my young family."*
—Excerpt from letter from former employee

My company "de-hired" employees who didn't perform. That is, we helped them find new jobs instead of firing them. The first employee we de-hired was smart and worked hard, but his experience and style didn't fit our projects. During the month he looked for a new job, we helped him prepare a resume and granted paid leave for him to interview. He was understandably uncomfortable with our help, but three years later he wrote me a letter that included the quote at the top of this vignette. In virtually every case, de-hiring advanced the career of the employees who left and motivated employees who remained.

When a relationship isn't working, how we change it is vital to our future success. Notice I said *"change it,"* not *"end it."* Ten years later, for example, I reconnected and had lunch with our first de-hire. He had become project manager for a large IT project at another firm, and he recommended me to the CEO of his company as a prospective client for the exit-planning consulting services that I offer.

Of course, we all want co-workers who produce superior results, but providing wake-up calls to underachievers is critical on high-performing teams. If you surrender to the *fear-of-confrontation* dragon by failing to replace employees who don't fit or to change processes that aren't working, your team's performance and your personal success are likely to deteriorate.

It is essential to build teams with people of diverse abilities, ideas, and backgrounds, but not at the expense of the organization's performance. So as you embrace differences, be sure the differences contribute to high performance. If you have workers who are not up to par, make changes. Like me, you probably will find that de-hiring such people may benefit both your organization and the workers who have to move on. Perhaps their skills and abilities aren't suited to your team, but they may be of use to another organization.

ARE YOU MY FRIEND?

We're all partners in the relationship economy,
even if your objectives are different than mine.

During a monthly billing cycle, the project manager for a large contract began a shouting match with the controller. The issue was the accounting department had rejected a subcontractor invoice claiming it contained insufficient data to justify the costs. The project manager said, *"Just process the* (expletive deleted) *invoice. I know they did the work, and the client liked the results."* The shouting match lasted ten minutes while each of them repeated their point over and over without listening to the other's viewpoint.

The project manager's objective was to eliminate delays in getting the subcontractor paid, while the controller's objective was to ensure the company had adequate records to survive the annual audit by the federal government. The two equally valid objectives collided in a near-violent argument. It was an example of how we frequently treat colleagues who think differently or have different objectives as if they were adversaries who threatened our very existence when, in fact, they are really partners in our success.

In the relationship economy, smooth internal interactions are more essential than ever because the business must focus on building external relationships. Internal relationships form the foundation for productive relationships with external (often global) partners. Even as you challenge your colleagues' assumptions and actions, which is a healthy practice in any organization, you must adjust to diversity in work styles, deadlines, priorities, objectives, and perspectives.

Melding diversity in your organization into an effective team is especially important when you introduce a new idea or change. You can expect reactions that vary from an open willingness to explore new possibilities, to a *wait-and-see* dragon that passively resists the change, to a hostile dragon that actively rejects the new idea. How well you handle those responses to change will govern your future success, but effective and supportive relationships within your team must be a given.

SINGING PIGS

If you force a pig to sing, he won't sing very well ... and
you'll probably have a very angry pig on your hands.

I worked for a vice president of an aerospace company who reported to the CEO and directed a division with 3,000 people. All of the management positions and most technical positions in his division were filled by males who had an engineering degree. Many also were military veterans. To the best of my knowledge, this vice president had never worked for a woman in his thirty-year career. While he outwardly supported the company's goal to advance women, he didn't believe any woman in his division—not even those with engineering degrees—was ready for a promotion. Even when the CEO set a quota for promoting women, he couldn't tame his *women-aren't-qualified* dragon. As far as embracing and using diversity was concerned, this vice president was a singing pig.

The *singing pig* metaphor describes an attempt to force someone to do something they either aren't suited to do or just refuse to do. It doesn't work. Believe me, I have tried. Neither my strongest coercive nor evangelical techniques were able to make an extrovert pay attention to detail, or change an introvert into a bubbly salesman. In short, I can't make a pig sing and you can't either. To be successful in the relationship economy, you must build a team of colleagues who have the knowledge, relationships, skills, and attitudes required to achieve the objectives, such as the ability and willingness to embrace diversity. So put people in positions where they can thrive.

Change is a door that can only be opened from the inside. As a leader, you may be so strong, so logical, and so persuasive that others choose to follow you, but it's their choice. They also could choose to leave. Since you can't force anyone to change, the only reliable way to improve your team is to change yourself. If you want your team to embrace diversity, demonstrate how to incorporate diversity when you make decisions. If you want your teammates to take more risks, then take more risks yourself. If you want thoroughness, be more thorough. You'll be amazed at how quickly changing yourself will change your team—everyone except the singing pigs.

CLOSING THOUGHTS ON DIVERSITY

Get the best from every member of your team, including the person whom you consider to be the least significant.

One cold January morning at Rensselaer Polytechnic Institute, I walked through snow to the building where my psychology exam was being administered. As I opened the door, I noticed that the steps were cleared of snow and a maintenance man was spreading salt. Once in the classroom, I worked through the exam and got to the last question with ten minutes left. The question was: *"Who shoveled the stairs so you could enter the building safely today?"*

I thought the question was a joke. Did he really expect me to know the man's name? Just then, another student raised his hand and asked, *"Is the last question for real? Does it count in our grade?"* The professor answered, *"Yes, it counts. You will work with many people in your career, and each of them is vital to your success. They deserve your attention and your respect."* Only recently, as I've watched the relationship economy unfold, have I begun to understand exactly what my professor meant over forty years ago.

Like flowers in a botanical garden, humans in the workplace and in society have different sizes, colors, and shapes. The bouquet of human diversity includes age, race, religion, gender, mental ability, analytical style, sexual orientation, educational level, native language, birthplace, family situation, and many other factors. The combinations of these diversities distinguish you from me, even as we all share life on Earth.

Embracing diversity is a dragon for many people, including myself. It is a challenge that forces me to let go of old biases and to modify longstanding beliefs about my identity and priorities relative to the needs of others. In the workplace, embracing diversity is a highly charged subject. Generally, when the concept of embracing diversity is first introduced in an organization as a value, the change meets resistance, skepticism, and sometimes even hostility. Taming such dragons requires respect, patience, and understanding.

What is your reaction when the word *diversity* is discussed in your workplace? Does it make you feel uncomfortable? Does it trigger resistance? Why?

Embracing diversity means giving respect and trust to co-workers, customers, suppliers, and competitors regardless of their backgrounds, positions, or ideas. In general, we've been taught that respect and trust are earned. But I would like you to consider an entirely different approach: *Give respect and trust unconditionally instead of insisting that your colleagues earn it first*. That shift was a huge change for me. I've lived most of my life doling out respect and trust conditionally. I gave or withheld them to help get what I wanted. In my experience, many of the most complex business issues could be resolved by simply embracing diversity; that is, seeking to genuinely understand and accommodate your colleagues' perspectives.

A war is raging in our minds—a war based on the illusion that we are all separate beings. Separate from our parents and children, separate from our spouse and friends, separate from competitors and clients, separate from people in faraway lands, and separate from our enemies. When we hold that belief, unfortunately our natural reaction to change is to protect ourselves from others. The protection manifests itself in behaviors that inhibit our success, from aloofness to competition to terrorism. The protection becomes a filter through which we evaluate unusual events and people.

> Embracing diversity is giving respect and trust regardless of a person's background.

The global relationship economy is forcing diverse cultures into direct contact with one another, including some cultures that may not be ready for such global intimacy. While most cultures thrive on collaboration, a few cultures feel inferior and are threatened by intra-dependency. The global intimacy of the relationship economy makes it abundantly clear where each culture stands in relation to the others. Unfortunately, that revelation may create the frustration and anger that fuel prejudices, withdrawal, and even terrorism. Our ultimate hope, of course, is embracing diversity on a global scale. It can begin with you and I embracing the diverse ethnic backgrounds, styles, backgrounds, and preferences found in our workplaces.

COLLABORATION

Tip #6: Collaborate, Collaborate, Collaborate

OVERVIEW

To thrive in the relationship economy, determine what others want, collaborate to help them get it, and achieve your goals as a by-product of the collaboration. The most successful people and most effective organizations you know are usually among the best collaborators. Collaboration has always been valuable, but today it is even more crucial because no single organization can stay on top of rapidly changing customer needs and emerging technologies, especially in volatile markets like energy, computing, telecom, manufacturing, and biotech. In such unsteady markets, the *go-it-alone* dragon can be fatal.

The fifteen vignettes in Tip #6 show that collaboration produces results that are far superior to any that can be achieved independently. As a change leader, therefore, you must assemble a collaborative team, make collaboration an accepted value, and lead in a way that encourages collaboration. Use collaboration to eliminate any obstacles you encounter; and, when you only have part of the answer to a daunting business issue, collaborate to get the missing parts.

OPEN SYSTEMS

*Collaboration is a powerful technique that quickly
eliminates obstacles and delivers superior results.*

In the late 1970s, I worked for a company that sold software for Wang computers. At the time, Wang Laboratories offered the premier word processing system on the market. I made a sales visit to a government agency with a seasoned Wang sales representative. After five minutes, it was obvious the agency was a year away from purchasing anything. The Wang sales representative handed her business card to the government executive and said, *"We sell the best word processing that money can buy. Call me when you're ready to make a purchase,"* and walked out of the meeting.

I was stunned. I had never seen a sales person treat a potential client with such arrogance. The *go-it-alone* dragon was a frequent guest in Wang offices, and the company's stubborn refusal to collaborate by offering their word processing software on other manufacturers' computers was legendary. A few years later, Wang was a casualty of the industry shakeout along with other firms like Data General and Prime that resisted the move toward open systems. That shakeout of computer manufacturers was an early indicator of the death of the industrial age and the emergence of the relationship economy.

The computer industry started as a band of renegade fire companies. Imagine that every neighborhood in your city used a different sized fire hydrant connection. That wouldn't be a problem as long as your fire company could fight every fire in your neighborhood. But a multi-alarm fire would be a calamity because the fire companies who came to help wouldn't be able to connect their hoses to the fire hydrants in your neighborhood. Obviously, a computer industry with such lack of collaboration couldn't survive long in the relationship economy. And it didn't!

The industrial age was based on a command-and-control thinking that depended on rigid, hierarchical separations. The relationship economy, on the other hand, is a collaboration that breaks down barriers, permeates boundaries, and penetrates walls wherever they exist. It pushes to connect everything including people, ideas, communications systems, industries, businesses, and cultures. The world has shifted from separation to collaboration.

So, to maximize your success, make collaboration a habit. Collaborate every chance you see, even when it seems at first glance that collaboration isn't really necessary.

The tools available today to facilitate collaboration are nothing short of fantastic. The value of the Internet *"word of mouse"* and other ubiquitous tools like cell phones, BlackBerrys, and Web sites such as Linked-In and YouTube increase geometrically as the size of their user base expands. Over one hundred million people use the Internet every day, and that number may double by the time you read this. Internet-based software like Enterprise Resource Planning (ERP) and Customer Resource Management (CRM) systems link customers and organizations into a unified, worldwide business network. Furthermore, the largest knowledge centers on the planet are plugged into the Internet and are available instantly to any user in the world. If terrorism and misplaced geopolitical fears don't interfere, this collaboration will produce unprecedented increases in worldwide prosperity.

> The collaborative relationship economy pushes to connect people, ideas, cultures, industries, businesses, and systems.

Similarly, your personal value is directly proportional to the size of your personal and professional networks coupled with the effectiveness of your collaboration. Today, you can collaborate or compete with more people, on more subjects, from more locations than at any other time in the history of mankind. The undeniable result of all the e-mails, cell phones, BlackBerrys, and Internet connections is an epidemic of global collaboration. You can share knowledge and work products in real time with little concern for distance or location. Tame the *go-it-alone* dragon and ensure your success by using these collaboration tools to extend your relationship network into the second and third degrees of separation.

ENOUGH BUDGET

*To find order-of-magnitude breakthroughs, look for ways
to fundamentally change how you collaborate with others.*

When I meet a government executive for the first time, I say, *"Your agency has enough budget to accomplish everything it needs to do ..."* I pause for a few seconds while they look at me incredulously and think to themselves, *"That's absurd. Dick doesn't understand."* I then continue by saying, *"but not working like it works today."* I cite a case in which three large divisions of a single agency spent millions of dollars to transfer their operations to the Internet. When they found that their approaches were incompatible, they spent millions more to integrate the three systems.

The most significant performance breakthroughs don't come from process re-engineering, reorganizations, or new technologies. They're produced by changes in relationships—a fundamental shift in how we collaborate. It happens in government, for example, when the U.S. Coast Guard tames the *I'm-unique* dragon and finds ways to collaborate with other Homeland Security agencies, the U.S. Navy, and international navies. You can make it happen in your workplace by collaborating with other departments of your organization and with people in other organizations around the world.

Orchestra conductors demonstrate collaboration when they combine instruments and musicians into a virtuoso performance. Inventors also display the ability to combine concepts that previously were viewed as separate. When you collaborate, you combine ideas and resources in exciting new ways to solve vexing challenges. Collaboration requires you to synthesize (put things together) instead of analyze (take things apart), to build productive relationships where none existed before, and to create solutions by integrating what no one else thought to combine. In a world overflowing with choices, ideas, and information, the ability to collaborate is an essential skill.

Some business leaders realize that today's business world requires different skills. Many more, though, have yet to see the light. The art of managing has become ever more complex as organizations move from command-and-control to relationship-centric management. For sure, the need for relationship-savvy leaders isn't new, but several new factors intensify the need for enlightened managers.

First, the compounded impact of years of rapid change has widened the gap between industry leaders and followers. For example, global supply chains have produced huge efficiency gains and new clients for some companies, but others haven't invested in such new production technologies. They find themselves falling behind in price competitions and don't know how to catch up. Collaboration is the answer.

The second factor is economic realities that add urgency to the need to change. Labor costs have leveled out recently, but the cost of health care and other benefits continues to spiral out of control. Cost control has always been essential, but today's economic pressures are forcing organizations to collaborate with external partners to develop joint solutions that were unthinkable a few short years ago.

The third factor, of course, is collaboration technologies that have reshaped how and with whom we work. It isn't like governments and businesses did not collaborate in the past. But the tools that are available today to integrate ideas, make global connections, and find resources have lifted the art of collaboration to a whole new level.

> To collaborate, put ideas together rather than criticizing them, and build effective relationships where none existed before.

Many leaders confuse collaboration with cooperation. To be sure, trust, shared objectives, and mutual benefit are essential for both. But collaboration is more powerful than cooperation because it can produce innovative solutions to multidimensional challenges, not just deal with shared issues. Cooperation integrates what you already plan to do with what I already plan to do. We usually can accomplish both with fewer resources. On the other hand, collaboration happens at a higher level: It integrates your objectives with my objectives. The result is often a new strategy that neither of us had thought of before (Stephen Covey refers to it as the *Third Alternative*). Collaboration uses complementary knowledge, relationships, and resources to tap the power of collective thinking. Do you cooperate or collaborate in your current business relationships?

DREAM HOUSE

The power of the Universe is at your fingertips. It will deliver whatever you ask for, if you'll collaborate to make it happen.

My wife and I started a notebook for our dream house soon after we were married in 1967. The book contained a section for each room we wanted in the house. When we saw something we liked in a magazine or at someone's home, we put a picture in the book. After my older brother died in 1999 at age fifty-nine, we walked out of his funeral, looked at each other, and simultaneously said, *"Why are we waiting to build that dream house?"* Of course, the problem was we didn't think we could afford a house with everything in our notebook.

I asked for ideas to finance the new house at my next CEO meeting. One CEO, owner of a construction company, reviewed the notebook and estimated the cost of the house. My *I-can't-afford-that* dragon tried to squash the whole idea, but collaboration tamed it. I met with another CEO who was a bank president and asked him, *"I need to borrow a lot of money. I know the group rules don't allow you to make the loan, but can you point me in the right direction?"* He looked at my personal financial statements, told me how to respond to the likely questions, and referred me to another bank that granted the loan. A friend who was a real estate agent helped sell our existing house and negotiate the contract to build our dream house. As I write this story, we've lived in our dream house for eight years. Big dreams can come true, but they will require big-time collaboration.

In the relationship economy, the power of the Universe is at your fingertips. You can have anything you dream by collaborating with the Universe. Ask the Universe for your equivalent of a dream house. It may take time to get a response, so be patient. However, don't let the futility dragon tell you it's impossible. That dragon is why you don't have it already. Whatever it is, all you need is support and collaboration from only a few of Earth's seven billion inhabitants. If you don't find them today, keep looking. Tomorrow may be the day you collaborate with the right person to achieve your dream goal.

A NEW BREED

The effectiveness of your collaboration skills will determine the magnitude of your success in the relationship economy.

I started my company in 1984 and grew it to about $20 million in annual revenue, an achievement I'm quite proud of. But I know three men who started similar companies in 1984. The revenue of one company reached $300 million, the second exceeded $100 million, and the third grew to $75 million during the same period. None of those founders worked as many hours as I did, and they didn't have the academic credentials or technical expertise that I have. How did they succeed at a level so much higher than I did?

The answer is collaboration. All three had partners while I embraced the *do-it-myself* dragon. They hired key executives based on relationships while I hired for skills. They risked collaborating with companies and people who had ideas out of the mainstream, but my strategies were predictable. They built partnerships while I operated independently most of the time.

Collaboration is an interdependent relationship that relies on trust. The relationship partners give and receive so that both achieve top-notch results. The other kinds of relationships, independent and dependent, aren't as effective. For example, my independent operating style frequently produced separation and a sense of competition.

Organizational structures are evolving as the relationship economy matures. Industrial age holdouts still are organized with a headquarters, and regional and international divisions linked by a top-down strategy. By contrast, forward-looking organizations organize as a synergistic set of joint ventures, minority ownership interests, and knowledge-sharing agreements. That kind of collaboration requires a new breed of executives whose skill is nurturing existing relationships and building new ones. Managers whose primary skills are limited to operations, production, or administration will still be important, but they will function as second-tier managers. Maximize your future success by cultivating your ability to collaborate.

THE TRIPLE BOTTOM LINE

Today's companies are measured by three
bottom lines: Profits, people, and the planet.

Early in 2007, Circuit City announced it laid off 3,000 highly paid retail employees to reduce expenses. Unfortunately, in April, the company reported a first quarter loss and large decline in sales. It also lowered its annual revenue forecast because sales of flat panel TVs were down. The Wall Street Journal analyzed the results and said the company had lost sales to competitors whose sales force was "better able to collaborate with customers." Circuit City cut expenses, but its bottom line was a loss because it threw away the ability to convince customers to buy big-ticket items. It also was in the red on the people bottom line.

Henry Ford said Ford Motor Company didn't need managers; it just needed a visionary like himself and a set of competent helpers. Some executives, unfortunately, still believe that today. The concept that he required people smarter than himself in specialty areas (e.g., finance, marketing, and sales) didn't occur to Mr. Ford. Arguably, his strategy worked in the early 1900s, but it's a formula for failure in the relationship economy. To sustain success, businesses must reach sales and profit goals, and take care of their customers and employees. People are the second bottom line of business.

But, on an increasing basis, consumers also are demanding that companies be sensitive about the environment—the third "bottom line." Today, corporate executives must balance the company as a business with three bottom lines:

(1) An economic bottom line that produces consistent profits;

(2) A human bottom line that takes care of its people; and

(3) A planet bottom line that is a steward of the environment.

In the industrial age, companies existed only to produce profits. In the relationship economy, corporations are expected to collaborate in the domains of social and environmental issues. Of course, a corporation can make social and environmental contributions only if it continues to be profitable. How does your company measure up against the triple bottom line?

THE COLLABORATION CHAIN

Collaboration produces unexpectedly favorable results.
It puts you into a chain of relationships that sometimes
can reach the third and fourth degrees of separation.

I joined a CEO group in 1998. One CEO in the group invited me to participate in a weekend retreat for men. During that retreat, I became friends with a lawyer who helped me sell my company and establish a trust for my family. He also introduced me to two other CEOs who became consulting clients. I referred the two CEOs to CPAs who subsequently introduced them to financial planners and new clients. Collaboration chains like this, which extended to the third degree of separation, are common in the relationship economy. The chain begins and grows by collaborating. I would have missed the entire chain if I said *NO* to joining the CEO group ten years ago.

Collaboration enables professional and personal associates to spread their strengths and resolve their challenges. You achieve your goals while you help others achieve theirs. Collaboration elevates networking, always an effective business practice, to a whole new level. Whenever you speak with someone, including the strangers (new friends?) you meet every day, determine what they want to accomplish, and ensure they also understand your goals too. Every member of your business and social circles should know how they can help the other members, and what kind of help they expect to receive when they need it.

As a collaboration leader, strive to optimize results on both an individual and collective level. You'll find that cutthroat competition still exists in the relationship economy, even among your closest business associates and strategic partners. Tame the competition dragon whenever it raises its head. Instead, use collaboration to answer the *"Why am I here?"* question when you're in meetings or having a casual business conversation. Collaboration gives you reasons to succeed beyond just a bigger paycheck to pay the mortgage, car payment, and your children's college tuition. Collaboration transforms work into fun!

10 PERCENT HUMAN

Our planet depends on collaboration to exist. Trees collaborate with humans by breathing carbon dioxide and emitting oxygen while we humans breathe oxygen and emit carbon dioxide.

You probably think you take pretty good care of yourself physically. But did you know you get help from trillions of microbes and bacteria that live in your body? Scientists say we couldn't live without the organisms in our intestines and blood, since they perform essential functions that human cells cannot do. On a cell-count basis, just 10 percent of our bodies are human cells. The rest is micro-life. Human cells are much larger, so microbes and bacteria contribute only about three pounds to the average person's weight. On a cellular scale, therefore, we are hybrid creatures whose continued existence depends on collaboration among human cells, microbes, and bacteria.

The same is true with the seven billion humans on Earth. We couldn't exist without the functions performed by others. Most of the time, we don't know who they are, where they live, or precisely what they do for us. For example, do you know the people who purify the water you drink or grow the fruit you eat? They are as different from us as microbes and bacteria are from human cells, yet each performs a vital function in the relationship economy. If collaboration works for such essential functions, doesn't it make sense for you to collaborate to achieve the success you want?

There was a time I thought it was easier to do things myself. I also thought the results would be better when I did it myself. Those were literally killer dragons. In addition to limiting my output and success, they exhausted me mentally and physically. I couldn't do everything myself. Even when I had the skills, I didn't have enough time. Today, I look for opportunities to collaborate. You shouldn't feel forced to do everything yourself either; just be sure it gets done. The relationship economy is so specialized and communications are so ubiquitous that it's often easier, faster, and more effective to find a collaboration partner to get something done than to do it yourself.

HIGH-PERFORMING TEAM

Encouraging collaboration improves team performance
while politics submerges the hard truths and limits growth.

My company supported a multibillion-dollar Navy acquisition program. The program manager said open and honest communications were a core value of his program. He encouraged collaboration and directed his staff to be open and honest with him, with each other, and with oversight authorities. One day he said, *"My staff isn't suggesting new ideas like they used to. Sometimes I feel they aren't telling me the whole story. Why?"* I shifted uneasily in the chair and wondered how to tell the emperor he was naked. Finally, I said, *"Remember the All Hands meeting when you told everyone that the new logistics strategy was the dumbest idea you had ever heard? That judgment shut off the team's creativity."* Outspoken members of his staff were unaffected by his judgment, but the mild-mannered people were afraid to suggest anything new. His staff meetings had become listening rituals instead of collaborative discussions of emerging issues and new solutions.

By comparison, my CEO group meetings certainly weren't rituals. They almost always were frank discussions of core issues. If a CEO presented a business issue but omitted facts or minimized his contribution to the problem, another CEO would call him on it. For example, at my first CEO meeting, an issue was being presented and the presenter resisted the group's recommendations. Another CEO halted the dialog and said, *"Wait a minute. You don't have to do what we recommend, but you do have to listen."* I knew I was with people who valued collaboration and were genuinely committed to resolving problems quickly.

In the relationship economy, speed wins. Collaboration accelerates solutions and creates opportunities for success. Behaviors that impede collaboration will slow decision-making and reduce team performance. The matrix on the next page lists ten traits of high-performing teams and contrasts each trait with behaviors by low- and average-performing teams. Ask yourself if you as a leader and your team as an organization operate in the high-performing category.

TEAM	PERFORMANCE LEVEL		
TRAIT	LOW	AVERAGE	HIGH
Prevailing Attitude	I'm here for the paycheck	The team shares success	I'm responsible for success
Ownership of Results	Managers produce results	The team produces results	I produce results
Discussion of Issues	Avoided if possible	Politely when comfortable	Directly when necessary
Goal Setting	Don't care about goals	Management sets goals	Collaborate to set goals
When I Don't Like Things	Ignore the issue	Complain to a manager	Collaborate to take action
Professional Growth	Expect to be spoon-fed	Take what is offered	Aggressively pursue growth
When Others Perform Poorly	I don't care	Report it to management	Push them to improve
Hiring New Employees	I don't care	Managers do the hiring	Everyone looks for team players
Business Setbacks	Leave the company	Feel bad about leaving company	Collaborate in the turn-around
Reaction to Problems	None	Slow	Rapid

Ten Traits of High-Performing Teams

Unfortunately, you may know of behaviors that are in the low or average categories in some parts of your organization. Those behaviors block collaboration, slow the response to change, and adversely affect growth. You may also find that an *us-versus-them* dragon uses actual results and unforeseen developments as a shield (*See, what we do works*) or a sword (*What they do doesn't work*). The goal of some people isn't to collaborate and resolve issues, rather it is to brand other parts of the organization as ineffective. If there are self-limiting behaviors in your organization, use this table to facilitate open and honest discussions that produce collaboration. Good luck!

GLOBAL REFERRALS

Referral networks are the heartbeat of the relationship economy. Keep everyone you meet in your network.

When my wife and I made our first-ever visit to Paris, the City of Light, our plan was to tour the city and take day trips to Versailles and Mount St. Michel. My wife found several excursion companies on the Internet. We were concerned about committing to an expensive tour with an unknown company, so we checked references thoroughly. We selected Paris Luxury Tours. Good choice! In addition to superb site visits, the drive into the French countryside and gourmet lunches at quaint restaurants exceeded our high expectations.

This would be a ho-hum story if it ended there. It doesn't. My wife and I told everyone about the wonderful day trips and referred three travelers to the owner of the tour company. He asked if I would share my experiences with a new client who lived close to us. I said *YES*. The contact actually turned out to be a potential client for me too. Collaboration had produced unexpected results.

To collaborate effectively, I must know your skills and needs so I can connect you to people who want those skills or can satisfy those needs. Likewise, I must communicate to you the value I offer and my needs. Later, when I discover the match of a skill with your need, I'll initiate the connection and risk my credibility by saying, *"I think she will help you."* That statement is a commitment, a promise to you and my referral that there is probably value in investing in this relationship. If possible, I like to participate in the first meeting, often at a breakfast or lunch meeting, or over coffee at Starbucks. If a three-way meeting isn't practical to arrange, a three-way e-mail is the next best introduction technique.

Referral networks are the cornerstone of the relationship economy. Judgments of value that exclude someone from your referral network are dragons. Contacts who may appear insignificant today may be stars tomorrow, potentially key relationships. They will remember that you respected them before they became stars. On the other hand, contacts who have weak *values* need to be excluded from your network no matter what their *value* may be.

HERO MODE

*Rescuing your staff from today's crisis may feel
good, but that behavior contributes to future crises
that force you to be a hero over and over again.*

A CEO client proudly told me that he had rescued a project manager from a difficult contract issue. It took two days to evaluate the issue, contact the client, define the recovery tasks, and assign them to the project team. When I asked, *"How did the project manager feel about receiving your help, and how much did he learn?"* the CEO looked at me as if I had asked the question in Greek. A few minutes later in the same meeting, the CEO complained that he was overloaded with problems to solve. Operating in hero mode may be ego-gratifying, but it is a dragon that limits growth and inhibits the collaboration that's essential for success in an organization.

In my experience, the five most common leadership behaviors that reduce collaboration and adversely impact team performance are:

(1) Impatience with how fast issues are resolved by others;

(2) Compulsion to control everything;

(3) Insensitivity to the emotional side of business problems;

(4) Inability to delegate authority and really let go of control; and

(5) Focusing on tasks instead of processes and results.

Control is the antithesis of collaboration. It's not that collaboration is good and control is bad. When the house is on fire, control puts out the fire quickly. But when the objective is to train the fire department, collaboration works better. Choose the appropriate style of leadership for the circumstances.

High-performing organizations in business, government, and sports share one common characteristic: Every part of the team contributes to success. But overall performance may suffer if one part is more efficient than the others. Paradoxically, team performance can improve if that segment becomes less dominant. To enhance the overall performance of your team, create a dynamic performance balance among all parts of the organization.

ASKING QUESTIONS

*Appreciative inquiry enhances collaboration while
judgments jeopardize the possibility of collaboration.*

As a director in a large aerospace firm, business development was my primary job. The Air Force issued a Request For Proposals (RFP), and I took the lead as proposal manager. The RFP requested a data system that converted operating plans into budget requirements. Phase I of the five-year project was system design. In total, the three phases were estimated to cost $350 million. The first line of the RFP read, *"The Air Force will make two Phase I awards totaling $15 million."* The proposal team concluded that our Phase I price had to be $7.5 million or less to win.

The team worked day and night for six weeks to write the proposal. Our bare-bones Phase I costs were $8.1 million. The vice president and I flew to headquarters to present the proposal to our CEO and get his approval to invest $600,000 of company funds to win the Phase I contract. The CEO didn't ask a single question during my hour-long presentation. At the end, he said abruptly, *"No. If the Air Force wants us they'll find more money,"* and walked out of the room.

We submitted our proposal at full price and lost. Two other bidders got contracts for $7.5 million each. I was frustrated, and the proposal team was angry because we worked so hard and long on the proposal. Since the CEO didn't ask questions and there wasn't any discussion, the team felt we lost because of a capricious decision. The entire team, including myself, left the company within a year.

Questions foster collaboration and strengthen relationships because they imply respect for the person who is answering. Asking questions may seem weak, but actually the questioner is directing the direction of the conversation, potentially toward new possibilities and conclusions. Find out what your relationship partners really want and help them get it. Asking questions is an effective way to identify those wants and to find mutually acceptable ways to satisfy them. You may even discover a possibility that neither of you had thought of before you asked the questions.

R-E-S-P-E-C-T

*Collaboration and mutual respect encourage everybody
from the mail clerk to the CEO to contribute to success.*

As the production engineer at Charleston Naval Shipyard, I managed the machines and tools used by 7,000 production workers. We spent nearly $300,000 per quarter on hand tools, and suspected that many tools were walking out the gate at the end of the day. So we conducted a procurement for an automated tool control system and awarded two contracts at a total cost of about $280,000.

The project goals were to save money and control tools. Two companies were hired: one for hardware and communications, and the other for software and training. They agreed to complete the project in eight weeks, living and working in a Winnebago seven days a week. On the Navy side, the team included the project manager from my staff, a tool shop foreman with over thirty years' experience, a union steward, and a group of tool room attendants who were among the lowest-paid workers in the entire shipyard.

In my forty-year career, this was the only software project that was completed on time and under budget. Why did this project succeed so much better than most? Simple. The tool room attendants who most people viewed as insignificant were respected and valued as members of the team. That respect motivated them and tapped into their creativity. They were proud to be operating a computer.

Late in the first week of operations, a machinist tried to draw a tool. The tool room attendant refused to issue the tool and provided a printed list of the twenty tools (maximum allowed by shipyard policy) the machinist had already drawn. News about the incident spread like wildfire, and tool replacement costs dropped to less than $50,000 per quarter in the second quarter of full operations.

During workshops and presentations on change, I've asked several hundred people, *"What is the most satisfying experience of your entire career?"* Every one of them has answered by describing a group of people who conquered a challenge through extraordinary creativity and collaboration. How would you answer the question? Do you stimulate that kind of environment in your workplace?

PARTNERING

Partnering is the lifeblood of the relationship economy. As Bill Gates says, "Sometimes lambs must lie down with wolves."

A friend managed the project to implement bar coding at the U.S. Postal Service's bulk mail centers. The complex project required collaboration among the Postal Service's management, supervisors, workers, and unions. Management guaranteed that there would be no job cuts, and anyone transferred to a new job would receive a pay increase. My friend met with workers in mail centers across the country to design new processes and get buy-in. He resolved worker concerns by incorporating them as process improvements. He also worked alongside gay men in some places, which was a challenge for him due to his beliefs. The project's success was built on conscious collaboration with all stakeholders regardless of differences.

My friend's experience parallels my own. As government projects grew larger and more complex, my company's success in winning contracts depended on knowing the client's requirements and constraints. In partnering with other companies, the question was who would be the prime contractor and who would become subcontractors. We all wanted to prime, of course, but the team based the decision on who gave us the best chance of winning, usually the company with the largest network of relationships and most influential connections with the agency's leaders.

A definite move toward expanded collaboration is happening; and boundaries among the public sector, private sector, and nonprofits are blurring. Governments at all levels are facing the reality that the key social issues of our time (e.g., increasing energy usage, education, anti-terrorism, and the revitalization of cities) cannot be solved by governments alone. Government's role is shifting from delivering services to governing the services. The private sector is doing more of the service delivery while governments are facilitating partnerships to support citizens more efficiently. Whether you are in government or industry, there are significant opportunities in this shift to improve your organization and meet its operating goals.

JUST SAY *YES*

When you don't know what to say, try saying YES.
YES *builds responsibility for results in the requestor,
which is one of your goals as a leader of change.*

In past years, my company held its Christmas Awards Banquet in mid-December. Last year, members of the organizing team wanted to hold it in mid-January instead. Their idea was that everyone would meet at the Washington waterfront for cocktails, take a boat ride on the Potomac, have dinner in Mount Vernon, and distribute awards on the return boat trip. Immediately, my control dragon shouted, *"That's crazy! Christmas is in December, and it could be cold on the river in January."* But I tamed the dragon long enough to just listen. The team leader said most places were booked in December, and the prices were lower in January. Reluctantly, I said, *"YES."* It turned out to be one of our best banquets of all. Everyone had a great time, morale was high, and more former employees were able to attend because there was no conflict with their company's December Christmas party.

The relationship economy generates ideas that, at first, seem off-the-wall. After hearing such ideas, you can respond in three ways:

- **NO!** Then further damage relationships by adding statements like *"That's a dumb idea!"* or *"Why would we ever do that?"*
- **YES.** Which supports the requestor but may be risky; or
- Ask questions to determine why the intelligent person standing in front of you would suggest an idea that seemed so outrageous.

When you ask questions and then say *YES*, you build responsibility for results. When you don't know what to say, try saying *YES*.

YES is a collaboration message. When you say *YES*, you strengthen relationships. *YES* empowers people to achieve more while *NO* is a message of rejection. *NO* forces your teammates to defend their ideas, or to find another way. Their loyalty to you will determine how many *NO*s they'll accept before seeking employment elsewhere. Based on the number of people who move from one company to another in the relationship economy, there are too many *NO*s and not enough *YES*es.

CLOSING THOUGHTS ON COLLABORATION

Your ability to reach out and get help is roughly equal to your willingness to reach out and collaborate with others.

While I was listening to a radio talk show during my drive to work one morning, the host said that his son was struggling with high school math. In particular, the problem was with quadratic equations. The host asked if any listener could help. I planned to call when I got to work, but before I arrived the host announced that the station had received two hundred responses in ten minutes and the telephone lines were swamped. That's relationship economy collaboration!

You might not be able to broadcast a request for help over radio or TV, but you can tap into the plethora of connections that are available in the relationship economy. I'm sure you already use a cell phone, e-mail, or a BlackBerry to collaborate with an ever-expanding network of people on new opportunities. You may even use YouTube, Linked-In, or another networking tool to maintain business contacts. But only the dragon that says, "*Nobody can help me*" or "*I don't want to appear weak*" stands in the way of reaching out even further. That dragon may be all that holds you back from being everything you can be in today's changing world. The number of ways to collaborate with the second and third degrees of separation is growing rapidly.

The reason you build relationships is to give them away. Just as you keep money in a savings account to use on a rainy day, nurture relationships to provide value to your other relationship partners. Over time they will add value to a new opportunity and be there to help you escape a crisis. Finding partners for business collaboration is usually easier than finding a new friend. In business, people know what they are searching for and are more likely to share their resource needs and goals. Knowing their needs and goals points you toward solutions and referrals that will be of value to them.

However, the realm of personal relationships is more complex. There are no sales brochures to tell you what motivates your personal relationships. Friends may not even know their own goals. Intimate relationships are more about chemistry than value, but collaboration is still an essential ingredient in those relationships.

In the industrial age, *quid pro quo* was expected when an introduction was made and the relationship produced value. Such expectations are taboo in the relationship economy. You don't want business partners worried about *quid pro quo* as they consider an offer of introduction. That concern could limit their willingness to accept your introductions, and shrink the size and effectiveness of your network. Reduce friction in brokering relationships. Disappear after you make an introduction. Such behaviors encourage people to accept more of your introductions, since they know you don't expect something in return. Even though immediate payback isn't expected, people will naturally want to do something for you in the future. *Pay it forward* by depositing collaboration savings into your relationships bank.

> As your network expands, your world will shrink. It becomes harder to avoid people and impossible to deceive them for long.

When your network expands, in some ways your world will actually shrink. It's more difficult today to avoid people, harder to ignore what they're doing, and nearly impossible to deceive them for very long. The world is tightly connected. When you take an action in one relationship (good or bad), it's likely that your other relationship partners will quickly know what you've done. Build your personal supply chain for information and support by collaborating with like-minded people in all areas of your personal and professional life. Use every tool, technology, and strategy you can think of to collaborate, collaborate, collaborate.

Part III

ACTIONS

Only Actions Change Reality

OVERVIEW

In the time-space realm of business, only actions produce success. Goals define possibilities and planning provides a direction, but actions change the reality of the world around us. Success requires two kinds of actions: actions to start new things and actions to stop doing some things you do today. The second is more difficult than the first. You must tame the dragons of change that resist letting go of what you have today to release the time and resources you will need to achieve what you want tomorrow.

At the beginning of each day, your success is bounded by the possibilities you visualize. The vignettes in this introduction to Part III: *Actions* show you how to take the first step toward those possibilities, and demonstrate that speed and commitment are crucial to success in the relationship economy. The action journey from possibilities to results has four steps:

(1) *Purpose* – Know what and why you want to change;

(2) *Planning* – Set goals and make plans to achieve them;

(3) *Innovation* – Be creative in your solutions; and

(4) *Execution* – Accomplish your plan effectively.

Tip #7 through Tip #10 present vignettes that address each of the four steps, respectively.

THE "KNOWING-DOING BORDER"

*Crossing the border between knowing and doing requires
you to take the first step, which is often the most difficult.*

T he Department of Homeland Security has undertaken a gargantuan
project called the Secure Borders Initiative (SBI). SBI's budget is
several billion dollars and it will employ thousands of new border
guards. When fully operational, SBI will integrate a network of sophisticated
technologies ranging from electronic fences, unmanned aerial vehicles, and
surveillance cameras to infrared detectors, seismic detectors, and motion
detectors. If anything even attempts to cross the border, the SBI sensors will
detect the change and immediately move to prevent the intrusion.

Functioning like SBI's technologies, many of us have a hoard of dragons
that guard the border between our *knowing* and *doing*. To name just a few,
there are the *wait-until* dragon, the *fear-of-failure* dragon, the *I'll-do-it-tomorrow*
dragon, the *lack-of-resources* dragon, and the *doubts-about-capabilities* dragon
that attempt to prevent you from taking action to change your organization
or your career. You probably already know most of the actions required
to succeed in the relationship economy. On the organizational side, it is
investing in efficient procedures, new technologies, and strategic partnerships. On the personal side, it is earning a technical certification or an
advanced degree, volunteering for a leading-edge project, moving to a more
progressive organization, expanding your relationship network, or starting
your own business.

But somehow it's difficult to leave the comfort zone and take those
actions. With surveillance systems as complex as the SBI, our dragons detect
thoughts of change and mobilize the *reason* guards to stop you from crossing
the border from *knowing* into *doing*. To push your organization and career
toward success, you must tame those dragons.

Unfortunately, we tend to change our actions only when the pain of the
status quo is substantially greater than the pain of change. However, the pain
of *status quo* may be years away, while you will feel the pain of change today.
For example, consider the urgent need to develop strategic organizational

relationships to succeed in the relationship economy. The pain of change requires you to invest your resources, time, and trust, all of which are in short supply. So you continue down the path that the organization is currently on, deluding yourself that you will make the necessary changes tomorrow.

The same thing happens on the personal side. As an employee, you may see your company struggling to survive in a changing market or falling behind the competition, or you know the future demand for your skills will decline. But the pain of a forced change to your career appears to be in the far-off future while the pain of acquiring new knowledge, moving to a new company, or starting your own business would occur today.

> As a knowledge worker, think and act like you are president of your own one-person company because, in fact, you are!

You must tame the dragons of change and take action because in the relationship economy you are responsible for your growth. In effect, each knowledge worker must think and act as if he is president of his own one-employee company because, in fact, he is. This is an about-face from the industrial age, when employees could depend on their companies to lay out a career-long strategy and provide training in new technologies as they came along. In the relationship economy, you'll probably switch jobs several times, and the organizations you work for will provide training to satisfy *their* needs rather than *your* needs. Therefore, it's up to you to build the portfolio of knowledge, skills, and relationships you'll need to succeed. It's up to you to cross the border between *knowing* and *doing* and enter the land of success.

WHAT WILL YOU STOP DOING?

*You probably think of action as doing more. But it
also takes action to stop doing things to release the
time and resources required for new possibilities.*

At a strategic planning retreat for a federal agency, I facilitated the
executive team through the process of identifying shortfalls in today's
results and selecting actions to improve performance. The list of
new possibilities was impressive. It contained nine great ideas that the team
prioritized based on estimated costs, risks, and return on investment. But
when the executives tried to allocate staff and budget to the new projects,
the process came to a screeching halt. There were not enough resources for
even the highest-priority new project.

Expecting that roadblock, I asked the next logical question: *"What will
your organizations stop doing so you can begin the new projects?"* The executive team agreed quickly on actions to improve results, but their inability to
agree on a single project to end was the dragon that ultimately limited the
agency's improvement. They compromised by agreeing to increase next year's
budget request to include the new items. Of course, Congress not only didn't
approve their budget request, it also reduced the agency's funding from the
previous year, which intensified their performance challenges.

Ending old actions is just as important as starting new ones, and it's
often more difficult. For example, New Year's resolutions generally are new
actions you commit to start (other than to stop smoking): dieting, a new
training program, exercising, or looking for a new job. But new starts can't
succeed unless you simultaneously stop doing something else.

One way to balance the time-resources equation is to set up a ledger
with columns for time and money. List your new starts, and the time and
money each will require. Do the same for the things that you plan to stop
doing. Since it's unlikely that you will have more time or money next year,
the amount you save from things you stop must at least equal the amount
you need for the new starts.

THREE DIMENSIONS OF POWER

*Influence is more powerful in the relationship economy
than control. Are you exercising all of your influence?*

A government executive took on the task of transforming his agency's workforce. Transformation included three initiatives: pay-for-performance, aligning competencies with mission, and increasing diversity. He developed a plan of action and identified the obstacles, which were formidable. Some were under his direct control within the agency while others needed support from the unions and action by the Office of Personnel Management (OPM).

The number and difficulty of the obstacles did not deter him from pursuing his goal. He formed a project office and allocated resources to manage day-to-day tasks. Those obstacles were under his direct control. Next he established liaison with union representatives to discuss and resolve issues, an area in which he had direct influence but no control. Third, he enrolled the department's Legislative Affairs Office to obtain OPM support for fundamental changes in personnel rules and practices. In that area, he had no control and only indirect influence. Today, as I write this vignette, this multi-year initiative is a work in progress, but so far the forward momentum is impressive.

This government executive understood that your power as a leader in the relationship economy has three dimensions. To achieve your truly big goals, you must exercise all three dimensions. The three dimensions of power are:

- ***Direct Control.*** Eliminating obstacles that you control directly, usually by allocating your personal time and attention, your staff, and other resources to areas that you manage. Eliminating such obstacles requires that *you change yourself.*
- ***Direct Influence.*** Eliminating obstacles over which you have firsthand influence but not direct control, such as actions by clients, suppliers, and competitors. This dimension is often a frustrating dragon because, despite your influence, they may make decisions you don't want or like. By using direct influence, you try to change someone that you deal with regularly.

- ***Indirect Influence.*** Eliminating obstacles over which you have no control and no firsthand influence. World events, laws, and regulations fall in this dimension. It may seem like you are powerless to change them. But, while your unilateral power is limited, you can band with others (e.g., in associations) who face similar obstacles and together eliminate them.

Most people focus on the first dimension, but actions in the second and third dimensions are really what will determine the magnitude of your success in the relationship economy.

> Exercise your power in all three dimensions to achieve your most important goals.

Notice that all three dimensions of power involve achieving results through relationships. In exercising direct control, you are leading the people whom you supervise, a significant task in itself. In exercising direct influence, you are enrolling clients, strategic partners, and other parts of your own organization to support your goal.

Many books have been written on the topics of strategic partnerships, negotiations, and customer care to help in the second dimension. The third dimension, indirect influence, is where the relationship economy provides opportunities and tools (e.g., blog sites and YouTube) that were not available in the past.

Your actions in the second and third dimensions will enable you to achieve your biggest goals. In the industrial age, it was difficult to accomplish changes through actions in these dimensions. But the relationship economy opened the floodgates to change by connecting like-minded people around the globe. The bigger the goals you set, the more your success will depend on exercising your personal power in the second and third dimensions.

THE PAIN OF CHANGE

*The journey to success frequently will require
you to endure the short-term pain of change.*

My sister-in-law is an animal lover who often keeps five or more dogs in her home. She protects them with an electric fence. But Hubert, a springer spaniel, was one dog she couldn't contain. Hubert knew the pain of the electric fence, but it didn't stop him. One day, I watched as he stood ten feet from the fence and focused on his escape. Then he sprinted as fast as he could go and leaped through the electric fence with a yelp. His momentum carried him through the pain to freedom. After brief adventures in the neighborhood, Hubert would return home and wait for my sister-in-law to let him in the front door. He wasn't willing to suffer pain to go back where he used to be.

Many barriers to success are like electric fences. To get where you want to go, you might have to endure transitional pain like Hubert jumping through a fence. Ever wonder how successful leaders always seem to be in the right place? It's because they put their organizations and themselves in position to succeed by taking action to prepare for new opportunities. They tame the dragon of short-term pain that holds their organization inside today's comfortable "box."

Psychologists say humans are driven more by pain-avoidance than by pleasure seeking. Therefore, to achieve the pleasure of future success, you must conquer a natural resistance to change (which, for the most part, is painful). Similarly, an organization moves forward when it consistently makes small changes to prepare for the future. When change becomes normal and comfortable, organizations increase their chances for success.

Successful leaders don't waste precious time trying to avoid the pain of change. Instead, they tolerate pain, and make change a habit in their organization and their personal routines. Your success momentum depends more on the actions you are taking today than on your past successes, your resources, or your luck. Don't avoid action because of the short-term pain of the first step.

IMAGINE THE UNIMAGINABLE

In planning your future, consider that in ten years the world
will be very different in ways you can barely imagine today.

In 1994, I helped to plan a large technology project for the Defense Department. The project stretched 1994 technologies by attempting to digitize and electronically distribute technical manuals, maintenance processes, and repair parts data for Navy, Marine Corps, Air Force, and Army systems. The project had the potential to revolutionize military operations. It was supported by everyone and was funded by Congress in the annual Defense budget. The project reached its zenith in the late 1990s, when then-available technology matched project requirements. However, the project was terminated in 2004 because its cumbersome development processes were too slow to exploit rapid advances in Internet capabilities and data management technologies that continue to this day.

The relationship economy is largely propelled by the creative use of new technologies. Since a technology generation is roughly two years long, we can only imagine what the world might look like in ten years, about five technology generations from today. Your business, project, and career plans must anticipate that the world will be a very different place in ten years. Your future success depends on your ability to imagine what the world might look like then and the actions you take to prepare your organization and yourself for that new world.

The winners in the relationship economy will be those who swiftly apply new collaboration technologies to build alliances. There are no guarantees that the winners will be American. They could be in Russia, China, India, or another country that is not encumbered by yesterday's technologies. For example, China doesn't have a landline telephone system like ours, but they have many more cell phones in use. We think of such countries as lagging behind, but they can implement new collaboration techniques quickly without depending on old systems that anchor us in the past. Scary thought? What actions can you take to transform that competitive reality into a positive instead of a negative?

CLOSING THOUGHTS ON ACTIONS

In a world that is changing faster than ever before, your success depends on how quickly you are able to sense a change and make an effective response.

Arguably, the world changed more on September 11, 2001, than on any other day in history. Everyone sensed the change. In the first year, the government responded with increased airport security, the Patriot Act, the Department of Homeland Security, and a jail for terrorists in Guantanamo Bay, Cuba. But in recent years, Congress has fallen prey to the *perfect-solutions* dragon, a paralyzing dragon that enables otherwise brilliant people to conceal their lack of action in an endless search for the perfect answer to a changing problem. But, action or inaction by an organization, even one as complex as Congress, is merely the sum of the actions by its members. On an individual basis, we sense change but sometimes place our response on hold while we search for the perfect solution.

The relationship economy is increasingly unstable because it is characterized by rapid and unpredictable change. The only strategy that can possibly succeed in such an environment is one that senses and adapts efficiently to changes in technologies, relationships, and markets. Adaptation, however, means more than just flexibility and agility. It also requires effective responses. If change is unpredictable, it follows that your responses will be unpredictable too—at least from the perspective that responses that worked last year might not work as well today. When the underlying reality is unpredictability, you must continuously re-examine habitual, comfortable actions to ensure that they are still effective in the new reality.

In today's ever-changing world, you don't need more data to succeed; you need more action. Don't wait for the *perfect* response or the *perfect* time. Now is the time to respond to the changes that you are already sensing. Make a small response, and then follow it with another. The response might not work very well at first, but you will avoid the paralysis of the *perfect-solutions* dragon. Don't waste time and opportunity searching for the ideal solution because one doesn't exist. Even if you find what appears to be the ideal solution today, it probably will be less than ideal by the time you can actually implement it because the world is changing so quickly. Sense the changes happening around you, and respond with action today.

> You don't need more data to succeed in a changing world; you need more action.

Actions that produce better results are simple, but not easy. The vignettes about action in Part III are presented in the following four tips, which describe the challenging journey from possibilities to results:

- Tip #7 – _Use Purpose to Set Your Direction._ Your vision for the future is the source of your organizational and personal goals, and the actions you take to achieve them. Know your purpose clearly.
- Tip #8 – _Plan to Achieve Your Goals._ Set lofty goals and make a thorough plan to achieve them. Communicate the vision and the plan to all of your colleagues.
- Tip #9 – _Reach the Top through Innovation._ Meet challenges with innovation. Try something radical, and look for ways to instill innovation into your team's culture.
- Tip #10 – _Execute to Produce Results._ Move smoothly and quickly through analysis into action. Measure your results, make corrections during the action, and persevere until you succeed.

These four tips address the four steps in the action process. Each tip has vignettes that provide pointers to tame the dragons that cause you to resist taking action even as you see the world changing around you.

PURPOSE

Tip #7: Use Purpose to Set Your Direction

OVERVIEW

Finding purpose is not only important for success, it is also essential for motivation. Purpose gives you and your organization a sense of direction, a feeling that your work matters for more than just "the numbers." In the short term, prospects for recognition, or a promotion, pay raise, or bonus may be motivating. But sustainable commitment requires that people see their work contributing to something worthwhile. Having a clear purpose is especially vital in large organizations where it's impractical for leaders to have a personal relationship with everyone.

Purpose infuses an organization with meaning. It lights a fire in the belly and tames the *it's-just-a-paycheck* dragon, the *dreams-never-come-true* dragon, and the *my-work-doesn't-make-a-difference* dragon. In the most successful organizations, purpose guides how people act, how they think, and how they treat each other. The vignettes in Tip #7 will help you discover your purpose, frame your team's purpose, make purpose come alive for everyone, and instill purpose into your team's culture.

SHAPING YOUR FUTURE

*If you don't know where you're going,
you're probably not going to get there.*
—Yogi Berra

Imagine you see your neighbor loading suitcases into his car. You walk over and say, *"Hi. Looks like you're planning a trip. Where are you going?"* He answers, *"I'm headed west."* Somewhat surprised by the vague reply, you inquire, *"Why are you going?"* And he says, *"Nothing better to do."* You follow up by asking, *"How long will you be gone?"* He says, *"I'm not sure. Just until something better comes along."* Most of us wouldn't plan a trip that way, but too many of us shape our organization's future and careers like that aimless neighbor planned his trip.

Having a clear purpose in the relationship economy is essential for success. No matter where you are, without a clear purpose it's easy to move in meaningless directions amid the profusion of information and tasks you face every day. Navigating without a clear purpose, you pursue short-term goals that seem worthwhile at the time. But soon years pass and you haven't advanced as far as you want to go. You see colleagues making extraordinary progress, and they seem to be doing the same things that you are. You attribute the lack of progress to bad luck when, in fact, it's a lack of clear purpose.

Possibilities in the relationship economy are endless: public service, management, the military, computers, sales, health care, law, education, and consulting, to name only a few. But none of them will produce success or happiness until they satisfy a *why* inside you. Your purpose is *why* you pick a goal: to serve others, to teach others, to cure others, to help others, to defend others. The *why* provides meaning for what you do and the decisions you make. You'll find—if you haven't already—that money by itself does not produce fulfillment. Instead, money is the by-product of doing an important *why* very well. When you make your purpose clear to yourself and everyone around you, you enable them to give you the help that you need to succeed.

THE JOURNEY

*A clear purpose provides criteria for making
choices on your journey toward success.*

One of my regular interview questions is: *"What's your career goal and how can we help you achieve it?"* Candidates usually answer with vague notions about rising to a management position or learning a new skill. However, one interviewee answered quickly and clearly: *"Government service is my purpose and my goal is to rise to a Senior Executive Service (SES) position. Working for your company, I expect to learn more about how government agencies operate."*

We hired him. He was an exceptionally effective leader, excellent at motivating people and satisfying clients. I helped him toward his goal by introducing him to SESes who had done what he planned to do: They began in industry and shifted to government service. After four years, he left the company for a GS-15 position in a government agency, one step below SES but well positioned to apply for open SES positions. I'm confident that he'll be an SES soon.

In my experience, only one in five people choose a position because it advances them toward a specific career goal. Most resumes I review list prior positions like steps on a ladder but rarely describe where the ladder is heading. Such candidates are generally job-hoppers who may be highly skilled, but they capitulate to the career-limiting dragon of a larger paycheck or a more interesting project.

My follow-up question during interviews sometimes is: *"What are your strengths, and how can they be expanded?"* or *"What are your weaknesses, and how can they be reduced?"* If the candidate looks back with a blank stare or answers in terms of improving their skills and diversifying their experience, I conclude that they have no idea what their strengths or weaknesses are. Are you aware of your strengths and weaknesses? Stop thinking of your career as a series of loosely related positions. Instead, view it as a progression of learning experiences that amplify your strengths, ameliorate your weaknesses, and enable you to fulfill your purpose.

In the relationship economy, you must set the direction of your team and your career. The gray flannel suit days of the industrial age when companies prepared people for lifelong employment are gone. Since people have different preferences, styles, and strengths, it follows that you'll need a specific type of workplace to achieve peak performance. It's essential that you understand yourself thoroughly, so you can find the working environment and the position where you will thrive and grow.

> View your career as a series of experiences that enable you to fulfill your purpose.

There are several elements in an ideal work environment. These days you may find yourself working at home or in the field as often as in an office. Do you learn best by seeing, by hearing, or by doing? Do you produce your best results with a team, or working alone? If it's with a team, do you like being the leader, a technical guru, or a supporter? Do you thrive in a structured work environment, or work better under the pressure of a tight deadline? Do you enjoy an environment of chaos and uncertainty, or not? When you can answer these questions, you will know a lot about the next position you should seek.

Today, the journey toward a successful career isn't based on luck or precise planning. Rather it's seizing the right opportunities as they appear. That being said, if your current position doesn't allow you to apply your strengths, to work in a stimulating environment that brings out your best, and to achieve your purpose, then look for one that does! That, of course, assumes you know your purpose. If you aren't sure what your purpose is, try:

- Writing down your personal definition of success;
- Stating why you are passionate about achieving that success;
- Telling yourself how it will be fun and how it will help others;
- Linking your vision of success to your unique qualities; and
- Identifying indicators that demonstrate you are succeeding.

Knowing this about yourself will help you evaluate opportunities and pick the best one *for you*. You will know when you have the right job because you will feel that you are making an essential contribution and a measurable difference to others. You will build a successful and rewarding career through a series of such positions.

GOLDEN HANDCUFFS

*Be careful what you wish for in
your career; you just might get it.*

For most of his thirty-five-year career, a senior executive was a leader in government consulting and worked directly with clients. He became CEO when his consulting firm spun out from its parent accounting firm and became a publicly traded company. Suddenly, he found himself responsible for managing a billion-dollar company with thousands of employees. A few years later, he resigned after reporting that quarterly and annual financial reports would be late because his company was using faulty accounting processes. Reflecting on his career, the executive said, "*I was thrust into the CEO position but that isn't who I am. First and foremost I'm a practitioner.*" He found more satisfaction in the short-cycle rewards of working with clients than the long-cycle rewards of executive management. Maybe he should have declined the CEO job. But how many of us could resist the enticing and ego-gratifying dragon of being the CEO?

Many people are trapped in jobs they don't like and don't want. But the golden handcuffs of lucrative salaries, bonuses, and benefits—and a matching lifestyle—deter them from leaving to find a position that is more attuned to their purpose. As this executive's experience shows, such people are neither happy nor successful even though they seem to enjoy the benefits of material success. Happiness and success arrive when you do satisfying work in a stimulating environment. The key question is: "*Where do I belong?*" If the answer is that you don't belong where you are, the follow-up question is *why?* Quitting is probably the right decision if you're in the wrong place or your performance makes little difference.

In my personal experience, the three most significant and often unexpected frustrations associated with being an executive are:

(1) *Sense of Obligation.* Mentally, an executive is always at work, even when he is at home or on vacation with his family. I often found myself awake in the middle of the night thinking of solutions to the challenges I would face at work in the morning.

(2) *Responsibility for the Lives of Others.* Executives frequently make decisions that affect many lives. No one enjoys laying off people

when the market shifts or counseling low performers, but those are essential tasks of an executive.

(3) *Larger Workload and Longer Workdays.* An executive's work often begins before employees arrive, and it ends hours after they leave. There seems to be no end to the help that people request or the tasks you know you *should* be doing.

If you're in management today or your goal is to become an executive, you are choosing these frustrations. Many people choose management for the wrong reasons. It isn't their purpose or their preference, but they think management is the only way to advance.

Career choices get more complex every day in the relationship economy. You purchase your future results with the choices you make today. Your choices may be conscious or unconscious. That's the first choice you make. You can establish a clear purpose and make choices based on that purpose, or you can put your career into autopilot and let it fly whichever direction the wind blows. Would career choices be simpler if there were fewer options? Actually, the variety of available choices is a source of limitless opportunity. However, it is also an opportunity to lose sight of your purpose. Make your choices simpler by having a clear purpose bigger than yourself on which you base your decisions.

> When you choose to become a manager, you choose new frustrations in addition to new benefits. Choose wisely.

CONFLICTS IN PERSPECTIVE

*These days, knowing your purpose is challenging because
you juggle so many conflicting roles and perspectives.*

I overheard a conflict between the controller and an employee in my company. The employee complained that he paid more toward family health care coverage than employees in other companies. The controller retorted that our bonuses and retirement contributions were superior, and the company couldn't afford more for health coverage. I empathized with both perspectives. The father and husband inside me wanted more health coverage at less cost. However, the taxpayer and executive in me wanted to reduce the costs to our government clients, while the shareholder in me wanted higher profits. Since 80 percent of the company's employees also were shareholders, the conflicting viewpoints I felt were shared by other employees too.

In the industrial age, the core conflict was between labor and management, and the issue was wages and benefits. However, in the relationship economy, the conflict is between consumers and workers, with companies caught in the middle. As consumers, we want more quality at a lower price. In response, the auto industry and global companies like Wal-Mart, for example, turn to employees and say, *"If we don't reduce costs, our foreign competitors will, and your jobs will be lost."* We find ourselves forced to choose between two crossed purposes: Are higher wages or lower costs more important? It's not that simple, of course.

Similar conflicts occur at all levels for governments that are pressured to provide more and better services without tax increases. Special interest groups have multiplied, and their logical but blatantly one-sided arguments have essentially frozen governments in inaction. Of course, the resolution of this conflict is squarely in your hands and mine as voters. The conflict is a multi-headed dragon that lures us into biased, dead-end thinking. Tame that dragon by sorting through your often conflicting perspectives as a taxpayer, citizen, parent, consumer, employee (or executive), and shareholder to be clear about what is most important to you.

WHAT ARE YOU DOING?

How you view the purpose of your work affects how you react to obstacles. The broader your view, the easier it is to overcome obstacles and the more complete the solution.

I asked several employees who were working on the same software project: *"What are you doing?"* One responded, *"I'm trying to build a C program to retrieve data from remote sites."* Another described her work as developing a system for a government client, and a third said, *"When we get them to agree on requirements, we'll implement a process to re-spare after an alteration is completed."* I would have said we were constructing a collaborative environment where multiple organizations could work together effectively. Your perspective about the work you do determines how you will react to obstacles that pop up along the way. The more you see your purpose globally, the more obstacles that you will be willing to overcome to achieve it.

Understanding the purpose of our actions is vital to success in the relationship economy. Without a clear purpose to guide our actions, we can easily get lost, choose incompatible paths, or find ourselves in conflict with one another. Even teammates who are well connected and skilled can be distracted by the endless administrative tasks they perform each day. Pulled in multiple directions without a clear purpose, they follow agendas that seem worthwhile but are disappointed when their efforts aren't understood or valued by others.

Lack of a clear purpose jeopardizes relationships. When teammates disagree on the purpose, they doubt each others' intention and commitment. Those doubts feed the dragons of resentment and confusion. Teammates might even start working against each other unintentionally. I have seen such stovepipe perspectives damage large change management projects. Project leaders think that the problem is immaturity or selfishness among the factions who refuse to cooperate. But the real problem is a lack of purpose. Does this sound like your team? Could it be that your team's purpose isn't clear to everyone?

THE FUNDAMENTAL QUESTION

Today's knowledge workers, more so than in any workforce in the past, require a clear purpose to motivate their best efforts.

Eventually, every organizational leader faces the fundamental question: *"What is our purpose?"* It is a complex question that few business leaders can answer. So the question goes unanswered and the organizational purpose defaults to more sales and profits. Fortunately, in the twisting kaleidoscope of life's events, I was able to find purpose for my company by asking:

- *What frustrates me and what fascinates me?*
- *How can my unique experiences be valuable to others?*

These questions were easier to answer than a blanket *"Why does my company exist?"*

I was frustrated that federal government operations, despite a $3 trillion annual budget, are often ineffective and inefficient. On the other hand, I'm fascinated by the new technologies of the relationship economy and the innovative ways they are used to promote teamwork. Therefore, my company's purpose became: *"To help government change through innovation & teamwork."* We didn't keep our purpose a secret. It was printed on our business cards and integrated into our bonus program, annual reviews, and strategic business plan. Although some employees didn't embrace it, that purpose became a beacon that guided our decisions and our investments.

Workers in the industrial age always knew what to do. Their role in the assembly line was clear. But for knowledge workers, *what to do* is the core question. Their work is creative, not repetitive. They control the work with their most valuable production tools: their knowledge and relationships. They use other tools, of course, like computers. But their knowledge determines how it will be used. Knowledge workers answer for themselves the questions: *Which tasks are essential? What results do we want?* and *What obstacles must be overcome to achieve those results?* But knowledge workers are able to answer those questions only after you as the leader clearly define and communicate the team's purpose.

BRANDING

*Your brand communicates purpose to customers and
employees, and differentiates you from competitors.*

A government services firm in Washington D.C. has branded itself as *The Project Management Company*. The truth is hundreds of companies in Washington provide project management (PM) services, many of them at least as effectively. But this company has clearly and consistently communicated to potential clients and employees that its corporate purpose is PM. When government clients need PM services, this company is among the first they think of.

Their clear purpose attracts employees whose goal is to work in PM. They instill PM in the culture by having a PM methodology and tools, by requiring employees to become PM-certified, by creating PM subspecialties, and by offering extensive PM training. Employees know the company's purpose and their role in its execution. The company has accelerated its growth by linking purpose with client and employee needs and to its strategic direction.

Customers and employees are attracted to companies that have a clear and relevant purpose—a purpose that's apparent in their brand. In the relationship economy, purpose is as essential to success for a start-up as it is for a Fortune 500 company because it strengthens relationships with customers and employees as much as superior service, quality products, and lucrative benefits. Companies that communicate their purpose in their brand create more perceived value than competitors, and they retain customers longer too.

In the relationship economy, like previous eras, the more you please customers, the more they buy and refer you to new customers. The difference is that the referrals proliferate (or not) through a global network. If your company lacks a brand that communicates purpose, you probably find yourself wrestling the *we'll-do-anything* dragon to grow. On the other hand, with a clear brand, your team's enthusiasm for work and productivity expand. What is your brand? Does it clearly communicate your organizational purpose?

LEGENDS

A team communicates its purpose to the members. When new members join, they either accept the purpose or leave the team.

A goal of my company was: *"Earn third-party recognition for our clients for the results we help them produce."* One project team pursued this goal especially vigorously. They researched awards given to government employees and correlated the project's results to award criteria. Four years into the project, the government's project manager was selected as one of the "Top 100 IT Executives in Government," a prestigious award. Several members of our project team attended the gala banquet where the client received her well-deserved award.

Every member of our project team received a bonus because of the award their client won. A few months later, the company won the five-year renewal contract and they earned another bonus. Needless to say, the project became a legend inside the company—a legend which made our purpose and our goals come alive. Recall your first experiences with your current company and team. What messages did you receive from your colleagues? What legends did they tell you about? Who were the heroes, and what did they do to achieve that status? What behaviors were considered to be acceptable and unacceptable? Those messages, legends, heroes, and behaviors are the culture of your current organization.

A team provides purpose for its members. When new members join, they either: (1) support the team's purpose, (2) reject the purpose and leave the team, or (3) in rare cases, motivate the team to adopt a new purpose. Team members need purpose to position their personal goals in context with the team's bigger purpose. They will adopt the purpose because of experiences, not because of any training lecture or employee manual. Any inconsistencies between a team's experiences and the purpose stated by management will erode the culture. Ask your team about its purpose and experiences. If members don't answer quickly and consistently, your team probably needs a few new legends.

RECONSTRUCTION

*Even as you pursue your purpose passionately, it's vital
that you continuously expand your relationship network.*

A friend was laid off when his company "right-sized" in response to Wall Street pressure to reduce overhead and increase profits. At fifty years old, he had been with the company fourteen years and was vice president of Gulf Coast Operations following Hurricane Katrina. He loved his job, and was widely recognized for planning and successfully completing several projects. I asked what he would do differently if he could rewind the clock fourteen years. He answered, *"I'd spend more time building a relationship network."* He added, *"I received several performance awards and became too comfortable."* His anger showed when he blurted, *"I can't believe the company threw me away after everything that I did for them."* He was confident in rebuilding New Orleans but doubtful about his ability to reconstruct his career.

His experience is common in the relationship economy: A successful career abruptly changed by events beyond his control. His purpose and passion was reconstructing the Gulf Coast, and he focused on them to the exclusion of critical career-building activities like networking and relationship building. Most companies don't train their people in relationship-building techniques. Fortunately, his clear purpose provides a happy ending to this story. After taming the anger dragon, he used one of the relationships he had nurtured and found a rewarding position that combined his reconstruction expertise with green initiatives (i.e., energy efficiency) in affordable housing.

There are several ways to build relationships while you follow your purpose passionately. For example:

- Shift focus from serving clients to caring about their success,
- Enroll your teammates in making every client successful, and
- Work hard to create value for clients, rather than to increase your revenue and profit (those increases will happen naturally).

Oh, one more thing: Change your view of the client. Treat everyone in your company and supply chain like a client because that's what they are!

GOVERNANCE

Government's role is to make decisions that resolve society's challenges and improve the quality of our lives. Its purpose, in short, is to govern, *which conflicts with large-scale* doing.

S pecialization in the form of outsourcing is growing in the relationship economy. Outsourcing changes relationships, yields large savings, and expands effectiveness in areas outside the core business of an organization. The move toward outsourcing non-core functions is likely to increase in the future and provide substantial opportunities for entrepreneurs who specialize in the outsourced areas. For example, outsourcing in supply chain, accounting, administration, and human resource areas are already major industries.

While outsourcing grows in industry, it's a ferocious dragon in federal agencies and Congress, despite undeniably favorable results. The General Accountability Office (GAO) has performed numerous evaluations of public-private competitions under OMB Circular A-76, first issued in 1966. One such study evaluated 286 A-76 competitions by the Defense Department over a five-year period. The government's Most Efficient Organization (MEO) team won over 75 percent of the competitions. Less than a quarter were won by industry. In cases where industry won, 30 percent of the displaced government employees were hired at a higher salary by the company that won the competition and almost all of the rest were reassigned to other government jobs. The competitions collectively save the government $290 million *per year.*

Surprised? Don't be. Government agencies are notoriously inefficient at large-scale *doing;* for example, consider Social Security and the Medicare program. The real purpose of government is to make decisions that solve society's basic challenges and improve the quality of our lives. Government's role is to dramatize vital issues, focus political attention on resolution, debate viable alternatives, and pick a course of action. In short, government's purpose is to *govern.*

Large conglomerates in the industrial age found that attempts to integrate governance and large-scale *doing* stifle decision-making and adversely affect the *doing.* Industry learned that top executives must be detached from *doing* because when decision-makers are held accountable for both governance and *doing*, they have difficulty making the tough governance decisions (i.e., changing direction), and the *doing* becomes inefficient. Industry resolved that challenge by decentralizing and outsourcing. Over 230 years ago, our brilliant forefathers labeled it "separation of powers" in the Constitution.

Decentralization in government doesn't mean delegating *doing* to lower-level governments. Instead, it is a systematic approach for engaging external organizations in the *doing*. The external organization could be another government agency or a company that specializes in the non-core function. Neither choice weakens the authority of the agency that outsources. Quite the contrary, it sharpens their mission focus, allows challenging decisions to be made decisively, and frees resources that were used inefficiently. The consequences of government continuing its current path are likely to be a catastrophic collapse in the execution of programs such as Social Security, health care, and the maintenance of our country's infrastructure. It will be the government equivalent of bankruptcy.

> Integrating governance with large-scale doing complicates decision-making and adversely affects doing.

It's time to choose between our current impotent government and a government capable of making the hard decisions and setting a clear direction. Of course, the downside is that jobs will move from federal agencies to other agencies and companies that have unique qualifications in the outsourced services. To make that shift, federal workers, unions, and Congress must tame several enormous dragons. You can push them to move in that direction with your votes and by voicing your opinions.

The change is not a *laissez-faire* approach to provide services to citizens. Instead, Congress would decide how to solve core issues and make the solution attractive to a government agency or company that would be willing to *do* the solution. Just as we reward a coach for getting the best from his team, we would reward our Congressional representatives and executive branch leaders for designing programs that resolve social challenges and operate efficiently. This is your purpose as a voter, and your job if you are a government employee.

GOING GREEN

*The roles of government and industry are shifting
with industry assuming more social responsibilities.*

America's capitalists seem to be going green. Two large private equity firms announced joint plans to purchase a utility company for $45 billion, among the largest acquisitions in history. But the real news is that those investment bankers intend to reduce construction of new coal-burning power plants, expand use of wind and solar power plants, incentivize clients who improve energy efficiency, and accept controls on greenhouse gas emissions. The deal shows a new corporate purpose emerging in the relationship economy. Protecting the environment isn't solely a governmental responsibility. Governments will continue to set standards, but industry is taking the lead in delivering the innovation and technology needed to "go green" and expanding its profits in the process!

The change from a regulation-driven to a market-driven strategy for environmental protection is allocating specific costs to pollution and energy efficiency, such as the taxes on greenhouse gas emissions. Those hard costs reward companies that develop solutions for environmental challenges and create strong economic incentives for new research. Companies large and small are expanding their environmental programs as demonstrated by the following examples in industries outside of energy:

- Financial: Bank of America allocated $18 billion in commercial loans for green projects over the next ten years.
- Technology: Dell uses "green" programs to increase recycling, reduce power consumption, and use Earth-friendly components.
- Retail: Wal-Mart has committed to sell sustainable products, reduce energy consumption, and impose environmental standards on its worldwide suppliers.

Critics label these initiatives as *green-washing,* claiming they are just a feeble attempt to polish tarnished corporate images. However, many environmentalists are jubilant that industry is addressing the challenge and making the environment part of their core purpose.

Former Vice President Al Gore, who has won the Nobel Peace Prize and an Academy Award, has been instrumental in increasing the awareness of the causes and effects of global warming. Companies that fail to react to this change put themselves at a severe competitive disadvantage. For example, American automobile manufacturers are on the brink of bankruptcy in part because they ignored the emerging demand for clean, fuel-efficient automobiles and trucks. At the same time, Japanese automakers earned record profits by making efficiency the expressed purpose of their car designs and by introducing hybrid engines, lightweight vehicles, and automated control systems.

"Going green" is just one example of how workplaces are changing in the relationship economy. As government and industry move from the adversarial relationships of the industrial age to shared purposes, the split of responsibilities is shifting. Industry is assuming social responsibilities as the effectiveness of government continues to be battered by political gridlock. Several companies have successfully balanced revenue and profit growth while protecting the environment and raising living standards.

> **What does your organization do to attract employees who are committed to more than just earning a salary?**

Today, many companies use innovation and the improved quality of their products and services as their core expansion strategy. Leaders are finding that productivity and profits grow faster in an atmosphere that fosters employee creativity and passion. And Wall Street is rewarding those companies with higher stock prices.

Most employees are unwilling to turn off their values and dreams to work like robots. They look for workplaces where their purpose is supported by the company and its executives. Interviewees frequently shared their values and purpose with me, and asked me about my company's mission and values. I found that such employees are committed to the projects they work on, and to the co-workers and customers they work with.

THE ECONOMICS OF SPIRITUALITY

*Since success in the relationship economy depends on
people-to-people connections, learn to appreciate the
value of each human spirit you meet in the workplace.*

In the movie *Jerry Maguire*, Tom Cruise plays the title role, a cutthroat sports agent who has an epiphany. One night he struggles to understand the purpose of his career. He works through the night to develop a passionate purpose statement that declares his intent to care for his clients and operate in integrity, accepting the fact that he might earn less money using that strategy. When the purpose statement is distributed throughout the office, his colleagues applaud and his boss fires him. Through that storyline, *Jerry Maguire* touches on several key issues regarding spirituality, integrity, and purpose, which are at the heart of the dramatic changes happening in the workplaces of the relationship economy.

In the industrial age, corporations proved themselves to be effective organizations for creating wealth and jobs. However, the relationship economy is challenging corporations to demonstrate their ability to produce social value. As corporations navigate the painful transition from the industrial age to the relationship economy, the nature of the workplace is changing, and purpose and values are becoming essential corporate tools.

Technology is, of course, fundamental to the relationship economy. However, there is a growing recognition that spirituality (not religion *per se*, but a deep concern for others and the purpose of life) is also essential to achieve top performance. Spirituality (i.e., an ability to tap into human spirits in the workplace) is especially vital in international projects. The human capacity for faith and commitment to a purpose larger than ourselves is wired into the right side of the human brain, which is the source of creativity. Spirituality satisfies our basic human needs. Indeed, the importance of spirituality may be rising precisely because so many people have super-satisfied their material needs (the left side of their brain).

Until recently, most workers hid their spirituality for fear of being judged as altruistic, impractical, or irrelevant. But spirituality is very important for millions of people in the workforce. They want to serve others, recognize value in others, and connect with others. Such workers are passionately committed to their work and co-workers. As the relationship economy spreads, they are connecting both within and across workplaces, supporting each other, and openly discussing their spirituality and their purpose. Such intimate relationships are an asset in any organization!

Spirituality is not the latest management tool, and corporations should not compel workers to participate in spiritual activities. On the other hand, corporations should encourage spirituality in their purpose and the workplace. Spirituality isn't a business issue; it is an intensely personal issue. So changes (if any) must originate inside of individual workers.

That being said, most effective leaders have a sixth sense about how to incorporate spirituality into their workplace. Leaders understand that organizations are just communities of human spirits bound together by a common purpose. When leaders define their team's purpose in terms of social responsibility, implement family-friendly practices, promote energy conservation and environmental protection, provide paid leave for charitable activities, or encourage work-life balance, they are injecting spirituality into their workplaces. Business studies have demonstrated that focusing on purpose and values rather than solely on profitability is good for the bottom line, revenue growth, and employee retention. Are you the kind of leader who accommodates and promotes spirituality in your workplace?

> **Spirituality is important for millions of people in the workforce who want to serve and connect with others.**

WHERE'S THE MISSION?

A clear mission statement is the basis for a company's competitive advantage and unique selling proposition.

After our annual retreat, executives in my company revised the three-year business plan. They gave me a draft revision to review over a weekend. Immediately I saw that the company's mission statement (*Helping Government Change Through Innovation & Teamwork*) had been omitted in Chapter One. I was furious. How could they leave out the mission, the heart of our competitive strategy? Then I realized the omission showed where the company stood relative to communicating its mission to employees and clients. The mission in last year's plan had been Dick's mission, not a collective mission. I expected them to be fired-up by our mission like I was, but they weren't.

It took the entire weekend to control my anger. On Monday, I spoke individually to the executives to determine why the mission had been omitted. Three executives were unaware that it had been left out, and they weren't particularly concerned. Another said, "*The mission is so abstract. It doesn't mean anything to clients.*" The executive who actually deleted it said he did so because, "*The staff doesn't see how the mission affects what we do.*" These reactions, of course, reflected the attitude of the executives themselves. Clearly, I needed to be more effective at communicating the value of the mission to my executive team and employees. I put that task on the top of my priority list.

A company's mission is its purpose, what it does best. The mission statement is the basis for a competitive advantage and unique selling proposition. Competitive advantage is the mission viewed by competitors, and selling proposition is the mission as seen by clients. Many companies are clueless about their selling proposition and how to communicate it to their clients. Such companies either don't have a mission or haven't made mission part of the culture. A company with a clear mission is more likely to succeed in the relationship economy than one with more resources that lacks a unifying purpose. Does your staff understand the mission (i.e., purpose) of your organization, and is it an integral part of their decisions?

CLOSING THOUGHTS ON PURPOSE

Purpose is a reliable navigational aid. It will tell you which way to turn when you are at an important crossroad.

A friend who worked with me at two companies left my company to start a B&B, a *boat* & breakfast. He had lived with his wife on a sixty-foot Trumpy motor yacht for a few years. At age forty-one, he decided to outfit it as a B&B for romantic cruises on the inter-coastal waterway. He invested his retirement savings to restore the boat, and worked for several months to prepare it for the first booking. My wife's fiftieth birthday party was held on the yacht. A few years later, my friend ended the B&B venture and became a landlord who repaired, rented, and resold properties in Baltimore.

When he decided to change careers, my friend said, *"Dick, government consulting isn't for me. It's not why I'm here."* Since that day, I have met with him often and he has never regretted leaving a six-digit salary to pursue new adventures. He says, *"I've stared failure in the face and walked through it. It's exciting!"* Hopefully, you enjoy your job. But if not, maybe you should switch to one that aligns with your purpose. Maybe you should take a chance and live your dream.

The relationship economy is not your father's business world. Today people who achieve lasting success are guided by a purpose that remains the same even as their career evolves in response to a changing world. Purpose is what you stand for, why you exist. It's more important to know *who you are* than *where you are going*, because *where you are going* probably will change frequently as the world changes at computer speed.

The same is true for organizations: Purpose is essential for success. You don't need brilliant men and women for routine jobs. Such jobs are likely to be offshored, outsourced, or eliminated altogether by new technologies. Instead, hire people with purpose who are comfortable with the unpredictable, willing to risk the impossible, and want to be part of creating the unimaginable.

PLANNING

Tip #8: Plan to Achieve Your Goals

OVERVIEW

Goals are essential for success because they establish a performance target. But goals without a specific plan to achieve them are hallucinations spawned by the *I'll-do-as-good-as-I-can* dragon or the *I'll-make-it-up-as-I-go* dragon. Goals define the destination and a plan is the course that guides you toward that destination. One without the other is pointless. A time-based plan provides quantitative milestones that allow you to measure where you are versus where you want to be, and to make course corrections to close the gap.

What are your major goals? Where are you today relative to the personal and organizational goals you set for yourself a year ago? Do those goals guide your daily decisions? The vignettes in Tip #8 will encourage you to set big goals, to develop a plan to achieve those goals, to use the plan in decision-making, and to measure your progress continuously.

SET BIG ONES

The goals you set today determine the pinnacle of your
success tomorrow. Are you setting them high enough?

My company was a platinum United Way participant for ten years, and I served as a United Way volunteer several times. One year, the regional director who knew my experience in effecting change asked, *"Our regional campaign grows about 3 percent each year. I think it's because we aim to grow that much. What can we do to grow 50 percent?"* I responded, *"We will need a strategy and a plan that produce 50 percent growth, even if some sectors grow more and others grow less."* He asked me to help develop the strategy and plan as my contribution to the campaign, and I agreed.

The regional campaign had four sectors: businesses, high net worth individuals, county workers, and the education department. We helped the leaders in each sector set their goal, select a strategy, and prepare a plan for their sector. I was leading one of the sector planning meetings on the morning of September 11th when American Airlines Flight #97 crashed into the Pentagon less than a mile from our meeting site. Contributions in many United Way regions declined in 2001 because people donated heavily to 9/11 funds. However, that United Way region grew 8 percent, its best year-on-year growth ever, a highly visible success. Setting big goals yields superior results even in difficult years!

Leaders sense the changes around them, and willingly accept responsibility for using that environment to generate extraordinary results. They seem to create goals from thin air, like the 50 percent increase in contributions. Albert Einstein doubted Newtonian physics, so he committed himself to discovering new physical laws. President John F. Kennedy announced, *"We will put a man on the moon in this decade!"* Martin Luther King told everyone, *"I have a dream!"* Where do goals like those come from? Leaders create them with no concern for how, when, or resources. Those are merely details to be ironed out during the planning phase. As a leader, when you set goals for your organization, you are creating its future.

Measurable goals are an essential prerequisite to developing an effective strategy and an executable plan. There almost always is more than one strategy available to achieve any goal. For example, for two of the four United

Way sectors the 50 percent growth strategy was to increase the number of donors. For two others it was to increase the size of the average donation. At first, the debilitating *we've-stretched-too-far* dragon led the sector leaders to think that a 50 percent growth was unachievable. But we helped them tame that dragon by selecting a viable strategy for the sector and by developing multiple techniques to support the strategy. The sector leaders left the planning meetings believing their goal was possible.

> Leaders create extraordinary goals from thin air, and willingly accept responsibility for achieving them.

In the real world, some techniques will work and others won't, and unpredictable events (usually not as catastrophic as 9/11) aren't unusual at all. In my experience (and probably yours too), unexpected events are more often negative than positive. But in any case, your results will always be directly proportional to the goals you've set, since such events affect big goals and small goals alike. The size of the goals you set today places a self-inflicted ceiling on the magnitude of success you can experience tomorrow. Do you set your goals high enough to achieve the success you really want for your organization and yourself?

SQUIRREL HUNTING

*If you don't set big goals, choose a strategy, and
make a plan, then you're likely to find yourself
squirrel hunting for someone who has a big plan.*

W hen I was a teenager, my goal was to earn a million dollars a year. To reach that goal, I needed a *big* plan and had to take *big* risks. But during the first sixteen years of my career, I worked hard to make small advances like a promotion or a few-thousand-dollar pay raise. Unfortunately, my goal was unachievable on that path. I was hunting squirrels. So I took a lesson from the Native Americans, who hunted buffalo because they couldn't feed the tribe with squirrels. I left the comfort of employment with a big business to start my own company.

During the twenty-two years I owned my company, I came close but never earned a million dollars in a year. But I didn't feel that missing my stretch goal was a failure because I succeeded way beyond what I could have achieved working for a big business. Where does the notion come from that if we set a big goal and fall short, we have failed? That *fear-of-failure* dragon limits our success by making us afraid to set big goals. But big goals and big plans usually feel uncomfortable because they require big risks. When you yield to the *fear-of-failure* dragon, you settle for mediocrity. In your heart, you can be so afraid of losing that you can't possibly win. Taming that dragon is a surefire escape from mediocrity.

You are an all-star player in the relationship economy. The game offers an unlimited spectrum of goals and strategies. But if you don't set big goals for your organization and yourself, choose a viable strategy, and make a plan, then you are likely to find yourself squirrel hunting for someone who has a big plan.

Renew your commitment to yourself. Go after what you want most. It really doesn't matter if you don't achieve your goal, because going for a big goal is energizing. No matter what happens, you will bring more joy and success into your life than by being afraid and doing nothing. So set your goals *BIG* and go for them with everything you have for as long as it takes!

THREE-LEGGED STOOL

Support and resources are everywhere in the relationship economy, so you don't have to achieve big goals all alone.

Starting a new business was an exciting roller-coaster ride in 1984 before the relationship economy. At first, my goal was to triple my income by providing engineering services. For the first two years, I was all alone; it was just me. My salary was down 50 percent, and I was afraid I wouldn't find enough clients. I returned the company car to my previous employer and leased a hatchback Mustang. My fears intensified when I lost a client after just six weeks. My workload was either feast or famine. And, after I did the work, I didn't get paid for ninety days. My first years in business were never boring or routine!

Fortunately, in the relationship economy, things aren't so grim. For those of you who are thinking about starting your own business, this may be the perfect time. The demand for innovative products and services, help from strategic partners, and the availability of financial resources today make this an ideal environment to start a new venture. Running your own business is a three-legged stool. You must: (1) find a stream of customers, (2) deliver a quality product or service, and (3) manage cash flow. Use the new tools of the relationships economy in all three areas, since your business will fail if any leg is weak.

If you're thinking about starting a business, ask yourself the following questions and write your answers down on paper:

- *Purpose.* Beyond improving your financial status, why are you starting a business? What human need will you satisfy?
- *Relationships.* Have you built mutually rewarding relationships with potential partners, clients, suppliers, and mentors?
- *Lifestyle.* Having your own business will occupy your mind 24-7-365. Does that fit your lifestyle and personality?
- *Resources.* Do you have the resources to support the company's growth and survive an extended dip in your personal cash flow?

Your answers will identify the help you'll need from the relationship economy. So *go for it!* But only when your business has all three legs.

GOLDILOCKS GOALS

Your goal is just right when you have: (1) a detailed plan
for achieving it, and (2) confidence that you can achieve it.

D uring my presentation at our annual shareholders' meeting, I described last year's results and accomplishments, and presented our goals for the new year. After I finished, a shareholder-employee raised his hand and asked, *"We didn't reach our goals last year or the year before. What will be different this year?"* I believe in stretch goals, but in that moment I knew that I had stretched too far. I had awakened the skepticism dragon and not built confidence in our ability to achieve the goals. When we began developing the plan to achieve our goals for the new year, I found that other employees felt the same.

The purpose of goal setting is to enhance performance, to find the amount of stretch that will motivate people to achieve their very best. A goal that's too easy doesn't push people or boost performance, so it is essentially useless. Studies show that performance increases as the goal becomes more challenging—up to a point. After that point, the skepticism dragon takes over, and the team's performance declines because it considers the goal to be beyond its capabilities.

But how can you tame the dragon and set a *"Goldilocks* goal" that's just right? After a goal is set and a strategy is selected, the next steps are to define and schedule tasks, identify milestones, and assign responsibilities. You have a realistic goal when: (1) you have a written plan to achieve it, and (2) the people responsible for each task feel they can finish them on time. The team's confidence grows when everyone knows exactly what is expected of them.

Setting a big goal, preparing a realistic plan, and getting buy-in are a good start, but accountability is also needed to reach your goals. Hold regular reviews to discuss and resolve issues. Adjust the plan for changes in the real world. Challenge your teammates and expect them to challenge you. Agree on the rewards for achieving the goal and the consequences for missing it. Do these things and, like Goldilocks, you too can live happily ever after relative to achieving your goals.

SCANDALOUS GOALS

Goals drive behaviors. So when you set them, be sure they are consistent with your organization's purpose and values.

Goal setting has contributed to the recent epidemic of corporate governance scandals. For example, a few years ago Fannie Mae set $6.46 as its target for annual per-share earnings. The head of Fannie Mae's audit department was quoted as imploring his staff: *"Every one of you must brand $6.46 in your brain. You must say it in your sleep, repeat it backwards and forwards. You must have a raging fire in your belly that burns away every doubt. You must live, breathe, and dream $6.46. After all, we have a lot of money riding on it."* Is it surprising that several years later Fannie Mae's financials had to be restated?

Goals drive behaviors, so be careful in setting them. Goals, and the strategies and plans used to achieve them, are controversial because they involve risk. Since goals are often backed by incentives, they merge the team's purpose with the needs of individual members. Goals become devious dragons if they conflict with purpose or values. Material-based goals like industry domination and ever-higher profits create a world of fierce competition and sometimes crime. Such goals are incongruous with the core of the relationship economy. When a leader focuses solely on revenue and profit goals, he surrenders to the insatiable quest for more. On the other hand, goals driven by a bigger-than-us purpose often produce the same or more revenue and profit.

Setting goals is among a leader's most important and riskiest tasks. Ineffective goal setting can damage a leader's reputation and his future. Bad goals are hatched and nursed by the goal-setter's dragons. For example, some leaders are very cautious, hedging their goals against unlikely events. Others are overly optimistic and don't see the challenges. And still others have memories of the past that limit their perception of how much is possible. Sooner or later, every leader will confront these dragons. Which of the three dragons is your personal challenge when you set goals?

UNCERTAIN TIMES

*Having a clear plan is essential in uncertain times, but
make it flexible enough to respond to emergent events.*

Anticipating instability in the Middle East in the mid-1970s, Royal Dutch Shell pioneered a technique called *Scenario Planning* to plot its future. Artfully constructed scenarios were defined to address potential future events. Each scenario linked possible events to actions Shell would take in response. In one scenario, for example, a pipeline rupture in Saudi Arabia disrupted oil supplies and greatly increased oil prices. The rupture never happened, but when OPEC announced an oil embargo and the price doubled, Shell already had a plan to react to the crisis. It responded faster and more effectively than competitors and, as the result, grew from the world's eighth largest oil company to the second largest. And oil was $12 a barrel in 1975!

In the relationship economy, your organization's future is every bit as unstable as oil prices. In most cases, your future is already happening. That is, events occur periodically that don't fit the basic assumptions of your current strategic plan. However, those events are creating new possibilities. Most of us were taught that new thinking always precedes a new reality. However, the exact opposite is usually true: Incongruous events occur, and *then* new ideas are developed to exploit them.

Knowing your strengths and sticking to them usually is a good strategy. But sticking with what you do well turns into a dragon when you continue doing it even after events tell you to change. At first, the sneaky dragon will say, *"Why change? What we're doing is working."* Next, the dragon will tell you, *"We don't have time to invent anything new. Let's work harder at what we do best."* And finally, the dragon will plead, *"In uncertain times, why introduce more uncertainty with something that's new and untested?"* If you let them, these persuasive arguments will cause you to miss new opportunities. What potential scenarios are you preparing for? Which ones are already happening in your industry? How will you address them?

READY. FIRE. AIM!

*Even after setting clear goals, initiating action without
a thorough plan often is a waste of time and resources.*

An executive started an innovative manpower allocation project
that promised to improve efficiency across his agency by more
than 15 percent. He made the project the agency's top priority
and assigned specific parts to eight executives who were his direct reports.
No project manager was designated, and no project plan was prepared. The
executives responded to their assignments eagerly. They worked hard to
generate innovative ideas and products. Unfortunately, several of their ideas
conflicted with each other, and there was no mechanism for collaborating
to make trade-offs. Chaos and frustration ruled even though the project's
goal was very clear. They were building pieces of a solution, but there was
no master plan for assembly.

Planning is the *aim* portion of the *ready-aim-fire* sequence. In this project,
the executive set a goal (the *ready* step), but surrendered to the impetuous
let's-get-started-now dragon by initiating action (he *fired*) before a plan or
control mechanisms were in place. Do you do the same thing in pursuit of
what seems to be an urgent opportunity? It is essential to have goals and, of
course, nothing happens until you take action. But planning is the process
that lets you to move quickly and efficiently from where you are today to
where you want to be tomorrow.

Any plan involves risk because it allocates resources to pursue an uncertain result. But the risk is minimized when your plan contains the essential
ingredients. You maximize the odds of achieving your goal by carrying out
the planning process faithfully and ensuring that your plan contains:

- Explicit objectives and measures of success,
- Defined assumptions and additional detail in risky areas,
- Interim milestones with clearly assigned responsibilities, and
- Flexible decision points to respond to changes in the real world.

So tame the *let's-get-started-now* dragon by developing a thorough plan for
where you want go in the relationship economy.

EXIT PLAN

You may be spending too much time planning how to start things and not enough planning how to end them.

business speaker challenged a dozen CEOs in a meeting: *"If a bomb exploded right here and you were killed, who would lead your company, and how well would they do?"* In most cases, there was no clear successor and, even when there was, the CEO had doubts about his ability to run the company. I was in the majority who didn't know who their successor would be. At that time, my company might have disintegrated if I had left abruptly.

It was a jolting wake-up call. I obviously focused too much on growing the company and not enough on my exit to retirement, which was about three years away. I returned to my office and e-mailed top people in the company to ask, *"If I got hit by a truck today, what part of our operation would worry you the most?"* We compiled responses in a plan and prioritized actions that resolved multiple concerns. After a year, I was able to reduce my workweek to four days, and a year later to three days. Employees joked that the company operated better than when I worked full time! Even if that was not true, clearly the company was stronger when it could operate without me.

It may seem paradoxical, but your organization would be stronger if it could operate without you. In the relationship economy, your career is likely to outlive the organizations for which you work. Statistically, the average person's work life exceeds forty years, while the average life of a successful company is less than thirty years and declining. For example, my company was twenty-two years old when I sold my interests.

Tame the *I'm-so-important* dragon by ensuring that your team can operate effectively without you; and concurrently prepare yourself for new opportunities that may come your way. Your ever-increasing success in a changing world depends on your answers to the following questions: *Why am I in this position? What must I learn? When should I leave?* and *What new opportunity should I be preparing for?* This is something that few people do, but everyone should be doing.

SHELFWARE

You may have a fairly good business plan. But do you
USE it to set priorities and guide your daily decisions?

Under contract to a government agency, my company worked eight months to capture user requirements, develop a design, and prepare an implementation plan and budget for a new Web-based records system. After approving the documents, the government's project manager put them in his bookcase and jokingly referred to them as his "million-dollar shelfware." Our team and his users were devastated. Seems his boss wanted the new system but left in the middle of the project. As I write this, the agency still hasn't achieved the new capability.

A plan is a set of decisions made in advance to achieve a goal, but it is useless until it's followed. Are any of your plans shelfware, or are they used regularly to make decisions and determine when you're off course? You can't foresee the opportunities or problems you may face tomorrow, or anticipate the decisions you will be forced to make. However, you can use your plan as a compass to guide impromptu decisions and as a chart to compare where you are today versus where you planned to be.

Plans should help you achieve stretch goals rather than being a compromise on easy-to-achieve goals. When you plan for a big goal, you prepare in advance to make important decisions and avoid results-limiting compromises. In developing a plan, you are determining how to achieve a goal and how you will measure progress along the way.

Base the compromises you inevitably must make on a clear goal and a written plan. The more thorough your plan, the more likely that compromises actually will help you reach your goal. Conversely, lack of clear goals almost certainly will produce mediocre results no matter how brilliant your plan. For example, consider a decision that you face today and ask: *What intermediate goal am I trying to reach in making this decision?* If you struggle to find an answer, it may be because you have put your plan *on the shelf,* or never had one to begin with.

PLAUSIBLE ASSUMPTION

*There are no perfect plans, since every plan
is based on a set of imperfect assumptions.*

One year we doubled the number of employees participating in our strategic planning off-site by inviting mid-level managers. They were eager to contribute and diligently researched and presented investment possibilities in their assigned areas. After the opportunities were presented in all areas, the total cost of the investments was seven times our budget. We did a return-on-investment analysis as a group and eventually chose a set of investments that fit the budget. When we completed the process, one mid-level manager exclaimed, *"We can't make such crucial decisions with so little information. We don't really know which investments will pay off."* He was correct, of course. It was a shocking entry into today's world of business, where even in the information age bigger and bigger decisions are made with less and less information.

In the relationship economy, successful people recognize a new pattern from only a few pieces of data. Such people seem to be far ahead of everyone else in exploiting opportunities. But how do they make decisions so quickly with such uncanny accuracy? They make decisions and take action based on an intuition that's rooted in past experiences—both good and bad—and an ability to discern minor risk from major risk.

Such intuition is difficult to teach, especially to those who are afraid to be wrong or are driven by the need for near-term economic rewards. Economic rewards are vital, of course, but are insufficient in themselves. Knowledge workers also need values, opportunity, and clear direction. In my experience, the fastest way to acquire intuition is through mentoring, by forming a symbiotic relationship with a seasoned executive who is respected for her intuition about today's business world. Ask her how she arrived at such risky decisions, what did she know that you didn't know, what plausible assumptions did she make, and what experiences did she have to support her assumptions.

OPERATIONAL PLANNING

In preparing for battle, I have always found that
plans are useless, but planning is indispensable.
—Gen. Dwight D. Eisenhower

Long before Hurricane Katrina struck, the Department of Homeland Security issued a 420-page "National Response Plan" as the script for the federal government's response to a man-made or natural disaster. After Katrina struck, its victims were frustrated by the large number of planning meetings that were held in the middle of the floods. Homeland Security may have had a written plan, but it was not an operational plan. It was merely a "plan for planning" that failed to describe what actions would be taken and by whom. And the heat of battle is an exceedingly poor time to begin detailed planning.

It's likely that your business plan accommodates events that you expect in the future. The plan is a guide for what you expect to happen. But when reality throws curve balls at you, as it often does, will your plan provide a point-of-departure for choosing what to do next? It should contemplate actions and set aside resources to allow you to make course corrections for the unexpected.

A plan is a commitment to future actions. But it's just a wish list until the actions become task assignments and deadlines are set. The people who must perform the tasks usually aren't the people who prepared the plan. Therefore, transforming a plan into effective action requires the planners to answer several questions:

- Who must understand the plan well enough to lead the actions?
- What priority actions must be taken when it is implemented?
- Who specifically will take those actions?
- Do they have the skills and resources required to take action?

In short, the plan must be appropriate to capabilities of the people who will execute it. This is especially important when people must change their routines, behaviors, or attitudes in order to put the plan into action. To be executable, your plan must contain operational steps, criteria to measure whether or not actions are working, and alternative actions when they're not.

REARVIEW MIRROR

*Where you are today is less important to your
future than your plan for the future and the
actions you are taking to implement that plan.*

B alanced Scorecard (BSC), originally developed by Robert Kaplan and David Norton in 1992, is a holistic approach for managing performance. BSC gurus say that financial statements, long a staple of management, are like a car's rearview mirror. They are essential for safety but insufficient to drive an organization's future performance. Typically, a BSC uses four measures: (1) client relationships, (2) financial health, (3) internal processes, and (4) innovation. These four measures are often tailored to suit a specific industry and company.

Too many performance systems still manipulate employee behavior by measuring and incentivizing actions that management wants them to take. Such performance systems are rooted in the control mentality of the industrial age. BSC, on the other hand, focuses on strategy and encourages employees to be innovative in taking action to achieve the organization's goals. In the relationship economy, conditions change continuously. So progressive executives are very clear about the goals they are pursuing, but grant knowledge workers wide latitude in determining how to achieve those results.

Everyone knows it isn't safe to drive a car without a rearview mirror; but if that's all you watch, you surely will have an accident. In a rapidly evolving business world, it's more effective to look through the front windshield to see the future than to know where you were yesterday (i.e., last month's financial statements).

On the personal side, the size of your house and bank account, the type of car you drive, and your current job are lag indicators. They reflect your past successes, but aren't reliable indicators of the future. Getting too comfortable with such lag indicators can undermine your future success. Instead, measure lead indicators of success like new relationships, expanding knowledge, and the ability and willingness to make a difference to others.

TAKING TIME TO PLAN

How can it be that, when there isn't enough resources and time to do it right, we find resources and time to do it over?

When the Department of Homeland Security was formed in 2003 to strengthen our domestic defenses, it began operations with an explosion of no-bid contracts awarded with very little planning. Three years later, federal auditors found that thirty contracts with combined costs over $34 billion were awarded with few controls or measures of success. The contracts experienced billions in overruns, mostly related to a lack of integration among the technologies, systems, and services that were purchased.

The contracts provided crucial security services such as airport screeners and luggage inspectors, radiation detection in harbors, and housing for Hurricane Katrina victims. The auditors found expensive systems that had to be entirely replaced. DHS's spending spree was expensive and only partially accomplished its objectives. One auditor said, *"A few months of planning would have saved billions of dollars and years of effort, and made America safer too."*

Effective leaders tame the hasty *do-something-now* dragon by taking time to plan activities that produce results. They establish clear goals, define measures of success, and engage the team's thinking to explore alternatives. For government executives facing the terrorist threat, this may have meant posting requirements publicly, soliciting several competitive strategies, and combining the best ideas in an integrated plan. Leaders know that the margin between superior and mediocre results is the thoroughness of the plan and the excellence of its execution.

In business, the process of measuring results is neither neutral nor objective. Results acquire special meaning and importance when they are designated for measurement. Effective leaders know the key question is not *"How can we measure results?"* rather it is *"What results should we measure?"* What results are you measuring, and are those results directly linked to your goals and your plan?

SMART SHIP

The most thorough plan for change is likely to encounter failures and resistance. Persevere through those difficulties to achieve success.

In test operations, the guided missile cruiser *USS Yorktown* (CG-48) went dead-in-the-water several times as a result of computer failures. The *Yorktown* is a test bed for the Navy's Smart Ship Program, whose goal is to use automation to reduce costs and the size of the crew. One newspaper reported: *"The ship had an engineering LAN casualty that caused it to lose control of its engines."* The Smart Ship Program manager responded, *"We pushed the envelope knowing something like this might happen."* Detractors of the program argued, *"Replacing vital systems on a Navy warship with patched together capabilities is just plain irresponsible."* Today, after almost ten years of controversy and further tests and modifications, upgraded control systems operate flawlessly on most Navy combat ships.

There is a practical limit to the advanced planning that can be done for a change initiative. Change requires contributions from many people, each with their own goals, ideas, and dragons. No matter how much planning is done, some team members will feel there wasn't enough planning, while others will think there's been too much. At some point in every change project, there comes a time when action is necessary. No amount of planning could avoid all of the problems or resistance. The Smart Ship Program, for example, had matured to the point in its development where field testing under the stress of actual operations was essential, and failures were an expected part of such stress testing,

A plan is just a tool for directing and motivating individuals and teams. As a leader, you have fulfilled the purpose of the planning process when the goals, milestones, and tasks are clear to your team members. If unexpected problems happen when the plan is executed —a common, almost inevitable occurrence—the important thing is to persevere through the failures until the goal is achieved.

CLOSING THOUGHTS ON PLANNING

*Plans are only good intentions unless
they degenerate into hard work.*

—Peter Drucker

In 1978, the Washington Bullets basketball team was behind three games to two to the Seattle Supersonics in the NBA best-out-of-seven finals. Dick Motta, the coach, inspired the Bullets to win the last two games and the championship by telling reporters, *"Don't count us out. It ain't over 'til the fat lady sings."* The scrappy Bullets used every known basketball tactic and invented several new ones. They tried unusual substitutions, in-bounds plays, intentional fouls, and full court presses. And they won! Like the Bullets, it's not over until you say it's over. Then, no matter what the real possibilities may be, *it isn't possible* because you mentally quit trying to plan ways to overcome the obstacles and achieve your goals.

I choose what is possible for me, and you choose what is possible for you. We each establish a mental get-off point, the point where we tell ourselves, *"It isn't possible,"* and stop searching for ways to make results happen. What is your biggest goal today? Do you or your team doubt the reality of that goal? Why? Consider that those *whys* might not be real at all; they may be your dragons talking. We each set a limit on our maximum success in the goals we choose and the plans we make to achieve them. Big goals produce big success while small goals add up to small success. Which do you want?

Nineteenth century military strategist Carl von Clausewitz argued that elaborate plans usually fail because circumstances change. And circumstances certainly change more in the relationship economy than during the Napoleonic Wars of von Clausewitz's era. But setting a goal without developing a thorough plan to achieve it is at best an idle daydream and at worst a failure that will generate cynicism and waste resources. In designing a plan for your organization, realize that the single most important factor that determines success or failure is not the plan itself, rather it is the confidence a plan produces that the goal can be achieved. Even the most thorough plan is secondary to the intangible, elusive motivations that it stimulates deep inside you and your colleagues. A plan that channels those motivations toward commitment and creativity will surely lead to your success in the relationship economy.

Remember that success is a journey. Your results will tell you when your plans and actions are taking you down the right road. Even though you might not reach your goals, when you operate at a higher performance level this year than in previous years, you are successful. Goals are statements of good intentions that are meaningless until they are supported by a plan that produces action. And plans always have—at least they *should always have*—specific outcomes, accountability mechanisms, and a defined time line. Of course, goals and plans are merely guesses and hopes about what *could happen* in the future. In today's relationship economy, don't count on the world to stand still while you execute a plan. It will change even as you are developing and implementing your plan! So ensure that your goals and plans give you the flexibility to respond to the ever-changing world.

> Big goals produce big successes while small goals produce small successes. Which do you want?

INNOVATION

Tip #9: Reach the Top through Innovation

OVERVIEW

The success you enjoy today could be the biggest threat to your continued success. When you are successful, the natural human tendency is to make just small adjustments and avoid risky innovations. Unconsciously, you assume that your future success is just an extension of today's success. Logically, it's easy to see the fallacy in that thinking, but you must tame the intoxicating dragon of today's success in order to create the innovations needed to produce tomorrow's success.

Paradoxically, success creates a new reality that often makes the actions that produced it obsolete. The vignettes in Tip #9 encourage you to meet new challenges with innovation—to start innovating somewhere, to occasionally try something radical, and to make innovation a habit by instilling it in your organization's culture.

NEWSPAPER SAFARI

*It's relatively easy to find an innovative solution once
you empty your mind of habitual thought patterns.*

When I find myself struggling to solve a problem, I treat myself to a newspaper safari. My habit is to read the front page and the business, sports, and metro sections of the Washington Post each day. But when I'm stuck on a problem or need a new perspective, I take a safari into the health, style, food, or apartment-living sections. Alternatively, I take an Internet safari by Googling a topic totally unrelated to my problem and being open to receive a new perspective.

Newspaper safaris work because the real challenge is not finding a new solution; it's emptying my mind of the old ideas that produced the problem in the first place. So for an hour or so, I browse through strange newspaper sections that I ordinarily would never read. I don't read every page. I just get a feel for the issues and solutions from the strange subjects and use them to find an innovative solution for my problem. Try a safari yourself.

Innovative people link old concepts together in new ways, often by adding just one small new idea. They have an uncanny ability to frame the problem in a way that leads to new alternatives. Then they find a creative solution by connecting ideas that others see as unrelated or useless. They find the missing links that connect jigsaw puzzle pieces into an exciting new solution.

In the relationship economy, innovations happen so fast in so many fields that many of tomorrow's innovations are likely to be the combination of smaller, specialized innovations from today. You may discover a new concept by combining several other innovations from your organization or other organizations. Turning your innovation into a major commercial breakthrough may require relationships with like-minded innovators in other fields. That's why it's so vital for you to build new relationships today to ensure your success tomorrow.

LOW-INCOME HOUSING

*Next time you're surprised, use it as an
opportunity to discover new possibilities.*

My wife and I live in an upscale community that has 900 homes worth an average of over one million dollars each. During the zoning phase of its construction, the developer was surprised when the county demanded that he build one low-income house for each other house. After a long battle, the builder transformed his surprise and anger into an innovative solution. He built all-brick, four-bedroom, low-income homes and subsidized their construction and maintenance with a surcharge on upper-end homeowners like myself. In return, the county reduced the required number of low-income homes.

Interest among low-income people in buying the new homes was so great that a lottery was needed to select buyers. One in twenty won the lottery and purchased a house for $70,000 in the early 1980s. The sale included a provision that low-income homeowners couldn't sell their house on the open market for twenty years. The twenty-year moratorium ended last year, and the homes are now selling for about $500,000. Everybody won with this innovation!

We usually brush off surprises as if they were nuisances, when in actuality they can be opportunities for innovation. A supervisor I worked for early in my career had a unique way to deal with business surprises. At our weekly staff meetings, he insisted that each of us report one case when our client surprised us. Not what went right or wrong, rather what was unexpected. Then we searched for, and often found, business opportunities in the surprises.

The relationship economy is the most surprising period in history. Nothing is immune to change. Actions by small groups of innovative people have triggered massive changes. Are you associated with such groups, or are you trying to succeed all by yourself? Next time you're surprised by what's happening around you, consider it an opportunity to discover fantastic new possibilities—an opportunity to make change work for you and your organization.

A LONG SHOT WINS

*Never give up! When the odds seem to be the
longest, call on your most innovative thinking.*

The first consulting firm where I worked processed claims for the New York State Medicaid program, at the time the largest Medicaid program in the country. Two other companies processed claims for California and Texas, the next two largest programs. The Texas five-year contract was up for renewal, and we were determined to win. But first we had to deal with the *we-don't-have-a-chance* dragon who said the odds were long because the other company's CEO was a friend and political supporter of the Texas governor.

The proposal team tamed the dragon by making an innovative offer: We bid zero cost! The caveat was that Texas would deposit quarterly funding for all claims in the commercial bank owned by the company for which I worked. Since interest rates were high, the interest earned on the funds was sufficient to pay all processing costs and produce a fair profit. Our innovative proposal won the award. How could Texas decline an offer that saved several million dollars each year? Politics being politics, the incumbent protested the award, and Texas upheld the protest. We were disappointed, of course, but our company was paid several million dollars in damages, which made our creativity and proposal quite profitable.

In the business world, it's remarkable how often breakthrough ideas are found not through extensive research but by accident or necessity. What appears to be brilliance to outsiders is actually innovation in the face of adversity. Large organizations often struggle to innovate since their strength is mass. Mass lets them use resources and infrastructure to solve problems more than a small company can. But mass can impede innovation and change because it usually applies scarce skills and knowledge skills in large profit centers rather than in growth areas looking for new possibilities. To succeed in the relationship economy, your organization, no matter its size, must sense emerging changes in the world of business and respond quickly with innovative strategies and effective strategic partnering.

EATING AN ELEPHANT

When you face an enormous challenge, start innovating on a piece of the problem, and soon the total solution will emerge.

One of the best compliments a client ever gave to my company was: *"When I don't know where to begin, I give them the problem because they'll come up with something."* The project that concerned him was acquiring business systems from scratch for a new naval base. The challenge was daunting. Where would he start? He needed answers to pivotal questions like: *What capabilities are required? By whom? When? Where? How much will they cost? And how long will acquisition, integration, implementation, and training take?*

We didn't know the answers either, so we approached the project as if we were eating an elephant. We broke it into bite-size pieces: user groups, hardware, software, security, communications, facilities, data, and interfaces. We interviewed people at other bases to determine requirements, develop specifications, estimate costs, and prepare a schedule. When the base opened four years later, all of the systems were installed and operational, the staff was in place and fully trained, and coast-to-coast communications were ready. Innovation started by breaking an enormous problem into manageable pieces.

Today, the federal government faces elephant-sized problems. To solve those problems, Congress and the President must cooperate to tame three ferocious dragons:
- Terminating marginal programs to free resources,
- Forming strategic partnerships to solve problems, and
- Overcoming entrenched organizational resistance to change.

The transformation will be forced by the extreme budget pressures of escalating Social Security and Medicaid costs, and crumbling national infrastructure. Government decision-making and funding methods are stuck in the industrial age. To enter the relationship economy, it must form creative partnerships with industry and not-for-profits. Congress should scrap its existing committee structure and oversee issues and outcomes, not agencies. How's that for an elephant-sized challenge?

GOING POSTAL

Since change never ends, the need for innovation never ends.

E ven as I get angry waiting in long lines at the post office during the holiday season, I admire the U.S. Postal Service's (USPS) resiliency. Few organizations face such powerful competition and pervasive change. First class mail volume falls steadily as we pay bills online, send *Evites*, and transmit documents electronically. But USPS still handles more than 600 million pieces of mail every day with an enviable on-time delivery record using one of the most automated operations in the world. The innovations pioneered by USPS include bar coding, *Click-N-Ship* online services, automated postal centers, and, most surprising of all, strategic partnerships with retail stores and competitors like FedEx. Their urgent need for innovations continues to grow. If junk mail disappeared, USPS might go belly-up!

Like the USPS, organizations must manage two concurrent streams of innovation: improving current products and services while creating new ones. The thinking behind the two streams is completely different, but both are essential for your future success. You must compete in today's markets with efficiency and quality, even as you develop the flexibility and speed that tomorrow's market will demand. As a change leader, you must pursue both innovation streams and resolve the conflict between exploiting the past and discovering the future.

The conflict is that the success of existing products and services can become a barrier that causes your organization to miss emerging opportunities and threats. The organizations that prosper decade after decade watch the market to find shifting demands and hot new trends by their customers, suppliers, and competitors. They know that being the world's best at what they do today can stifle innovation. Pursuing innovation aggressively while you're on top is not an act against expanding today's success; instead it is an act against short-sightedness. Are you cultivating both streams of innovation in your organization?

JUST DO IT!

When your world is undergoing earthquake changes, gradual change inside your organization is a one-way ticket to oblivion.

When the Berlin Wall fell, our country essentially stopped building submarines. My company was subcontractor on a submarine contract that was cut from $90 million a year to $18 million. At first, the government-industry team resisted the cut and protested with safety-of-ship and other boogeyman fears. After a while, we tamed the *catastrophic-change* dragon, accepted that there was no alternative to a reduction, and committed to find innovations that cut costs. But how could we ever deal with the earthquake tremors of an 80 percent cut? Obviously, incremental change wasn't an option.

The breakthrough occurred when a team member asked, *"What can we just stop doing?"* We examined every task we performed to support the ships and their crews, and found innovative cost-cutting measures in three categories:

- *Just Do It* ideas that should have been implemented years ago, including eliminating tasks whose purpose had disappeared;
- *Process Improvements* that accomplished essential tasks faster and better, which is always cheaper too; and
- *Investments* in new technologies with high return on investment.

One idea led to another like snowballs rolling down a hill. All it took was starting. Each innovation, no matter how small, began a chain of innovations. We met the budget reduction target early!

In the relationship economy, no matter what industry you are in, long periods of incremental change are periodically interrupted by earthquake changes that wipe out entire business lines. During times of incremental change, the most efficient organizations prosper. But when dramatic change happens, incremental improvement of services, products, and relationships is a one-way ticket to oblivion. However, organizations that recreate themselves to exploit the new environment will thrive. Are you pursuing innovations and creating relationships that will thrive after the next earthquake in your industry? What will that earthquake be?

FUZZY FUTURE

In planning for tomorrow, don't underestimate the power of innovation by assuming that things will be like they are today.

In 1982, I bought my first home computer, a Commodore-64, to play games like *Donkey Kong* and *Q*Bert*. When I used the C-64's 64,000-byte memory to process a spreadsheet or a word processing document, my frustration pushed me to conclude that computers in the home would never be anything but toys. Ten million C-64s were sold. Most of them are in landfills today, their tiny memories replaced by megabyte Pentium computers linked to the Internet. I didn't grasp what Gordon Moore, who gave us Moore's Law in 1965, meant when he predicted that computing power would double every two years.

Your mental picture of future possibilities is fuzzy as well. It is easy to assume the future will be an incremental improvement over today, which underestimates the power of innovation to change the world. If you let it, that fuzziness can cause you to miss possibilities that are just over the horizon and be ineffective in your preparations for the future. To maximize your opportunities for success in the relationship economy, stretch your imagination to visualize the future. But how can you know which new ideas will produce results?

The short answer is you can't. But creative minds understand that innovative ideas that are like newborn babies. They are immature, vulnerable, and their future is uncertain. An innovative mind doesn't ignore such fledgling ideas as useless. Instead it asks three questions:

- *How could this embryonic idea be an opportunity for the future?*
- *What would it take to transform it into something that works?*
- *How can I exploit my answers to the first two questions?*

Even though a majority of new ideas die, consistently search for ways to convert ideas into new services and products. Since it's just as hard and risky to transform a new idea into a small success as it is to make it into a major breakthrough, don't aim for incremental improvement. Instead, aim to create a new way of doing business or an entirely new business. To innovate, think big!

ACCELERATING INNOVATION

As the use of collaboration tools proliferates, innovation is accelerating and creating exciting new business possibilities.

In 1970, my billet on the *USS Farragut* (DLG-6) was as the main propulsion assistant who supervised operation of the ship's two main engines and four 1,200-pound steam boilers. Whenever we encountered a maintenance problem, we filled out and mailed a paper Feedback Report (FBR) to headquarters. In eighteen months on board that ship, I submitted over twenty FBRs but didn't receive a response to a single one. The average FBR response time was over two years.

In the 1990s, ships used a computer to prepare FBRs, but the response process was essentially the same as in 1970. My company received a Small Business Innovative Research contract to improve the shore-based response process using automated workflow tools to pass FBRs ship-to-shore electronically and track them through the response cycle. By 2000, that system cut the average response time to weeks, a major improvement but still archaic by today's standards.

By 2005, just five years later, Internet communications had eliminated FBRs. Sailors now receive responses to queries in minutes, not weeks. Sometimes they get feedback before they know they have a problem. Some equipments send data (when ship operations permit) about their condition and performance to shore-based experts in real time. The experts analyze the data for anomalies, remotely diagnose problems, and transmit recommendations to the ship's crew.

The FBR process confirms that incremental improvements that took decades to develop in the industrial era have been replaced by sweeping changes implemented in just a few months. In particular, the relationship between people and equipment is changing. For example, you speak to your car and it answers, and some cars park themselves. Your car also can warn you about a traffic jam ahead and suggest an alternate route. Ships still have crews, but we already have remote-piloted airplanes and soon will have autopilot vehicles of all types. How will the accelerating pace of innovation boost your success?

WHO PAYS WHOM?

The relationship economy is flipping the business model in many mature industries and creating new opportunities.

One night, I watched an hour long TV show in thirty-three minutes on TiVo by skipping commercials. I saved time, but I also wondered what will happen to the economic model of TV. Will advertisers continue to pay to produce TV shows if nobody watches commercials? Will I be forced to pay for TV shows I select when I use TiVo? Interestingly, I don't reject advertisements from Amazon or Google because they're usually tailored to my unique preferences.

For decades the TV industry has produced shows, put them on TV, and prayed that we would watch. But as many of us order shows through season passes, how will that business model evolve? Who will be paid for what? Will consumers pay for shows individually, or buy access to channels that offer the programming they like? Will shows be aired at scheduled times, or reside in an on-call library? How will the revenue from these services be shared?

The fundamental ingredient of any business model is *who pays whom*. For TV, the path to new business models is fraught with power struggles among the companies who produce content, networks who broadcast and market it, and Internet and telecom companies who compete with cable and satellite companies to deliver content to the consumers. It isn't unusual for some strands in this spaghetti bowl to be separate divisions in the same Fortune 500 company.

The same trends are occurring in music, communications, and other areas. The relationship economy is forcing new business models based on the ubiquitous connectivity provided by cell phone networks and Voice-Over-Internet-Protocol (VOIP). By the time you read this, sixty years of TV economics may have been replaced by an innovative model created by an entrepreneur who made tons of money. But don't feel like you have missed the boat, because the same kind of change is probably occurring in your industry too. Are you seeing a shift in who pays whom in your industry? How can you get paid for using things that you pay for in your current business model?

BROWNFIELDS

*To produce breakthrough innovations, reshape
the basic relationships of your industry.*

An unsavory by-product of the transfer of U.S. manufacturing jobs overseas has been thousands of abandoned industrial sites in and near big cities. Many of these "brownfields" could be brought back to life if the uncertainty and liability of the environmental contamination from prior uses was eliminated. Without such assurances, developers build in previously undeveloped areas rather than endure the higher risk and costs of cleanup and redevelopment in cities. They make that choice even though building in undeveloped areas often makes it hard to hire and retain the skilled workers who live in and around cities.

Responding to pressure from city mayors in the mid-1990s, the Environmental Protection Agency (EPA) created the innovative Brownfields Economic Redevelopment Program under the Super Fund. Recognizing the developers' dilemma, the EPA made grants to cities to evaluate brownfield sites so the developers would know the cleanup and pollution challenges they faced in redeveloping inner-city properties. Furthermore, EPA indemnified developers from lawsuits related to contamination from prior uses of the brownfield sites.

The brownfields program reinvented relationships between the EPA and cities, and between cities and developers. Previously, EPA had been the regulatory enforcement dragon. But the EPA changed its role from enforcer to collaborator. So far, the program has addressed over 20,000 brownfield sites and cleaned up many of them. It has fostered several billion dollars of private investment in inner-city redevelopment and created tens of thousands of inner-city jobs. Those extraordinary results were produced by looking at vexing problems in new ways, by realigning old relationships, and by taking actions that at first seemed radical. Most people view the Brownfields Program as government at its best.

On the other hand, government at its worst becomes paralyzed by a plethora of special interest groups and fails to take effective action in a timely manner. The government's top current challenges—arguably stimulating the economy, developing new energy sources, protecting the environment, and controlling terrorism—will require more, rather than less, government. But those challenges require a cooperative brand of governance and different relationships among federal, state, and local governments; between the government and industry; and between the government and citizens.

Since the time of ancient Rome, mankind has been obsessed with top-down control and enforcement. However, a legacy of the relationship economy will be a transfer of power and enforcement to peer groups. There is a mother lode of untapped potential to be gained by pushing action to the bottom, rather than by focusing on what can be done at the top of government.

> **Tap into the mother lode of creativity at the bottom rather than expanding what is done at the top of your organization.**

Governments must change how they face challenges. Effecting change in any organization—be it government, business, non-profit, labor union, or association—requires three concurrent actions:

- Terminate programs that aren't working and those which are no longer relevant to the organization's priority mission;
- Focus on programs that produce results and those that enhance the organization's ability to deliver results; and
- Restructure marginal programs to move them into either the first or second category above.

One common contributor to almost all major performance advances is new and more effective relationships. Invent new ones frequently.

Government executives have a unique innovation opportunity in dealing with special interest groups. Today, special interest groups get intense oversight and mostly adverse media publicity. In the future, government leaders, special interest groups, and industry must realign their relationships and coordinate their strategies to implement innovative solutions such as the EPA's Brownfields Program. The same applies to those of you who aren't in government: Lucrative opportunities lie in realigning your relationships in a radically new way. Reinvent the fundamental relationships in your industry.

DISAPPEARING OFFICES

Innovations often succeed in unexpected ways for unexpected reasons. Look for such benefits from your next innovation.

When my son-in-law moved to North Carolina, he kept the same job he had in San Francisco. He develops software from the office in his new house. In the early days of computers, programmers had to work in the building that housed the mainframe computer. Today, thanks to client servers, laptops, the Internet, wireless networks, BlackBerrys, and e-mail, people like my son-in-law can process, transmit, and collect data from anywhere in the world.

Telework is redefining the concept of an office and the relationship between employers and workers. From the employer's viewpoint, the advantages of telework include:

- Reduced office costs and enhanced worker productivity;
- Uninterrupted operations during bad weather or traumatic events;
- Global recruiting with no relocation costs; and
- New sources of free agents and employees (e.g., the handicapped and mothers at home) who can't travel to a central office.

There is a similar list of benefits from the workers' viewpoint.

The U.S. Census Bureau reported that in 2005 about 4 percent of the workforce worked full time from home and another 12 percent telecommuted part-time. Despite the significant financial, productivity, and recruiting benefits of this innovation, control dragons born in the industrial era make managers reluctant to implement the infrastructure and policies required to promote and support telework.

When telework finally succeeds, it probably will be because employers find reasons beyond what we know today and because they won't be able to hire enough skilled employees any other way. Most innovations produced benefits that their creators didn't imagine. So innovative teams must begin knowing that any new product or service probably will find users in markets no one thought of, for uses no one envisioned at the start. In any case, given the rosy future of telework, I don't plan to invest in any new office building projects.

SKUNK WORKS

*Innovation teams are more productive when
they are separated from mainstream activities.*

A government executive who was a client of my company received a charter from top management in early 2000: "*Start a skunk works. Let's see if there's anything useful we can do with that Internet stuff.*" It was an unusual mandate, since applying computer technology wasn't in his unit's mission. But he accepted the task and contracted with us to identify new possibilities, implement new capabilities with willing users, and build the system incrementally. He instructed us to take risks and try things that might not work.

During the September 11th crisis, the fledgling system was tested and passed with flying colors. Easily accessible from anywhere, the system became a trusted source of accurate and timely information for users in the larger organization. After four years of development and refinement, responsibility and funds for the new system were transferred to the technology division of the organization where it originally belonged.

Innovation teams are usually more effective when they are separated from mainstream activities. Like white blood cells in our bodies that quickly destroy foreign material, most organizations have people who staunchly resist new ideas that are outside the norm. By setting aside the pressure of daily routines and internal criticisms, innovation teams are free to adjust their strategy, align their roles, and set their priorities to reshape the organization's future.

Skunk works, a term coined by Lockheed-Martin in World War II, often can produce a stream of innovations that alters the basis of competition. By contrast, the mainstream of most organizations thinks in terms of incremental changes. When facing an urgent need to innovate, the danger is that a successful organization may succumb to the inertial dragon that pushes them to defend yesterday's success and reject any radically new ideas. Given the freedom to be creative, most people enjoy the challenge of being innovative.

The progress of skunk works is discontinuous. Breakthroughs occur one day, and embarrassing failures happen the next day. Skunk works are normally small, avoid centralized structure, have loose procedures (if any at all), and experiment with things that may seem irrelevant. The key people in such units are often inexperienced, brilliant, and technologically savvy. On the other hand, the team leader is often a respected veteran who knows how the mainstream operates but doesn't feel bound by its norms. Almost without exception, effective skunk works teams are committed to do whatever it takes to produce innovative new products or services.

Skunk works people work in isolated facilities because the mainstream organization will try to squash, discredit, or ignore them. In contrast to the mainstream, skunk works people are inefficient and expensive. They generally don't care if they violate tried-and-true rules revered in the mainstream. Skunk works people gain experience from experiments, and learn from failures and false starts. Executives shouldn't be discouraged by such difficulties, nor should they be overly excited by early successes. After a major success, a skunk works team often is disbanded, and the new product or service is transferred into the mainstream for implementation.

> **Consistently communicate a vision for the future, even if the vision is a moving target!**

Transitioning an innovation from a skunk works to the mainstream for implementation is a turbulent and chaotic event. Many times, existing business strategies and processes must be dismantled before the innovation can be taken to the market. Executive attention during this fragile transition period is essential for success. They must maintain control by:

- Communicating a clear vision for the future;
- Promoting the innovation broadly across the organization;
- Adjusting the organizational structure for the innovation; and
- Being open to feedback and taking corrective action if needed.

Change leaders will be required to consistently communicate a vision for the future even as the vision itself is a moving target. Look for an opportunity to join a skunk works team or to start such a team in your current organization.

RISING TAXES

*The practice of government must be rebuilt to perform
in the relationship economy's unique environment.*

Maryland, my home state, just implemented the largest tax increase in its 200-year history, including a 20 percent increase in the state sales tax. Why? We aren't receiving better services. In fact, our services have been cut. The answer is the state operates a cornucopia of programs each designed to address a specific social need oblivious, for the most part, to other programs that address related issues. As a group, the programs are economically unsustainable, so our taxes rise and rise and rise. Similar overlaps exist in federal programs and in the integration of federal, state, and local programs.

The argument for integrating government programs isn't new. For decades, governments have searched for a holistic approach to the diverse challenges of defense, social services, education, land use, and the environment. But the integration is more urgent in the relationship economy because everything is connected. Some government agencies have won "Innovation In Government" awards for holistic thinking. They deserve our congratulations and thanks. But such programs are rare because of the parochial dragons of special interest groups, and Congressmen and women who continue to support pet projects.

In the relationship economy, governments must operate more like businesses. Businesses have three advantages over governments. First, they are adept at pursuing strategic partnerships. Second, they can terminate a product without a public outcry; indeed, to survive businesses must end products and services when demand falls. And lastly, businesses face a brutal performance test: Before making a purchase, consumers ask, *"Is this worth what I'm paying?"* If the answer is *"No,"* they don't buy it. But there is no alternate supplier for government services, and government agencies are hear-of-hearing when it comes to feedback about their performance gaps. If you're in the business of government, make joint programs part of your plan for success. If you're in business, be sure that you exercise all three of your major advantages.

CLOSING THOUGHTS ON INNOVATION

In the industrial age, big usually crushed small; but in the relationship economy, flexible and fast beat stable and slow.

During the years from 1983 through 1986, IBM had the highest profits among Fortune 500 companies. By 1995, IBM had slipped to ninth, but it still was an icon in the world of business. In 2007's rankings, IBM's profits sunk to sixteenth. Microsoft was tenth in profits, so IBM did not fall because of a collapse in the computer industry. What causes once successful organizations to fall behind their competitors?

Success followed by decline, and dominance followed by stagnation is a pattern that occurs regularly in organizations. To achieve No. 1 status and stay there requires an extraordinary blend of execution discipline in today's operations and innovation to create tomorrow. Unfortunately, today's success is a playground for the insidious dragons of stability that can undermine growth. Innovation is the magic sword that slays those dragons.

Innovation isn't an accident. Actually it is a response to one of three challenges. The first challenge is *the unexpected*: unexpected events, unexpected successes, or unexpected failures. The unexpected may be the first warning that innovation is required to continue your success. The second challenge is *need*: An emerging problem requires its first solution or an old problem needs a new solution. The third is *external change*: The market wants a new product and service, or the world is changing (e.g., demographics of baby boomer generation). Consider the three challenges to be three doors to the future. While the view is different through each door, the environment for innovation is similar.

To be innovative, an organization must genuinely value innovation and willingly accept its liabilities. The values typically found in innovative work environments include:

- **Risk-Taking:** Experimentation is encouraged, and it's okay if a reasonable attempt at something new falls short of expectations;
- **Change:** An eagerness to try new things based on the belief that change is essential for survival and growth;

- **Trust and Honesty:** People feel comfortable expressing ideas and concerns, even when they're at odds with popular thinking;
- **Diversity:** Differences in culture, experience, and style are not only accepted; they are actively sought after on project teams;
- **Resources:** Time, facilities, and financial backing are provided to explore new possibilities;
- **Freedom:** People have the freedom to decide *how to* be creative and how do their jobs and reach their goals; and
- **Commitment:** People are challenged by their assignments, and emotionally and intellectually committed to producing results.

Values are positive things, but occasionally they will conflict with one another in a world where you can't have everything you want. Your most important values show up in your daily choices. Building a culture of innovation requires that you value innovation more than you value the characteristics that compete with innovation, like order, efficiency, and predictability. Where do the seven innovation values rank among your values?

> To build a culture of innovation you must value innovation more than you value characteristics like order, efficiency, and predictability.

Leading innovation and radical change must be anchored in today's success because, if an organization isn't successful today, there may not be a tomorrow. The real leadership test is to compete successfully in today's market through continuous improvements in efficiency while stimulating innovation to develop tomorrow's services and products. Leading an organization through short-term and long-term success simultaneously is like a juggler working with a set of sharp knives. How well are you juggling your organization's current and future successes?

EXECUTION

Tip #10: Execute to Produce Results

OVERVIEW

The wide gap between the goals an organization sets and the results it achieves is a dragon that frustrates leaders. They preach change, but change doesn't happen until the quality of the plan is matched by the quality of its execution. Without effective execution, breakthrough thinking breaks down, deadlines pass by unnoticed, and stretch goals are forgotten. The organization is in worse shape than if change had never been attempted in the first place because the performance gap creates cynicism and drains energy. Lasting change can be produced only through excellence in execution.

The vignettes in Tip #10 are about execution. They will encourage you to move rapidly from planning into action, show you how to make effective decisions in the heat of battle, help you make course corrections when things get off-track, and push you to persevere all the way to success.

THE GAP

*There is no more dangerous matter to conduct, nor more
doubtful in its success, than to lead the introduction of change.
For he who innovates will have for enemies all those who are
well-off under the old order of things, and only lukewarm
support from those who might be better off under the new.*
—Niccolo Machiavelli, Italian Philosopher

L ate one afternoon, I met with a government executive in his corner
office. He looked tired and angry as he said, *"I'm frustrated. It's been
a year since we held that strategic planning off-site, but there is still a
huge gap between our plan and our results."* My company had helped arrange
the off-site in an ideal setting away from everyone's offices, and retained
two world-class facilitators to prepare for and conduct the three-day event.
The two facilitators briefed each flag officer and civilian executive who
participated, and the meeting agenda clearly addressed the organization's
core challenges.

The executive was at a loss to explain why the strategic imperative had
stalled. The off-site had included stakeholders from headquarters and field
commands. Everyone knew the urgent need for change and embraced the
strategic plan for the enterprise. It was a solid plan, and it was the right time
for change. He lamented, *"Our top leaders were there, our best and brightest. They
felt motivated and empowered to do what had to be done. We aligned our resources
and rewards with change. Our commitment and energy were high. But nearly a
year has passed and we aren't close to meeting our goals. What did I miss?"*

Unfortunately, I have heard the same frustrations far too many times from
capable, experienced, committed leaders who understand the challenges of
change and seemingly have done all the right things to make change happen
in their organizations. They have a superb staff and clear vision for the future
but consistently fail to realize the results they have every right to expect.
When the shortfall becomes common knowledge, they lose credibility inside
and outside of the organization, and people in the organization become cynical
about change. Of course, what they're missing is effective execution.

The worlds of government and business are full of enterprise change
initiatives that failed. The initiatives are launched with great enthusiasm and

fanfare, but a year later (or less) the changes succumb to the stonewall dragon and are forgotten. Executives and managers return to their old agendas, and the last thing workers want is yet another doomed-to-fail change program. The bottom line is the that organization wastes money and time, and everyone thinks they would have been farther ahead if the organization had never attempted the change in the first place.

In helping organizations change, I've found that leaders spend too much time developing a brilliant strategy and insufficient time to plan its execution. Executives participate in stimulating off-sites and leave in full agreement about what must be done. But change never occurs. Lack of execution is the root cause of this pattern every time. Execution is more than a thorough plan, a detailed schedule, and control and accountability mechanisms, although those are essential. Execution is a discipline embedded in the organization's culture that is invoked whenever goals are set and plans are made.

> **Execution is a discipline embedded in the culture that is invoked when goals are set and plans are made.**

To avoid the horrors of a failed change, consider that a culture of execution is a mandatory prerequisite for any major change. If your organization hasn't built a culture of execution and accountability, it would be better served not to initiate change at all. That being said, if you decide to pursue change, declare the change, establish the urgency for change, and describe the post-change vision of your organization. Form a team to direct the change, preferably not as collateral duty. As the change leader, follow through with personal attention, regular reviews, and other actions that send the clear message: *"This change is our No. 1 priority."* Then follow up consistently to ensure everyone from top to bottom executes his portion of the change.

ECONOMIC DARWINISM

If you don't lead or respond rapidly to change in the
relationship economy, your organization may not survive.

A government executive was particularly direct with me about his worldwide change program. He said, *"I expect implementation will take years,"* as he pointed to a schedule on the wall. He continued that he wanted performance metrics and also thought his program needed a sustainment plan. He requested that my company assign a consultant to handle these matters. When I returned to my office, I e-mailed his concerns to the project team. But our execution was inadequate, too slow, or both. Within two months we lost the contract to a competitor who responded more rapidly to that client's needs.

The fast-paced relationship economy can be thought of as an economic Darwinism—only the fit survive. Like Darwin defined it in *Origin of the Species*, fit doesn't mean biggest and strongest. Rather, fit means responsive and adaptable to change. Small organizations actually have an advantage over big ones in responsiveness. If your organization isn't responding to the changes around you, at the very least you are throwing away a competitive advantage and you may be compromising your survival.

To execute effectively, be the first to know when and how your market is changing. Keep your finger on the pulse of change by using a four-step process:

- *Monitor Relationships.* Maintain a two-way information flow with your key clients, prospective clients, and strategic partners.
- *Analyze Information.* Share findings and ideas throughout your organization. Get everyone's perspective on what events mean.
- *Take Action.* Incorporate the findings and perspectives into your strategies, your plans, and your actions.
- *Obtain Feedback.* Tell the source of the information what you are doing with it, and ask them how well it is working.

In short, gather, share, and act on strategic information to respond to your market's long-term agenda, not just its immediate needs.

DEAL WITH THE DRAGONS

Change leaders look at things from the perspective
of their people so they can clear the path to change.

When Dwight D. Eisenhower was elected president, President Harry S. Truman said, *"Poor Ike. As a general, he gave an order and it was done. Now he'll sit in the Oval Office, give an order, and not a damn thing will happen."* President Truman was referring to the dragons that cause people to resist change. It isn't that generals have more authority than presidents. Rather, military leaders learned long ago that orders alone won't accomplish change, so they use techniques like after-action reports and bomb damage assessments to verify the execution. Execution suffers in organizations that don't have effective ways to find and eliminate the resistance to change.

Resistance is a normal human reaction to change, so don't be angry or surprised when it happens. Instead, deal with the resistance by: (1) anticipating resistance, looking for it in every change initiative; (2) identifying the sources of, and reasons for, resistance; (3) listening to and empathizing with the resisters; and (4) taking timely action to deal with their concerns and recommendations. To achieve change in your organization, you must tame all of the many resistance dragons.

People resist change for a variety of reasons, including:
- They don't believe the need or urgency for change;
- They resent not having a role in planning the change;
- They don't understand exactly what the change will be;
- They doubt that the change will be an improvement;
- They're uncomfortable because change disrupts the *status quo;*
- They disagree with the change and want something different; and
- They are afraid of failing or losing status after the change.

Most resistance to change actually can make the change work better if it is dealt with correctly. Open, two-way communications is a vital tool. Explain as many times as is necessary why the organization must change to survive, grow, and prosper; why this particular change will be effective; and how their personal future will look after the change is implemented.

Logic rarely works in eliminating the fear of change. Instead, fear can be reduced by listening and asking questions such as, *What is the worst that can happen? How do we ensure that doesn't happen? What do you suggest?* Let people voice their fear of change. Many times they will answer their own questions, and their concerns will dissipate without any help from you. Furthermore, sometimes they will suggest valuable improvements for the change initiative. Act on those ideas and be sure they know you used their ideas.

On the other hand, two stubborn dragons will erode support for the change if they aren't dealt with early and decisively. They are:

- *Victim Dragons* who deny responsibility for their actions and the organization's performance. They blame others, won't take the initiative, and expect management to resolve every problem.
- *Insurgent Dragons* who aggressively resist the change, refuse to follow the new procedures, and enroll others in resisting change. Insurgents are hazardous to the health of your organization.

These behaviors are dangerous because they are contagious. To tame the victim and insurgent dragons, confront them and explain that such behaviors are unacceptable. Request them to change their position and support the change. If they refuse, encourage them to be childish in somebody else's organization. Your decisiveness in dealing with these two dragons before it's too late is vital to the success of the change.

> If it's dealt with correctly, most resistance to change will make the change more effective.

Successful execution of a change hinges on how effectively you can anticipate, identify, and deal with resistance. By embracing resistance, understanding it, and leveraging it to improve the change process, you increase your chances for success dramatically. Every change is about relationships, even when it doesn't affect the organizational structure. Practice seeing the change through your people's eyes. Use your heart as well as your head. That insight will chart the course for managing resistance, executing the change, and reaching your organization's goals. By understanding your people's needs and having compassion for the challenges they face, you will be able to implement changes that are a win-win for everyone.

MAKING IT PERFECT

If you wait until all the lights are green before you leave home, you'll never start your journey to the top.
—Zig Ziglar

O n the fifth anniversary of the September 11th terrorist attacks on the World Trade Centers, members of the government commission that investigated the attacks blasted both the Bush administration and Congress for inadequate progress in executing their recommendations. The commission felt the president and Congress had procrastinated in several areas vital to protect the country from another attack. The commissioners issued a report card with far more *F*s than *A*s relative to their execution of the recommendations. The commissioners issued an emotional plea for bipartisanship to enact change in areas such as protecting our boarders, preventing the spread of weapons of mass destruction, and allocating homeland security funds.

Since change is always uncertain, trying to make things perfect is a mortal enemy of change. There are several similarities between the lack of action by the president and Congress, and lack of action to change ourselves and our organizations. Too often we:

- Substitute debate and planning for action;
- Search for the perfect answer in fear of doing something wrong;
- Do nothing when we aren't sure what is the best alternative;
- Rationalize inferior results by blaming external factors;
- Avoid accountability for the lack of measurable results; or
- Fall into the *working hard* trap by letting activity replace action.

The *making-it-perfect* dragon can cripple your ability to initiate action for change.

Tame the *making-it-perfect* dragon by aiming for success, not perfection. Don't surrender your right to be wrong, because in doing so you will lose the ability to learn and modify your direction. When you pursue perfection, you actually invite failure because nothing is perfect. When you set an unattainable goal, you're guaranteed to be disappointed. *I'm waiting until I'm 100 percent ready* is a dragon that will block your path to success, because you'll never truly be ready for anything new.

THE MOMENTUM OF SUCCESS

*The irony is that it's easier to execute change in
the middle of a crisis than at the peak of success.*

Executing change in a successful organization is like changing the direction of a fast-moving freight train. Successful organizations have momentum that carries them in the direction they are going even if it isn't the best direction for the future. For example, the challenge IBM faced when personal computers first became popular wasn't the technology. IBM already knew how to build PCs better than anyone else. It was the hugely successful marketing strategy, sales staff, and management processes that were based on selling "big iron." They couldn't change the size of the computers they sold without changing their strategy and their staff. Those are difficult changes for anyone, but they're nearly impossible in a successful organization.

The more successful the organization, the stronger the *I-don't-have-to-change* dragon that resists change. Unfortunately, that causes successful organizations to be especially vulnerable to performance deterioration in times of rapid change. Success makes it easy to deny that the world is changing. It's not an accident that today's business world has so many successful start-ups. In many ways, it's easier for a start-up to create and introduce a new product or service than it is to transform a successful company infested with resistance dragons.

Incremental improvement improves the execution of today's strategy, but it limits an organization's ability to react to big changes in the market. To continue success tomorrow, organizations that are successful today must invest in the development of new products and services in skunk works outside of the mainstream. Organizations that aren't proactive in making strategic changes often find themselves making changes in reaction to increasing competition, declining sales, and shrinking margins. It is much better to act before being forced to do so. The irony is that it's easier to execute reactive change in the middle of a major crisis than it is to proactively change at the peak of success. Are you proactively changing your organization and yourself, or waiting to make reactive changes?

NEGOTIATING EXECUTION

Excellence in execution is built on clear commitments formed through negotiation and appreciative inquiry.

In setting goals and budgets for the new year, the director of a field activity told his headquarters sponsor that he would eliminate the backlog of quality deficiency reports and reduce the time to process new ones by half. The sponsor, excited by the director's goals but skeptical about their execution, asked, *"The goals are great. How do you plan to achieve them? What resources do you need to change the process?"* The director provided clear answers but the sponsor pressed further: *"Are your people behind the change? How long will it take? What are the intermediate milestones?"* The sponsor didn't just accept the goals and approve the budget request. Instead, as a change leader he encouraged everyone in the room to contribute, and used the forum to build their commitment to the aggressive new goals.

The challenge of execution is getting to the heart of issues with constructive and persistent negotiation. Since most negotiations begin in partial ignorance, the following guidelines are useful:

- Set the tone of the negotiations in opening statements: helpful or challenging, whichever is more likely to produce results.
- Ask questions to gain understanding: *What do you mean by …?*
- Don't argue, since arguing serves no useful purpose.
- People always take action to satisfy their agenda, not yours.

Use these guidelines to negotiate agreements on goals, the strategy to achieve them, the measures of success, and the resources (including time) that will be required.

Negotiating is collaborating to gain the favor of people from whom you want something. As an exercise in relationship building, negotiation is a vital skill in the relationship economy. You negotiate all the time in your professional and personal lives. Whenever two or more people exchange information for the purpose of implementing a change, they are negotiating. For example, you and I are negotiating ideas as you read this.

THE NEW REALITY

America has become addicted to high salaries and a high
standard of living. The new reality is that now we have
to earn them in competition with a globally connected world.

A ccording to the Commerce Department, U.S. manufacturing grew from about $1 trillion in 1975 to well over $4 trillion in 2005 (in 2005 dollars). With only 5 percent of the world's population, the U.S. produces one-fourth of the world's goods and has done so consistently for the last several decades. The U.S. has the largest manufacturing economy in the world by far. Japan, our nearest rival, has been losing ground recently. While China's manufacturing capacity is growing, it still produces about one-tenth of the world's goods with 17 percent of its population.

But the employment outlook in manufacturing is unfortunately dismal. U.S. manufacturers have invested heavily to redesign their production lines to replace people with computer-controlled machines wherever possible. When that wasn't profitable, they offshored work to China, Mexico, and other places that have much lower labor costs. While the value of U.S. manufacturing continues to rise, employment in manufacturing has dropped from a peak of 20 million in 1979 to just 14 million workers in 2005, the lowest number of manufacturing workers since 1950.

On the other hand, business-friendly North Carolina is typical of the new trends in U.S. manufacturing. They effectively executed changes that recovered part of the loss. According to reports by the North Carolina Commission on Workforce Development, the state lost 72,000 manufacturing jobs between 2002 and 2005 in textiles, electronics, and furniture making. In the same period, several thousand new jobs were created in profitable areas such as specialty textiles, pharmaceuticals, and biotechnology produces. That is still a net loss of many jobs, but experts view North Carolina's successes as a model for U.S. manufacturing: produce high-value products that apply our technological expertise and highly skilled (but expensive) workforce.

The new reality for the U.S. economy is that manufacturing will decline as a source of employment for the foreseeable future. The blue-collar manufacturing jobs created in the industrial age seem to be gone forever, and only some of those jobs will be replaced by high-tech manufacturing jobs. We are only just beginning to grasp the full implications of this shift and other new realities of the relationship economy including:

- The world economy is growing rapidly and consistently;
- Most markets are expanding to encompass the entire globe;
- The buying power of other countries in the world is increasing faster than our buying power;
- Personal income is up and prices are down in real terms;
- Productivity gains are outpacing labor cost increases; and
- High quality is no longer a luxury; it is expected.

Manufacturers in the U.S. are working hard to control costs, but world markets will determine if our efforts are sufficient. The key challenge for the U.S. is: *Can we produce superior products and services at a price that the world is willing to pay?* The answer to the question has both innovation ramifications and cost-control ramifications.

If a company can buy five workers in China or India for the price of one in the U.S., as consumers we expect them to buy the five. But as citizens we get angry that, in the long run, the U.S. is losing much of its industrial capacity. The only way to satisfy our conflicting needs as consumers and citizens is to find ways to develop a highly educated workforce that not only produces a piece of the economic pie that

> Producing products and services at a price the world will pay requires both innovation and efficient execution.

is in global demand, but also produces more than it consumes. We also must invent new products and services that the world is eager to buy from us. How have the new realities listed above affected you and your organization? What new opportunities do those new realities create for you?

COURSE CORRECTIONS

*Adapting effectively to unexpected events is more
important in execution than having a perfect plan.*

My first duty as a midshipman was a ten-week deployment to the Mediterranean Sea on board the aircraft carrier *U.S.S. Intrepid* (CVS-11). During my first week on the ship, I worked with the navigator to plan our trip from Norfolk, Virginia to Naples, Italy. We plotted the course in hour-by-hour detail, including time for training exercises and flight operations. I was reassigned to the engineering department when we left Norfolk, but in the evening I would visit the navigator's shack to check our position. I was shocked to find that we were off course every day. We were never where we were supposed to be according to the plan that we worked so hard and long to prepare.

Several unexpected events occurred as we were crossing the Atlantic. We circumnavigated a fishing fleet, which added 100 miles to the trip. One of the four main engines failed, which reduced the ship's top speed. And we lost a plane, but fortunately a helicopter rescued the downed pilot. That incident delayed us over four hours. But such unexpected events didn't upset the navigator. He and the quartermasters determined the ship's position several times each day with radio triangulation and star sights (there was no GPS in 1964). Knowing our location, destination, and target time of arrival enabled the navigator to recommend a new course and speed to the captain. As scheduled, a week later we passed through Gibraltar and entered the Mediterranean Sea despite having been off course every day.

Your organization and possibly your career are similar to that ocean crossing in two respects. First, unexpected events often occur to disrupt execution of your plan, and push you off course. How well you react to those disruptions for the most part determines your long-term success. A second similarity is that measuring results against the plan ensures that you won't get too far off course, or stay off course as long. Even though you find yourself off course more often than you'd like to be, you still can achieve your goal by executing the appropriate course corrections. Being off course is not the real problem. In fact, deviations from a plan are normal, but unfortunately unpredictable events. Instead, not knowing when you are off course or failing to execute the necessary course corrections are contributing causes of most failures.

Knowing he had a reliable navigating capability and flexibility to make course corrections easily allowed the ship's captain to adopt an aggressive ocean-crossing plan. Likewise, your plan isn't viable until you make sure that your team has or will obtain the capabilities and resources required to execute the plan.

> For the most part, how well you react to unexpected developments will determine your future success.

Change leaders develop plans that are more like road maps than a path etched in stone. Their plans are fine-tuned for execution. That is, they include provisions to adjust quickly when the unexpected occurs, as it often will. Tactics are an important part of execution, but execution is much more than tactics. Execution must be an essential consideration in planning. Indeed, in many cases, the inherent capacity of your team to execute will shape your plan.

BLOODY FINGERS

*Examine your mistakes and the mistakes of
others, not to fix blame but to fix the problem.*

Safety was a top priority during my days in the naval shipyard. Safety posters were plentiful, and mandatory safety lectures were held at least weekly. Reports were prepared whenever an injury occurred and a formal inquiry was held for serious injuries. Inquiry results were distributed as additional lectures. The burdensome nature of the safety program led to the "bloody finger syndrome." When a worker cut his finger on machinery, rather than report the injury and suffer through an inquiry, he would simply put the bloody finger in his pocket, his colleagues would treat it in the bathroom, and the incident would go unreported. Such behaviors may have avoided short-term hassles, but they enabled conditions to persist that could have produced serious injuries. The *bloody-finger* dragon prevented organizational learning.

Peer pressure caused the bloody finger syndrome. As workers helped their co-worker treat his injury, they also pressured him not to report it. The pressure people receive from their colleagues determines what behaviors are acceptable and what behaviors are unacceptable. Peer pressure reflects the culture of an organization, which in this case was to hide mistakes rather than to learn from them. Peer pressure doesn't mean that people will ignore management initiatives like the shipyard's safety program. Rather, it determines how they will react to deviations from the expectations (i.e., mistakes) of such programs.

Unfortunately, the English language has no synonym for a mistake characterized as a positive experience. In an organization, making a mistake can be an organizational learning event or a time to fix blame. Your people can learn from their mistakes and the mistakes of others, or give into the blame dragon and hide them. But correcting mistakes is frequently the difference between success and failure in a relationship economy that won't tolerate the same mistake twice. Does your team learn from mistakes, or hide them as if they were bloody fingers?

TOO LITTLE, TOO LATE

When an economic bubble bursts, the best execution in the world won't substitute for diversified strategic partnerships.

A large government contractor with a golden history recently was sold under unfavorable conditions. For thirty years, the company had won contracts with federal and state agencies to build computer systems. In the 1990s, the company focused on software services for the telecom industry. When the telecom bubble burst, their revenue and profits dropped. Unfortunately, it wasn't ready for the next bubble in government contracting: the spectacular run-up in intelligence and defense spending after the September 11th terrorist attacks. The company had not invested to build strategic partnerships required to win contracts in those areas.

The company hired a new president in late 2001 and tasked him to change direction. He laid off hundreds of employees and offshored software development to cut costs. Then he purchased a company that provided technology to intelligence agencies. But it was too little, too late. Competitors had been making those changes years ago. The big contracts never came and time ran out. After reporting an eight-digit loss to Wall Street, the company was sold to competitors.

The relationship economy is a series of bubbles and crashes. More lie ahead. So, to be successful, you must anticipate change when possible or, at a minimum, respond quickly. Playing catch-up with change is usually a losing strategy. Relationships are the only insurance that protects you from every bubble: relationships with customers, with employees, and even with competitors.

When your organization is an industry leader, you have special challenges. You will be forced to make on-the-spot decisions even if circumstances are so radically different from the past that your experience seems useless. But you will still be held accountable for the results of those decisions. President Harry S. Truman said, *"If you can't stand the heat, stay out of the kitchen."* Prepare yourself and your organization to endure the heat of a major change, especially if you're on top of your industry today.

GET REAL

*Realism is essential in execution. Force realism into the
culture of your organization and your business processes.*

Navy officials seem to have salvaged the LPD-17 amphibious ship class construction program. The lead ship experienced nearly a billion dollars in cost increases and schedule slippages totaling several years. Lead ship funding was included in the FY96 budget and the ship was finally commissioned in 2006. For years, Navy executives claimed that the program was on track. But problems with the new computerized design system meant drawings had to be redone and steel that had been cut had to be scrapped. One official acknowledged, *"We're working out problems that have been there for years, and we are finally beginning to make real progress."*

Effective execution regularly exposes reality and acts on it. Unfortunately, many organizations are staffed with people who avoid reality. Why? Because reality is uncomfortable. People would rather hide problems and buy time to find a solution than admit they don't know what to do. They avoid confrontation. To inject realism into an organization's culture, its leaders must be realistic. They must make realism part of every discussion, every meeting, every decision, and every plan. Embracing realism requires frank assessments of your performance and your results, and a comparison of your results against the results of other people and other organizations.

Denying problems when the fundamental indicators are unmistakable is a sure path to failure. You may hope working harder will save the day, but projects fall years behind one day at a time when the team doesn't finish what was scheduled each day. Most organizations don't face reality very well, which is why they can't execute. They ignore reality. To tame the *rose-colored-glasses* dragon, get real. Force realism into all of your business processes and inject realism into the culture. Your execution strategies must include ways to re-examine your assumptions and upgrade your organization's ability to respond to changing conditions.

TWENTY-TWO TOUCHES

*Perseverance is the heart of execution. Do whatever
it takes, for as long as it takes, to achieve your goals.*

D uring my first year in government services, my boss sent me to
a sales training program. The instructor told us that, on average,
twenty-two touches were needed to win a contract with a government client. A touch is a meeting, phone call, or e-mail in which critical
information is exchanged about the client's problem or its solution. During
each touch, I must deliver value to the client: a unique idea, a referral to an
expert, a white paper with a recommendation, or a cost estimate. Otherwise,
the client won't want me around.

The instructor emphasized the need for perseverance by asking me, *"What
happens if you quit after just ten contacts?"* Of course, if I quit I've wasted the
time I invested in the ten contacts. He continued to push the challenge: *"How
long will twenty-two touches take?"* I did some math and figured that, at one
touch per week, it would take me roughly five months to win a contract.
At one touch every two weeks, it would take ten months to win. I left the
training with a lesson that has served me well for thirty years: perseverance
and execution are synonymous.

A substantial amount of time may be required to build a high-value
relationship, possibly twenty-two touches. Keep in mind that your relationship partner is acquiring knowledge about you at the same time. Persistence
pays off. Your return on investment may not come from the person in whom
you invest twenty-two touches. It may come from someone that he or she
refers you to.

Sometimes you may think you've failed and give up before you've solidi-
fied a relationship. But the depressing *let's-quit* dragon may be the only thing
standing between you and your goals. Failure is a key ingredient in success
in many fields. Failure helps you to grow and leads you to new knowledge.
Eastern philosophies teach us that each arrow that strikes the bull's eye is a
result of a thousand misses. Tame the *let's-quit* dragon. Persevere.

WACK-A-MOLE

Superior results are the difference between a culture
of execution and a culture of frenzied activity.

When I walk the boardwalk in Ocean City, Maryland, one of my favorite pastimes is playing an arcade game called Wack-A-Mole. The game board has nine moles arranged in three rows of three. The moles pop up their heads in random order, and I score a point each time I hit a mole on the head with a long-handled wooden mallet. The game is one minute of frenzied activity. I'm exhausted after the game, but my intense activity produced no results. The moles are ready to exhaust the next player. Ever notice how some people work hard but produce little in the way of results? Activity, no matter how intense, may not lead to results. When defending their weak results, activity junkies recite a long list of activities they performed.

Change leaders build a culture of execution that tames the activity dragon. A culture of execution isn't like a culture of frenzied activity. It seeks to prevent problems, rather than fixing them in a crisis. It uses repeatable processes and promotes people who produce results. In the industrial age of mass production, companies were able to focus on activities because, in general, more activity produced more results. In the relationship economy, however, organizations must focus directly on results because situations change and activity by itself may be like "wacking a mole" (i.e., it produces no useful result).

Given that execution is the foundation of extraordinary results, pay more attention to your people's results than to their activities. To build a culture that produces world-class execution, measure results and hold people accountable, but give them freedom to decide how to achieve those results. When you measure results like sales, customer satisfaction, and product quality, you'll be able to manage execution and be confident that things are getting done in the prescribed way. This will allow you to identify deviations early in the process, isolate weak spots, take corrective action, and reward the high performers in your organization.

AN ALL-STAR TEAM

Hiring the most talented performers doesn't ensure success.
Execution is essential for the team to realize its full potential.

Among the thirty major league baseball teams, the New York Yankees have had the highest payroll for the last seven seasons. In 2007, the team payroll was a record $218 million. Ten players had salaries over $10 million. They had a current or former all-star at almost every position, but they did not win a single World Series in those seven years. Individual performance can be a dragon, because even a team of all-stars must execute to realize its full potential.

On the other hand, the decades-long success of Silicon Valley isn't the result of a monopoly on creative people and venture capital. Silicon Valley's success grows from the network of companies and people in the region who know each other from previous ventures. They share ideas and possibilities in a connected *e*-culture. This microcosm of the relationship economy is a well-lubricated execution environment, one that leverages small advantages and new ideas to produce large opportunities. If the U.S. expects to compete favorably with China, India, and Mexico in the future, our businesses must look more like Palo Alto than Detroit.

Superior individual performances don't guarantee a team's success. Most managers have metrics that measure the performances of each team member and the team's collective performance. When team performance falls below expectations, they try to upgrade results one position at a time, usually focusing on the weakest unit or weakest person first. They either improve that person's performance or replace them. The underlying assumption being that all a manager has to do is hire an expert team and results will take care of themselves. It isn't so. The team needs direction and coordination, especially when it faces a significant market or technology change. How frequently do members of your team operate independently? How much of that independence could be harnessed by an environment suited to execution, one where team members knew their role in supporting the team's success?

CLOSING THOUGHTS ON EXECUTION

Don't blame results on an immature strategy or a weak economy. Instead, find ways to improve your execution.

In a chili-cooking contest, ten chefs were provided the same ingredients: beef, tomatoes, jalapenos, green peppers, cayenne, chili powder, onions, salt, pepper, etc. They were asked to prepare their best chili, but weren't required to use all of the ingredients. One chili was judged as the unanimous winner. But how could one chili be so obviously better when the chefs used the same ingredients? It wasn't a recipe that won; it was execution. In our projects and careers, we all have access to the same ingredients (e.g., relationships, information, and education), but results vary widely. Execution is the difference. How effectively are you using the ingredients?

The relationship economy has a tough standard for execution. The performance of every organization and every individual, not only businesses, is measured against benchmarks set by industry leaders around the globe. Even though your operations and markets are local, information about extraordinary successes or failures travels rapidly to remote locations. The Internet tells potential customers, competitors, employers, and employees about the products, services, and benefits available anywhere in the world, and at what price. The availability of such information has created enormous global opportunities.

Your organization probably has a pretty good strategy. So the difference between winning and losing isn't strategy; it's your ability to execute. If your competitors execute better than you do, they'll beat you every time. And vice-versa. Execution is the stealth dragon in the business world today. It's not discussed very often, but the absence of effective execution is the biggest single roadblock to success and the cause of mediocre results that are often blamed on something else. So don't blame your lack of results on a struggling economy or a strategy that hasn't reached its full potential yet. Instead, find ways for you and your team to improve your execution.

In Closing
FUTURE CHANGES

Change is an equalizer that reallocates
advantages to those who adapt quickly.

In the Wild West settlers relied on Army forts as safe havens. When times were dangerous, they felt safe in the fort because soldiers would protect them. Similarly, in the industrial age, large corporations became safe havens for workers by giving lifelong employment and generous benefits. During the information age, computer skills were a safe haven that guaranteed lucrative employment. But in today's wild world of business the safe haven is relationships. When things change, an organization may disappear. But people with whom you have built trusting relationships will help you thrive in times of change, just as you will help them. We are living in the relationship economy.

As I studied the organizations and change leaders who are successful in the relationship economy, I felt like Dorothy from *The Wizard of Oz*. I expected to find a brilliant wizard behind the curtain of success. Instead, there was just a hardworking businesswoman or businessman who had connected ideas and relationships in a visionary way to benefit people. Maybe that is wizard-like after all.

The emergence of the relationship economy is as revolutionary as the invention of the printing press, the computer, or the Internet, each of which radically changed how people interacted to conduct business. Whether you're a giant redwood in the Fortune 100 or a bonsai tree in the garden of small businesses, the effectiveness of your relationships will determine your future success.

You might say, "*Relationships were vital in every economic era. What's new?*" And I would agree. Relationships were critical to Christopher Columbus on his voyages to the new world and to John D. Rockefeller when he built the Standard Oil empire, a precursor to the Exxon-Mobil Corporation. However, three fundamental shifts are unique to the relationship economy of the twenty-first century:

(1) Creativity replaced productivity as the driving force behind profits, thus pushing relationships to the forefront of business.

(2) An ability to communicate instantly from anywhere with anyone at any time has enabled global relationships to blossom.

(3) Computer chips control everything we touch, from luggage to automobiles, from music to art, from toys to toasters.

Entrepreneurs have combined these three shifts in imaginative ways to produce earthshaking social, political, economic, and organizational changes. And the changes are only beginning!

The rising relationship economy is unlike anything we've ever seen before. When I looked for common threads among the vignettes in this book, I found ten "future changes." That is, changes that are already in progress but won't reach their peak impact for years. Think of the ten future changes in two ways. First, they are business opportunities in themselves for creative entrepreneurs; and second, they will deeply affect how your organization operates in the future.

Future Change #1 – *The Rise of Free Agent Workers*

Hierarchical organizations thrived when business changed slowly, but they are too rigid and slow to survive rampant change. To adapt to rapid change, industrial age conglomerates flattened their operations and gave autonomy to operating units. Centralized control is not a viable business model in today's fast-paced business world.

Knowledge workers have become the engine of production. Their knowledge is a valued asset, and they often move from project to project. In the industrial age, blue-collar workers relied on their company more than their company relied on them. The reverse is true today. Organizations depend on knowledge workers more than free-agent knowledge workers depend on any organization.

This startling development profoundly changes the employer-worker relationship. More and more workers aren't employees at all. Instead, they are 1099 consultants that work concurrently on multiple projects. The organization of the future will be virtual. It will perform a set of core tasks (its competitive advantage) and outsource the rest. If you are a knowledge worker, this phenomenon will forever change your career options. If you manage a large staff, it will change your personnel strategies. You must offer a customized employee-worker relationship (e.g., number of days per week, travel or no travel, unique benefit packages) and accommodate highly skilled people (e.g., baby boomers) who only want to work part-time on interesting projects.

Future Change #2 – *Customers Replace Employees*

The ultimate virtual organization would be staffed entirely by customers. Companies will never reach that utopia, but pumping our own gas, checking food at the grocery store, and making purchases on the Internet demonstrate how rapidly seller-consumer relationships are changing. When customers do what employees once did, costs decline and satisfaction increases because customers are able to do things their own way.

Soon we'll buy custom automobiles, appliances, and furniture online instead of in malls and mega-stores. We'll choose options, see products, negotiate price, and submit orders directly into the seller's supply chain. Then we'll monitor our purchases through the supply chain like we track shipments online today. Transactions will be transparent, with sellers and consumers each knowing a lot about the other. Every action you take to move your organization closer to its customers will be a significant step toward its future success.

Future Change #3 – *Communications Eliminate Jobs*

In the industrial age, machines replaced humans: the cotton gin on farms, process controls in manufacturing, and the assembly line in factories. In the information age, computers performed jobs that were previously done by humans. In today's relationship economy, e-mail, BlackBerrys, cell phones, and instant messaging are wiping out more jobs. Communication devices allow us to eliminate the middlemen and have direct relationships with business associates whom we rarely, if ever, meet face-to-face.

Any task that has repeatable steps and structured rules is a candidate for automation or offshoring to areas with low labor costs. For example, *TurboTax* and $10-an-hour accountants in India have transformed the tax return preparation business. But *TurboTax* and the Indians aren't safe either. It won't be long before, instead of merely accepting electronic tax returns, the IRS will move closer to taxpayers by allowing them to prepare and edit tax returns on-line, get a refund on the spot if they are entitled, or withdraw cash from their checking account if they are not. Whether you're a free-agent consultant or an executive, if you want to thrive, put yourself and your organization on the creation side and not the elimination side of such job redefinitions.

Future Change #4 – *High-Skill Professions Are Redefined*

High-paying professions that prospered in the industrial and information ages such as law, engineering, architecture, accounting, and software are evolving. Their income stream is vulnerable because advice and products that earned high fees just a few years ago are now available free via the Internet. On the other hand, those who lead the change by creating new ways to help their clients are being rewarded handsomely. Similarly, consumer demand in professions like health care, education, law enforcement, and mortuaries will remain steady. But the entry-level skills, relations with other vocations, and tools used in these professions will become more complex.

The industrial and information ages moved from one stable state to another over several years, but the relationship economy is stability in constant motion, like riding a bicycle. No matter what your profession, you'd better be close to your customers since they access the Web every day. They know what they can get for free and where they can locate cut-rate professional services if that's what they want. Customers will reward you with high fees for innovation solutions, but not for just doing a job. Organizations, no matter their size, will be forced to respond to this new challenge by creating new services and products, forging strategic partnerships, and building innovative teams to serve their current customers and find new ones.

Future Change #5 – *Creativity Is More Valued than Analysis*

The industrial and information ages were dominated by people who analyzed and resolved problems: executives who organized business operations, accountants who evaluated financial transactions, programmers who wrote software, engineers who designed machines, and lawyers who avoided or resolved conflicts. But the relationship economy is ruled by people who, in addition to those left-brained analytical skills, are able to incorporate relationships, new ideas, and new technologies into their solutions.

For roughly a hundred years, managers in government and business were promoted because of proven experience and advanced academic degrees. While post-graduate degrees are still valuable, long experience in how things were done in the past may be a big liability. Today, instant communications, global markets, and powerful new technologies fertilize the creativity of a new breed of leaders. They build unconventional alliances, find hidden possibilities, and combine unrelated concepts into amazing new products and services. To thrive in today's relationship economy, continue developing your analytical skills but, more importantly, let your creative juices flow freely!

Future Change #6 – *Social Change Is Rampant*

Social change is spreading in the relationship economy at a rate that is unprecedented. Communications enable the champions of social reform around the globe to unify their messages and share their resources. Social change stretches our ability to deal with change in general. On top of adjusting to a global economy and a plethora of new technologies, we also must live in a world where gay marriages, gun control, abortion pills, DNA manipulation, global warming, and government eavesdropping are controversial but common practices.

People think differently today. The end of the Cold War has allowed historically repressed peoples to seek freedom. Chaos theory, new-age thinking, the ecological movement, and a renewed interest in understanding other cultures have enabled us to recognize how tightly people, animals, and our Earth are connected. Industry's contribution to social change, especially in ecological areas, is expanding to the point where industry may soon be more important than government in implementing social change.

Social change thrives in the relationship economy for four reasons. The first, of course, is that technology touches every area of our lives, even affecting how church services are conducted. Second, ubiquitous communications connect like-minded people no matter where they live or work. Third is a growing awareness of how much we depend on the Earth for life, and a realization that we might be destroying the planet we live on. The fourth factor is an increase in international cooperation driven by a frustration with the ineptitude of governments. The wonderful news is that not only are social changes a boon for society, they're also a growing source of exciting business and career opportunities for you.

Future Change #7 – *Economies Are Interdependent*

In its first hundred years, the U.S. led the world in mega-farming. In its second hundred years, the U.S. built mega-factories. But the world is catching up. Despite having the most efficient farms and factories in the entire world, those industries aren't an engine of economic growth and are declining as a source of employment. The economic drivers today are relationships and ideas. Unfortunately, the transition from farms and factories to relationships and ideas has been painful for workers in several industries.

Many people are afraid that offshoring manufacturing jobs to China and service jobs to India will cause irreparable damage to the U.S. economy. For sure it is causing major changes, but our economic history has been to respond to such challenges by reallocating and reinvesting resources. Given our country's high salaries and benefits, trying to resist offshoring in labor-intensive industries is like trying to swim up a raging river. Instead, the path to tomorrow's success lies in upgrading our capabilities to claim a slice of the growing but very competitive international business pie. But how can we do that?

The good news is that offshoring has built new markets and opportunities by stimulating the appetite of Indian, Chinese, and other global consumers. They want high living standards, not slums. They want world-class goods, not junk. They want advanced technology conveniences in their workplaces and homes. And they're willing to pay for them! Like us, the more they have, the more they want; and the more they earn, the more they spend. Their increased disposable income and expanding desires have created a demand for travel, and the innovative high-end products and services that the U.S. produces.

As we continue in the twenty-first century, relationships and ideas are replacing products as the driver of U.S. economic growth. Today, your business challenge is to mass-produce relationships and ideas like we mass-produced agricultural and manufactured goods in the nineteenth and twentieth centuries. In the end, the interdependent global economies will be an economic windfall that will increase our quality of life above the high standard that we enjoy today.

Future Change #8 – *The World Is Shrinking*

The world is small. Transportation advances have been shrinking the globe for centuries. The steam engine replaced the sail and shrank the oceans. Locomotives replaced wagon trains and the Pony Express, and reduced the travel time between the Atlantic and Pacific coasts. Today, UPS, FedEX, and others move things in jet planes from your workplace to any other place with guaranteed next-day delivery! Information transfer is instantaneous. We don't have the transporter technology that Captain Kirk and Mr. Spock used to move objects in *Star Trek*, but even that is getting closer to reality.

Global trade is now about one-quarter of the world's economic output, compared with less than one-tenth at the start of the industrial era. The rise of China, India, the former Soviet-bloc, and other small countries as active trading partners means a majority of the world's people now buy and sell in the global marketplace. Unfortunately, the explosion in trade has amplified the economic gap between the *haves* and the *have-nots*, and spawned social unrest. Ironically, the same instruments that shrunk the globe have helped to spread the unrest and become tools of terrorism (e.g., crashing planes into buildings). In a small world, we're all tightly connected economically, ecologically, and socially. How does the shrinking world make ideas that once may have seemed impossible into viable ways to expand your success?

Future Change #9 – *Global War Is Archaic*

Fighting for resources and land may have produced economic benefits in the industrial age, but today countries co-exist in a very fragile ecosystem. Whether they are big or small, countries' economic healths are tightly coupled. If one gets sick, they all suffer. Cultural infections like terrorism and aggression by rogue nations weaken the entire ecosystem so, to preserve their collective health, countries will band together to eradicate the disease and inoculate future generations against such viruses. The collaboration will be tense and characterized by suspicion and resistance. But in the end, responsible governments will prevail and negotiate a healthy economic environment for all.

Governments, even the powerful U.S., are slowly learning that war is not effective as an instrument of national policy because of its devastating impact on the economy. Since war and threats of war are intolerable, governments will behave more like businesses and resolve differences on the basis of economic benefit. Furthermore, the tools of major warfare (e.g., tanks, bombers, and warships) are unaffordable and marginally useful. The companies that manufacture them will be forced to shift to a different business base in the next twenty years.

At the same time, tools and technologies for law enforcement and intelligence gathering are rising in value, not because of military uses but because of their vital economic importance. Electronic and robotic warfare

223

are replacing bombs and bullets as the weapons of warfare. For example, the Chinese are among the most aggressive users of electronic warfare tools for economic espionage. How does such a gigantic resource reallocation affect your economic future?

Future Change #10 – *Uncertainties Are Increasing*

It used to be that if you researched a market, prepared a good business plan, assembled the resources, and built a solid management team, your new business venture was virtually guaranteed to succeed. Changes occurred slowly, and you could adjust to them when they happened. Companies could be managed with the principles described in thirty-year-old business books. But change isn't like that any more. You still must plan thoroughly to succeed, but you will also need to be creative and agile. Monster changes will happen even as you execute your thorough business plan. Your natural tendency will be to work harder to make your plan succeed, even though it grows less and less appropriate to market conditions. On the other hand, new concepts like the ten tips in this book seem risky, awkward, and altruistic.

The relationship economy is like being on a rope bridge in a Tarzan movie. The flimsy bridge spans the dangerous jungle between yesterday and tomorrow. Many organizations and people share the bridge. Some say the trip to the relationship economy is a mistake, and they want to return to yesterday. But there can be no turning back. Those who cross the bridge first will be the most successful, and those who try to return to yesterday will be left behind.

When you enter the relationship economy on the far side, you may expect a land of milk and honey like the dot-com era. That might be true in a few cases, but the landscape also has false peaks and dead ends. A business chasing what looked like a lucrative market may find itself alone on an isolated hill. For example, Detroit once boasted it had the top automakers in the world, but today competitors deliver more desirable luxury cars and more affordable family cars. Similarly, IBM was king of the mainframe mountain until Dell and others built a PC mountain that was the Himalayans compared to IBM's mainframe market. When you find yourself in one of these dead ends, the only way out is to turn around and try another hill! The sooner you realize your plight, the greater your chance of survival.

§ § §

Faced with these ten future changes, I'm changing, you're changing, our customers are changing, and our local and international competitors are changing. No business, government, or not-for-profit is immune to the ten changes. But some won't have the flexibility and leadership necessary to succeed, not because they resist change but because change happens so fast it passes them by. The rewards will go to those who move with speed and agility. The relationship economy glitters with opportunities, but it is ruthless with organizations and people who are oblivious to change, rigid of mind, or slow.

The relationship economy doesn't change business basics: serve your customers, deliver quality, be first to market, and cut costs. But success is different today. It doesn't last as long. Success often breeds more success, but it can just as easily breed complacency and decline. Being on top of your market is an unstable and unsafe place because competitors aim at you with new technologies and business practices, some of them highly innovative. Bringing new products and services to market is just half the solution; letting go of old successes is the equally important other half. For those who truly understand the relationship economy, success breeds a healthy paranoia about success and a proactive eagerness to search for change.

Change is uncertain, painful, and risky, but it is unavoidable. Unless you accept your role in leading change, you may be relegating yourself to chasing others who lead. A change leader expects to find opportunity in change, and recognizes the difference between strategic change and a passing fad. While it may be risky to lead change, it's even more risky to follow change. If you aren't willing to change, you probably won't get things that you don't already have today.

The ten tips in this book equip you to be a change leader. They encourage you to examine your beliefs, build your relationships, and take action. The ten tips might be different from the practices used in your workplace today. So if you go back to your workplace and try to implement the tips, you may encounter a few resistance dragons. The initial reaction of your co-workers might be apathy, surprise, rejection, or even hostility. But change in the world of business begins and grows with leaders like you. Regardless of your organization's history, you are its future.

> If you don't become a change leader, you will find yourself chasing others who lead.

I'd like to close by predicting that twenty years from today, you will look back at the early twenty-first century as a turning point, the time when organizations first understood the tremendous power of change and used it as a strategic ally. By mid-century, the relationship economy will produce a world where:

- Supply chains link virtually every business in the world;
- Joint ventures between government and industry are the norm;
- Governments integrate their programs and share resources;
- Governments actively support multinational ventures;
- African nations are key players in the world's economy; and
- Industry is the primary caretaker of the environment.

You may say I'm a dreamer. *I am!* I acknowledge it. I enjoy being a dreamer because it's more stimulating and rewarding than worrying what will change next and feeling powerless to do anything about it.

The world changes faster than ever before in history because the number of people who anticipate, embrace, and use change is larger than ever before. They are a team of men and women who have a vision for the future of our world and take action to make it that way. The team doesn't compete, at least not in a conventional sense. Each member is a leader for bigger-than-me goals. *Join the team* if you aren't already a member. Your organization will follow you if you change yourself and lead the way. Furthermore, find leaders in other organizations (maybe in other countries) that have goals consistent with yours, and work with them to achieve big goals that would be impossible alone. The ten tips in this book give you the tools and the inspiration you'll need to reach the top in the relationship economy. It's simple, but it isn't easy!

ACKNOWLEDGMENTS

This book is the product of many relationships. The writing required thousands of hours, but it was my relationships with mentors, colleagues, customers, and competitors that made it possible. They were the source of the two hundred vignettes in this book, even though they probably weren't aware that they were helping me tame my dragons so I could achieve success. But that's typical of the fast-paced relationship economy.

Many people contributed to the development of this book—thanks to you all. I sincerely appreciate the gift of your time and energy, both of which are very precious. Several deserve special acknowledgment because without them this book might never have been finished. First, thank you to my wife, Mary Ellen, for supporting me as I spent hours and hours in my cave (my office) writing and rewriting the manuscript. Next, thank you to the business leaders who reviewed the manuscript, provided frank feedback, and suggested ways to increase the book's quality and usefulness. That group includes Jim Schecksler of the CEO Project, Clyde Northrop of Vistage, Bob Busch of Busch Change Solutions, Tom McMahon of RGS Associates, Earl Smith PhD, Archie Tinelli PhD, and Nathan Zee and Bill Stieglitz who are senior government employees. And thanks to Ellen Reid (the "Book Shepherd") and her team for the fantastic assistance they delivered to transform my rough manuscript into a quality book.

I also want to acknowledge the authors I read in preparation for writing this book. In the two years it took to write this book, I've read over twenty business books. The four that influenced me the most in defining the relationship economy of the future were: *The World is Flat* by Thomas Friedman, *A Whole New Mind* by Daniel Pink, *Leading Change* by John Kotter, and *Unleashing the Idea Virus* by Seth Godin. I thank these men for their insightful perspectives about our changing world, and I appreciate the gift they gave by offering those perspectives in a way that ordinary business people can understand and apply. My purpose is to make *Taming the Dragons of Change in Business* that kind of book.

Additional information is available at:

www.dickstieglitz.com
www.dragonsofchange.com

CONTACT INFORMATION

I sincerely hope this book was insightful and useful to you. If any vignette was especially inspiring or valuable, let me know via e-mail at: dick@dragonsofchange.com. I look forward to hearing from you.

If you want to learn about changes in government and business on a regular basis, I invite you to subscribe at www.dickstieglitz.com for a free copy of my monthly e-newsletter, which is three or four pages long and contains articles on change topics related to current events. The newsletter is distributed monthly via e-mail.

If you need help accelerating change in your organization, I'm available for consulting. Send an e-mail with as much information as you'd like, and I'll contact you. The initial phone consultation is free. I also offer presentations and workshops on change including these:

Taming the Dragons of Change—Keynote Address

Is your organization facing a significant change?
Are your people apprehensive about that change?

If these questions describe your organization, this presentation will set the tone for a productive conference or strategic planning meeting. This flexible keynote address will entertain the audience and provide tips to deal with an ever-changing world.

Leading from the Middle—Interactive Workshop

Are your organization's middle managers on divergent paths?
Do they complain about each other, instead of working together?

If these questions describe your management team, this workshop is for you. Pick a current issue for them to resolve during this four-hour to two-day workshop, while at the same time learning to work effectively with senior executives and each other.

Future Changes—Presentation

Is your company looking to lead the next bubble?
Are you wondering what that bubble might be?

If these questions describe your company, this presentation very well may point you in the right direction by expanding on the closing section of this book.

ABOUT THE AUTHOR

Dick Stieglitz's groundbreaking work in change management and his success in helping executives, corporations, and government agencies use change to achieve success have earned him the title of the "Change Doctor."

Dick pioneered the Integrated Change Management (ICM) methodology to help Federal agencies (the largest business on earth) transform how they do business. He recently sold his company to devote time to writing, consulting, and speaking. He publishes a monthly e-letter called "*The Change Challenge*," and frequently speaks at industry and government forums on the topic of change and new trends in a changing world.

After earning a PhD in nuclear engineering, Dick served ten years in the U.S. Navy refueling nuclear submarines before moving to the corporate world. He was VP of a software company, then Director of Defense Consulting for an aerospace firm. *Taming the Dragons of Change in Business* is based on his thirty-five years of experience working with business and government leaders to make change work in complex environments. Dick and his wife, Mary Ellen, live in Potomac, Maryland.

www.dickstieglitz.com